Sacred Interconnections

David Ray Griffin, editor, *The Reenchantment of Science:
Postmodern Proposals*

David Ray Griffin, editor, *Spirituality and Society: Postmodern Visions*

David Ray Griffin, *God and Religion in the Postmodern World:
Essays in Postmodern Theology*

David Ray Griffin, William A. Beardslee, and Joe Holland,
Varieties of Postmodern Theology

David Ray Griffin and Huston Smith, *Primordial Truth and
Postmodern Theology*

David Ray Griffin, editor, *Sacred Interconnections:
Postmodern Spirituality, Political Economy, and Art*

SACRED INTERCONNECTIONS

Postmodern Spirituality, Political Economy, and Art

DAVID RAY GRIFFIN, *Editor*

STATE UNIVERSITY OF NEW YORK PRESS

Published by
State University of New York Press, Albany

© 1990 State University of New York

For information, address State University of New York
Press, State University Plaza, Albany, N.Y., 12246

Library of Congress Cataloging-in-Publication Data

Sacred interconnections: postmodern spirituality, political economy,
and art / David Ray Griffin, editor.
    p.   cm. — (SUNY series in constructive postmodern thought)
Includes index.
ISBN 0-7914-0231-2. — ISBN 0-7914-0232-0 (pbk.)
1. Postmodernism. 2. Spirituality — History — 20th century.
I. Griffin, David Ray, 1939-   . II. Series.
B831.2.S23   1990   89-34234
200'.1—dc20   CIP

10 9 8 7 6 5 4 3 2

For Marcia Doss,
secretary extraordinaire

All things are implicated with one another,
and the bond is holy.

—Marcus Aurelius

CONTENTS

INTRODUCTION TO SUNY SERIES IN CONSTRUCTIVE POSTMODERN THOUGHT

The rapid spread of the term *postmodern* in recent years witnesses to a growing dissatisfaction with modernity and to an increasing sense that the modern age not only had a beginning but can have an end as well. Whereas the word *modern* was almost always used until quite recently as a word of praise and as a synonym for *contemporary,* a growing sense is now evidenced that we can and should leave modernity behind—in fact, that we *must* if we are to avoid destroying ourselves and most of the life on our planet.

Modernity, rather than being regarded as the norm for human society toward which all history has been aiming and into which all societies should be ushered—forcibly if necessary—is instead increasingly seen as an aberration. A new respect for the wisdom of traditional societies is growing as we realize that they have endured for thousands of years and that, by contrast, the existence of modern society for even another century seems doubtful. Likewise, *modernism* as a worldview is less and less seen as The Final Truth, in comparison with which all divergent worldviews are automatically regarded as "superstitious." The modern worldview is increasingly relativized to the status of one among many, useful for some purposes, inadequate for others.

Although there have been antimodern movements before, beginning perhaps near the outset of the nineteenth century with the Romanticists and the Luddites, the rapidity with which the term *postmodern* has become widespread in our time suggests that the antimodern sentiment is more extensive and intense than before, and also that it includes the sense that modernity can be successfully overcome only by going beyond it, not by attempting to return to a premodern form of existence. Insofar as a common element is found in the various ways in which the term is used, *postmodernism* refers to a diffuse sentiment rather than to any common set of doctrines—the sentiment that humanity can and must go beyond the modern.

Beyond connoting this sentiment, the term *postmodern* is used in a confusing variety of ways, some of them contradictory to others. In artistic and literary circles, for example, postmodernism shares in this general sentiment but also involves a specific reaction against "modernism" in the narrow sense of a movement in artistic-literary circles in the late nineteenth and early twentieth centuries. Postmodern architecture is very different from postmodern literary criticism. In some circles, the term *postmodern* is used in reference to that potpourri of ideas and systems sometimes called *new age metaphysics,* although many of these ideas and systems are more premodern than postmodern. Even in philosophical and theological circles, the term *postmodern* refers to two quite different positions, one of which is reflected in this series. Each position seeks to transcend both *modernism* in the sense of the worldview that has developed out of the seventeenth-century Galilean-Cartesian-Baconian-Newtonian science, and *modernity* in the sense of the world order that both conditioned and was conditioned by this worldview. But the two positions seek to transcend the modern in different ways.

Closely related to literary-artistic postmodernism is a philosophical postmodernism inspired variously by pragmatism, physicalism, Ludwig Wittgenstein, Martin Heidegger, and Jacques Derrida and other recent French thinkers. By the use of terms that arise out of particular segments of this movement, it can be called *deconstructive* or *eliminative postmodernism.* It overcomes the modern worldview through an anti-worldview: it deconstructs or eliminates the ingredients necessary for a worldview, such as God, self, purpose, meaning, a real world, and truth as correspondence. While motivated in some cases by the ethical concern to forestall totalitarian systems, this type of postmodern thought issues in relativism, even nihilism. It could also be called *ultramodernism,* in that its eliminations result from carrying modern premises to their logical conclusions.

The postmodernism of this series can, by contrast, be called *constructive* or *revisionary.* It seeks to overcome the modern worldview not by eliminating the possibility of worldviews as such, but by constructing a postmodern worldview through a revision of modern premises and traditional concepts. This constructive or revisionary postmodernism involves a new unity of scientific, ethical, aesthetic, and religious intuitions. It rejects not science as such but only that scientism in which the data of the modern natural sciences are alone allowed to contribute to the construction of our worldview.

The constructive activity of this type of postmodern thought is not limited to a revised worldview; it is equally concerned with a postmodern world that will support and be supported by the new worldview. A postmodern world will involve postmodern persons, with a postmodern spirituality, on the one hand, and a postmodern society, ultimately a postmodern global order, on the other. Going beyond the modern world will involve transcending its individualism, anthropocentrism, patriarchy, mechanization, economism, consumerism, nationalism, and militarism. Constructive postmodern thought provides support for the ecology, peace, feminist, and other emancipatory movements of our time, while stressing that the inclusive emancipation must be from modernity itself. The term *postmodern,* however, by contrast with *premodern,* emphasizes that the modern world has produced unparalleled advances that must not be lost in a general revulsion against its negative features.

From the point of view of deconstructive postmodernists, this constructive postmodernism is still hopelessly wedded to outdated concepts, because it wishes to salvage a positive meaning not only for the notions of the human self, historical meaning, and truth as correspondence, which were central to modernity, but also for premodern notions of a divine reality, cosmic meaning, and an enchanted nature. From the point of view of its advocates, however, this revisionary postmodernism is not only more adequate to our experience but also more genuinely postmodern. It does not simply carry the premises of modernity through to their logical conclusions, but criticizes and revises those premises. Through its return to organicism and its acceptance of nonsensory perception, it opens itself to the recovery of truths and values from various forms of premodern thought and practice that had been dogmatically rejected by modernity. This constructive, revisionary postmodernism involves a creative synthesis of modern and premodern truths and values.

This series does not seek to create a movement so much as to help shape and support an already existing movement convinced that modernity can and must be transcended. But those antimodern movements which arose in the past failed to deflect or even retard the onslaught of modernity. What reasons can we have to expect the current movement to be more successful? First, the previous antimodern movements were primarily calls to return to a premodern form of life and thought rather than calls to advance, and the human spirit does not rally to calls to turn back. Second, the previous antimodern movements either rejected modern science, reduced it to a description of mere appearances, or assumed its adequacy in principle; therefore, they could base their calls only on the negative social and spiritual effects of modernity. The current movement draws on natural science itself as a witness against the adequacy of the modern worldview. In the third place, the present movement has even more evidence than did previous movements of the ways in which modernity and its worldview *are* socially and spiritually destructive. The fourth and probably most decisive difference is that the present movement is based on the awareness that *the continuation of modernity threatens the very survival of life on our planet.* This awareness, combined with the growing knowledge of the interdependence of the modern worldview and the militarism, nuclearism, and ecological devastation of the modern world, is providing an unprecedented impetus for people to see the evidence for a postmodern worldview and to envisage postmodern ways of relating to each other, the rest of nature, and the cosmos as a whole. For these reasons, the failure of the previous antimodern movements says little about the possible success of the current movement.

Advocates of this movement do not hold the naively utopian belief that the success of this movement would bring about a global society of universal and lasting peace, harmony, and happiness, in which all spiritual problems, social conflicts, ecological destruction, and hard choices would vanish. There is, after all, surely a deep truth in the testimony of the world's religions to the presence of a transcultural proclivity to evil deep within the human heart, which no new paradigm, combined with a new economic order, new child-rearing practices, or any other social arrangements, will suddenly eliminate. Furthermore, it has correctly been said that "life is robbery": a strong element of competition is inherent within finite existence, which no social-political-economic-ecological order can overcome. These two truths, especially when contemplated together, should caution us against unrealistic hopes.

However, no such appeal to "universal constants" should reconcile us to the present order, as if this order were thereby uniquely legitimated. The human proclivity to evil in general, and to conflictual competition and ecological destruction in particular, can be greatly exacerbated or greatly mitigated by a world order and its worldview. Modernity exacerbates it about as much as imaginable. We can therefore envision, without being naively utopian, a far better world order, with a far less dangerous trajectory, than the one we now have.

This series, making no pretense of neutrality, is dedicated to the success of this movement toward a postmodern world.

David Ray Griffin
Series Editor

ACKNOWLEDGMENTS

In somewhat different form, Richard Falk's essay has been published in *Alternatives* and as an occasional paper for the City University's Center on Violence and Human Survival. Somewhat different versions of Frederick Turner's essay were published in *Harper's* magazine (November, 1984) and in his book *Natural Classicism: Essays on Literature and Science* (New York: Paragon House, 1985). Earlier versions of the contributions by Bernard Lee, Catherine Keller, John Cobb, William Beardslee, Suzi Gablik, and Steve Odin were presented at events sponsored by the Center for a Postmodern World.

I wish to thank the various contributors to this volume for advice regarding the introduction. I am grateful to President Richard Cain and the trustees of the School of Theology at Claremont for a leave of absence during which this book was completed, and to John Cobb and Nancy Howell of the Center for Process Studies who made this time away possible. I am also grateful to William Eastman of SUNY Press for continued support of this series, and to Elizabeth Moore for efficiently guiding these volumes through production. Finally, my thanks to various secretaries at the School of Theology, especially Ginny Hodges and Kathy Deskin, for typing some of the chapters.

This volume is dedicated to Marcia Doss, who has been the secretary to the dean of the School of Theology at Claremont since 1973. Over the years I have thanked many secretaries in the acknowledgments at the front of the books. But these secretaries have come and gone, while Marcia remained, and during all that period it has been Marcia who, as supervisor of the faculty office, has seen to it that things were done, and done well. This dedication is thereby a belated expression of thanks with regard to those earlier books as well. I make this dedication, however, not simply because of the importance she has had for my individual work, but because of her importance to the spiritual-intellectual community to which I have belonged since 1973. We often joke that everyone at the school is dispensable except Marcia, and, like many jokes, this one is not far from the truth.

1

INTRODUCTION:
SACRED INTERCONNECTIONS

David Ray Griffin

In the introduction to a previous volume in this series, *Spirituality and Society: Postmodern Visions,* I noted that "no feature of postmodern spirituality is emphasized more than the reality of internal relations." This assessment is borne out by the present essays. Two of them (those by Falk and Turner) were originally published elsewhere, and the others were essentially completed before the decision was made to use "interconnections" in the title. And yet, the idea that all things are interconnected, and that these interconnections are internal to the very essence of the things themselves, is the central thread running through all these essays. They are interconnected by the theme of interconnections.

Catherine Keller, for instance, says that "interconnection is the cosmic case," and that "No one and no thing is really separate from anything else." Bernard Lee says: "We are interconnected in a system in which whatever happens to any part of the system reverberates in small or large ways throughout the system." Joanna Macy speaks of "interexistence," of "a vision of radical and sustaining interdependence," of an "experience of profound interconnectedness with all life," and of our

1

selves as "inseparable from the Web of life in which we are as intricately interconnected as cells in a larger body." Steve Odin speaks of an "aesthetic continuum of harmonious interpenetration between the many and the one," while Suzi Gablik advocates an "aesthetics of interconnectedness" based on a paradigm shift "from objects to relationships." Matthew Fox speaks of "an interdependent universe," and Joe Holland of "ecological communion." Richard Falk points out that postmodern religion is "richly relational." Frederick Turner says that matter's "only existence was and is in its relations, internal and external. The universe is made up of the differential sensitivities of its components to each other." John Cobb speaks of "God as interconnected with the whole interconnected creation."

Postmodern spirituality rejects dualistic supernaturalism, on the one hand, and atheistic nihilism, on the other, in favor of some version of nondualistic spirituality. The reality of spiritual energy is affirmed, but it is felt to exist within and between all nodes in the cosmic web of interconnections. It is thus dispersed throughout the universe, not concentrated in a source wholly transcendent to it. Postmodernists who speak of God generally affirm a naturalistic panentheism, according to which God is in all things and all things are in God. In any case, the relations between things are not thought to be imposed upon them from without, as in the supernaturalistic theism and deism of early modernity (the collapse of which led to nihilistic atheism). Rather, the relations between things are regarded as internal to them, and as their participation in the universal web of interconnections, which is itself holy or sacred, being the source of all value and power. This receipt of valuable empowerment is grace. Joanna Macy, from a Buddhist perspective, speaks of it as grace without God. When the reality of God is affirmed, our relations with God are taken to be examples of, not exceptions to, the universal system of internal connections. Because empowering grace comes through the web of our interconnections, this web is sacred.

The present book can be considered a sequel to the aforementioned *Spirituality and Society.* Although it stands on its own, and can be read independently, reading it in conjunction with that earlier volume will be helpful. Obviously, the positions of those authors who are in both volumes (John Cobb, Richard Falk, Joe Holland, and Catherine Keller) will be understood more fully if their present essays are read in the light of those previously published ones. But also, in the briefer introduction here I do not repeat the extensive and heavily documented comparison between modernism and postmodernism which I gave there.

Besides the notion of internal interconnections, already discussed, the present book illustrates the other themes lifted up in that introduction as characteristic of postmodern spirituality and social thinking. These themes are: a nondualistic relation of humans to nature and of the divine reality to the world; the immanence of both the past and the future (albeit in different ways) in the present; the universality and centrality of creativity; postpatriarchy; communitarianism (*versus* individualism and nationalism); the "deprivatization" of religion, meaning the rejection of the autonomy of morality, politics, and economics from religious values; and (specifically) the rejection of materialism, in the sense of economism, meaning the subordination of social, religious, moral, aesthetic, and ecological interests to (short-term) economic interests.

What is most new in the present book, besides the new perspectives brought by seven new authors (William Beardslee, Matthew Fox, Suzi Gablik, Bernard Lee, Joanna Macy, Steve Odin, and Frederick Turner), is the focus on the place of art within postmodern spirituality and culture. Gablik deals with the visual arts; Beardslee looks at literature and literary criticism; Fox and Odin focus on the centrality of art within religious meditation; and Turner's essay deals more broadly with the nature and role of art within the emerging nondualistic postmodern culture. Through these essays one of the gaping lacunae in the earlier volume is partially filled in. The present volume also goes beyond the previous one in relating postmodern spirituality to further sociopolitical issues—war and nuclearism (Lee and Keller), family and work (Holland)—as well as focusing more explicitly on the relation between religion and political economy (especially Falk, Turner, and Cobb).

At the heart of all these explorations of art, spirituality, and political culture is the theme of the interconnections among all things. That this universal connectedness is a fact can be said to be the first thesis of this book. The second thesis is that our problems arise largely from the human failure to recognize, both in theory and in our conscious experience, this fact. Macy speaks of the notion of the "skin-encapsulated ego" as a "pathogenic notion of the self," saying that it is basic to our planetary ecological crisis. Keller sees war and nuclear terror as rooted importantly in the "nuclear ego," meaning the idea and experience of the self as separate, as independent from its relations to others, which especially characterizes men in modern culture. She suggests that part of the allure of nuclear weapons may lie in their power to wreak vengeance upon all the connected life from which modern men have felt alienated. Turner makes a similar suggestion: the materialistic worldview of modernism alienated us from the really real, declaring the personal to be a second-class reality. The technological monsters of Communism, Nazism, and the hydrogen bomb perhaps reflect the final upshot of this suspicion of the personal by promising "to eradicate persons from the face of the earth." Fox regards most of modernity's distinctive problems, such as the extreme violence, and the extraordinary levels of drug abuse and suicide, especially among the youth, as significantly rooted in modernity's lack of a cosmology that stresses the ecological interdependence of all things and mystical relations between the microcosm and the macrocosm, between the self and the Divine Mystery. Turner uses quite different language to make the same point: that the worldview and resulting materialistic religion and ethic of modernism have starved people "of the pleasures of the mind and spirit and soul." Holland sees the modern crises as resulting from the fact that the techno-scientific economy, which is the most powerful aspect of modern society, is "autonomous from ecological, social, and spiritual communion." Cobb shows how the modern vision of human beings, as substances with only external relations to each other and to nature, has contributed to the destructiveness of modern economics.

This modern nonrecognition, or denial, of essential interconnections is, in part, a matter of theory. A significant feature of this theoretical denial was Descartes' definition of a substance—and the human soul was one of the two earthly types of these—as that which requires nothing but itself to exist. But neither the human soul, nor a material substance, was a full-fledged substance, under this definition, because both of them do require God to exist, Descartes said. But God, according to the traditional supernaturalism accepted by Descartes, did not require them or anything else. God alone, therefore, was truly a substance. This idea of God lay behind the modern view of matter and of the self. As Turner points out: "Like God, the atom of matter was indivisible, eternal, invulnerable, and responsible for all events in the world." And Keller adds: "The atomic ego is created in the image of a separate God."

In Keller's view, this separate God is a patriarchal deity. The modern "ideology of separation" is therefore a product of a patriarchal image of God. Fox agrees, seeing the modern denial of creativity and interdependence as reflective of the one-sided focus at the outset of modernity on a masculine "sky god" over and against the divinity of "Mother Earth." In contrast with the Goddess and the Cosmic Christ, each of which symbolizes the immanence of divinity in all things, modern theism taught that God was "out there somewhere." This split between God and nature, between God and us, says Fox, is the "dualism of dualisms that the modern era has bequeathed to us," which lies behind our other uniquely modern problems. Joe Holland sees this dualism, already present in classical spirituality, as the "deep root" lying beneath the modern degradation of the family and of work, because religious contemplation of a masculine, wholly transcendent deity led to the desire to be free from the feminine webs, cycles, and creative energies of nature, which were declared by that vision of deity not to be holy. Turner points out that modernist art has been exclusively masculine.

The modern nonrecognition of essential connectedness is not simply theoretical, however; it is also experiential. The conscious experience of modern human beings, especially modern men, is of being a separate self, separate from nature, other people, and God (if the reality of God be accepted). To some extent, this problem is rooted in the nature of consciousness itself, according to Alfred North Whitehead, whose analysis is presupposed by many of our authors. According to his analysis, our "stream of experience" is comprised of a series of momentary experiences, each of which is a process of becoming. Each momentary experience arises out of, and is internally constituted by, its relations to the entire past world. As Odin points out, Buddhists and Whiteheadians agree that the many literally become one: the one (for example, my present experience) is formed out of the past multiplicity of beings. But consciousness, which arises only late in each momentary experience, if at all, tends to illuminate only the more self-created, seemingly independent products arising at the tailend of each moment of experience, leaving the relational origins of each experience largely in the dark. Our essential connectedness to our bodies, the rest of nature, other people, and with God therefore tends to be vague and fuzzy, or even wholly unconscious, while that aspect of our selves that is clear and distinct in our conscious self-perception gives us the impression that we approximate one of those mythical Cartesian substances that requires nothing but itself to exist. Buddhism likewise, as Macy points out, regards human consciousness itself as prone to the notion of a separate, abiding self, which is "the foundational delusion of human life."

This universal tendency of consciousness, however, is not fulfilled to the same extent by all people. Most premodern peoples have not had our modern sense of separate individuality. Macy therefore speaks of the boundaries of the modern self as "culturally defined." Keller sees the separative self which she calls the "nuclear complex" as rooted in the early childhood relationships of males to their parents, especially in the modern nuclear family. The separative self of the modern man is therefore not universally human, being less characteristic of women in general and of premodern (and, it is hoped, postmodern) men. Turner speaks of the sense of alienation from nature as a "cultural illusion" of modernity.

While this cultural conditioning is in part a matter of the practices and institutions of a society, such as the nuclear family and its childrearing patterns, it is also significantly constituted by the aforementioned theoretical beliefs. We tend consciously to notice things our theories tell us to expect, and to ignore things they tell us to be nonexistent. And we tend to become, especially at the conscious level, what we believe we are. Fox says, accordingly, that the "disenchantment of the world" could also be called "the death knell of mysticism"; in other words, the denial of a living cosmos, and of the possibility of a direct experience of the link between the self and divinity, led to the loss of consciousness of that experience. For Keller, the image of the disconnected self led to the warrior's "aesthetics of disempathy." For Turner, the illusion of alienation was due to "the worldview of Modernism," according to which the world is "reduced to a valueless collection of objective facts."

The various essays in this book reflect a sense that a postmodern age is dawning, in that the fact of interconnectedness, which occurs willy-nilly at the unconscious depths of our selves, is being increasingly experienced at the conscious surface. The feminist spirituality described by Keller is an important example. The ecological self described by Macy is another. The creation spirituality outlined by Fox is a third. The reenchanting art pointed to by Gablik, Beardslee, and Turner is yet another manifestation. Falk and Turner point to more sweeping illustrations of a sea-change in human consciousness in our time, with Turner giving central attention to the developments in science. He marks the beginning of the end of the religion of materialism with the dissolution of the presumably indivisible atom "into event, relation, and information," and the extension of evolution to so-called physical matter, which implies that "all of the world is alive," and that "the whole world is made up of such as we are." The interpenetration of Christian and Buddhist sensibilities manifested in Cobb, Macy, Fox, and Odin is itself a sign of the times, as is the fact that these various authors not only stress interconnection but also seek to get the realization of it incarnated in our social, political, and economic structures.

Besides stressing the interconnection of all things and reflecting the increased awareness of it in our time, these authors also point to ways to increase this awareness still further. Because modernity with its discontents was partly the product of a way of thinking, a new way of thinking is essential to this conscious awareness of interconnection. Fox, equating theism with the dualistic God "out there somewhere," calls for a panentheistic vision, in which God is in all things and all things are in God. This panentheistic vision is central to many of the other authors too, especially Beardslee, Cobb, Lee, Holland, and Keller. Closely related is the call, most explicitly enunciated here by Fox, for a living cosmology, a reenchanted world, an emphasis upon the creativity in human beings and throughout nature, and a reverence for the webs and cycles of nature. Turner, like Fox, sees a postmodern version of this living, animistic cosmology already implicit in twentieth-century science. Besides the fact that matter has been dissolved into relational events, taking evolution seriously implies that life and even matter and energy are simply unorganized, undeveloped forms of that self-reflection which blossoms in human awareness. The universe is thus rife with value and meaning, and human beings, insofar as we are machines, are machines whose purpose is to produce spirit, soul, and value. Gablik enunciates a theme common to all the authors in speaking of a shift of focus "from objects to relationships." Macy, a Buddhist, and Lee, a Christian, both employ the relation of the cells to their body as a metaphor for thinking of our relation to the world as a whole; both point out that, insofar as we attain this consciousness, right action need not depend upon a victory of moral duty over inclination. Turner uses the discovery of endorphins to make a similar point: the universe and our place in it are such that our greatest rewards come naturally from acting in accord with the standards of moral and aesthetic excellence discovered and taught by the great religious and artistic traditions. In reaction against the model of domination in patriarchal thinking, Gablik calls for a participatory "aesthetics of interconnectedness." Keller similarly speaks of an "aesthetic of the panempathic field." Macy sums up much of the basis for postmodern theory by referring to the coalescence of three influences: ecological and pacific thinking evoked by the contemporary planetary crisis; nondualistic spiritualities, such as Buddhism; and systems ways of thinking, among which she would include Whiteheadian philosophy.

At the heart, or the base, of this Whiteheadian philosophy, which lies behind more than half the essays, is the concept of "prehension" as the fundamental form of perception. It is more fundamental than sensory perception, being presupposed by it, and is in fact exemplified by organisms that do not have sensory organs. Each event is a unification of many prehensions, and each prehension is the taking in of causal influences from previous events. Prehension is indeed simply the reverse side of causal influence, and is therefore synonymously called "perception in the mode of causal efficacy." This is the basis in Whitehead's philosophy for the claim that all things are internally related to other things, and that the interconnections within nature in general are not different in kind from the interconnections between our experience and our bodily cells.

Of central importance for the present volume, given the centrality of mystical experience for many of the authors, is the realization that to speak of prehension is to speak of mysticism. A mystical experience is, most fundamentally, an experience in which there is a direct, unmediated contact with another experience. This is precisely what prehension is, in distinction from sensory perception. Sensory perception involves a very indirect, mediated contact between the experience and the object. For example, my sensory image of the tree outside my office depends upon a very long chain of photonic events from the tree to my eye, and then upon a long chain of neuronic events in my eye, optic nerve, and brain. Literally billions of events separate me from the life of the tree itself. I do not, therefore, directly feel the values enjoyed by the tree. In seeing it, I do not feel its feelings. But my prehension of my brain cells, through which I receive the sensory data from the tree, is *not* mediated; I am directly in contact with those living cells. Through this direct, unmediated relationship to my body, I share with sympathy or compassion the values enjoyed by my bodily members, both their pains and their joys. The mind-body relation is thus our primary example of mystical connection. But it is not the only one. What we call "memory" is another example: our direct perception of our own past experiences.

This memorizing perception is not limited to our immediate past; we remember events that occurred several minutes or even several years ago. This direct experience of noncontiguous events extends beyond what we usually think of as our "own" past: as Macy points out, the interactions between things in general can operate at a distance. Aside from what we call memory, we normally are not consciously aware of these experiences of events that are remote in space and/or time. What parapsychologists call "telepathy" and "clairvoyance" are therefore considered unusual. According to Whiteheadian and Buddhist thought, however, what is unusual is not the interconnection or perception at a distance but only the consciousness of it. The mystical prehensions of remote events are occurring all the time at the unconscious level. This provides, for those forms of postmodernism that speak of God, an analogy for that special mystical experience which involves a direct intuition of God. Assuming that there is an all-inclusive experience in which we live, move, and have our being, we would be prehending it all the time. The only thing special about what is usually called mystical experience, meaning a conscious experience of the holy reality as holy, would be that the continuous prehension of God had finally erupted into the conscious dimension of our experience. To speak of a mystical experience of God, as does Fox for example, is therefore not to move beyond the theme of the universal interconnection of things; it is instead to speak of an experience of the most inclusive form of this interconnection.

In any case, this mystical connection between experience and experience, referred to rather prosaically by Whitehead as "prehension," provides a naturalistic basis for the universal connectedness spoken of by the authors in this book. Because this prehension involves a sympathetic reception of the values experienced by the prior experiences—which

Whitehead calls the "initial conformity of subjective form"—it also explains why the conscious experience of this interconnection can be such an emotional, ecstatic experience. (This is not to deny, of course, that the endorphins of which Turner speaks in describing "natural highs" are contributors to the ecstasy—to exclude them would be to return to the dualism of soul and matter that postmodernism rejects.)

Reference to experience brings us to the next point, which is that these authors speak not only of new ways of thinking but also of methods for inducing an *experiential realization* of sacred interconnections. Macy points out that meditation upon our own pain and despair in the face of the planetary crisis evokes recognition of the existence of this larger, ecological, compassionate self already present in the depths of our being. Falk likewise sees reverence for the sacred energy of life itself, and empathetic identification with the suffering of fellow humans and the rest of nature, as fundamental to a postmodern spirituality. Fox says that creativity is the basic spiritual discipline for a postmodern era, and says in particular that art as meditation, in which we come to grips with our images, is the primary spiritual practice for a creation spirituality. Gablik suggests, in contrast with those relativistic postmodern artists who have given up all hope of changing the world, that a reenchanted, shamanic art may play a significant role in awakening a sense of responsibility for the fate of the earth. Beardslee calls for a recovery of overarching, orienting stories. Turner reinforces these calls by Gablik and Beardslee, adding that we need to educate the young to administer their own higher brain rewards, by teaching them the pleasures of honor, insight, love, beauty, and excellence of all sorts. Lee calls for a world construction based upon the intuition of our equal existence in relation to the parenthood of God through which the texture of the relational web of existence becomes transformed in the direction of a single body in which the pain of one is the pain of all. Keller speaks of "ritualistic affirmations of interconnection," through which we can cultivate the "courage of our connections." And Odin, drawing upon Whitehead's observation that sensory images can usually evoke deep religious experiences better than words, suggests that Shingon, an esoteric form of Buddhism whose practices are only now becoming known to the West, may provide in its contemplation upon mandala art a method for us to realize experientially the value-laden interconnectedness of all things. Whitehead's idea that the basic causal and prehensive process of dependent arising, or the many's becoming one, involves the transference of aesthetic emotion from experience to experience, and that this process is presupposed in sensory perception, is fundamental to Odin's analysis of the truth-function of maṇḍala art. This function, he suggests, is "to manifest the beauty of hidden depths." That beauty is nothing other than the "aesthetic continuum of harmonious interpenetration between the many and the one" which lies at the base of every moment of our experience but is, in our "ordinary" consciousness, especially in the modern West, largely hidden.

The vision of interconnection described and advocated by these authors leads them toward a postmodern vision of the interconnection of religious spirituality and politics. This is the central theme of Falk's essay. Whereas the modern world, in both its capitalist and socialist versions, declared religious identity irrelevant to the political organization of society, this modernist orientation has suddenly been challenged by a variety of attempts to "recast politics" in the light of religious convictions. After speaking of anticapitalist, antisocialist, and fundamentalist forms of this challenge to modernist politics (which Turner also notes), Falk explores the emerging postmodern sensibility and mentions some movements that may provide "a partial revelation of what a fused religious and political postmodern consciousness imagines an alternative, preferred world might be." Falk is not alone, however, in thinking that the postmodern "needs to be both a political way ... and a religious reawakening." Macy says that the ecological sense of selfhood "combines the mystical and the pragmatic." More pointedly, she challenges the notion that Buddhism necessarily leads to nihilism and escapism, saying that it "can bring the world into sharper focus and liberate one into lively, effective action." Fox argues that a society's renaissance must be a "rebirth based on a spiritual initiative," that we need a rebirth that "regrounds humankind's politics in the laws of the universe." Holland, likewise criticizing the autonomy allowed to the "techno-scientific economy" by modernity, calls for "the birth of a new political economy" based on the emerging postmodern vision of interconnection. Cobb provides a sketch of the direction such a political economy might take. Turner joins Holland and Cobb in anticipating a greatly decentralized political economy.

One aspect of the postmodern vision of religion and politics that separates it decisively from premodern forms is exemplified especially well by Lee's emphasis on "the only survivable world." In premodern versions of the union of religion and politics, the question of the survival of the world itself was not a political concern. In Jewish, Christian, and Islamic cultures, this was because the end of the world was considered to be solely in the hands of the omnipotent God. This attitude is still reflected in many modern "nuclear theologians" who hold that political responsibility extends only to concern for freedom and justice, not to concern for global survival. We can therefore, they believe, with impunity engage in nuclear brinkmanship for the sake of defending human freedom from totalitarian tyranny (not to mention the present economic arrangements from which we benefit). This attitude seems intelligible only against the backdrop of centuries of moral-political thought in which an eschatology of omnipotence took this concern in principle out of human hands. In any case, this attitude, and the theology on which it was based, plays no role in postmodern spirituality, as illustrated by Lee. Saying that he was brought up on the image of the inevitable coming of the divine reign, he says: "In my honest moments today I know that the reign of God may not come, that we human beings, as necessary agents in the co-creation of history, may terminate rather than propagate human life if we do not with God protect the preciousness of our shared existence on this planet." It is this radically new sense that we human beings genuinely have our own power *vis-à-vis* the creative power of the universe, and that we could use this power to destroy the portion of the creation that is our home, that most centrally motivates the postmodern fusion of political and religious consciousness.

The remaining question is the role of art in this postmodern effort to shape a survivable world. As Gablik and Beardslee show, there are two radically different versions of postmodern art, literature, and artistic and literary criticism: a deconstructive and a reconstructive version. Deconstructive postmodernism carries modernity's disenchantment of the world to its nihilistic conclusions. Pluralism means complete relativism, with no culturally transcendent standards of aesthetic or moral criticism. The web of interconnection, whether in reality or in language, is understood in such a way as to exclude human creativity and originality, at least of any significant degree. At the same time, there is a loss of temporal connectedness, a loss of the sense of connection between the present and the future. Most inclusively, this deconstructive postmodernism in the artistic-literary world means *resignation*—resignation to the unredeemed world as irredeemable. This resignation translates into the artist's decision to attempt nothing more than to mirror the hollowness and inauthenticity of contemporary culture, and in fact to benefit personally from it. If you can't beat 'em, join 'em—with ironic detachment to be sure, but join 'em nevertheless. The task of art is simply to mirror, not to shape.

This deconstructive postmodernism has thus far been the dominant form of postmodernism in the world of art and literature, in fact the only visible form. Indeed, while writing this introduction I heard an essay on the *MacNeil-Lehrer Report* (November 24, Thanksgiving Day, 1988) in which the points made by Gablik and Beardslee about deconstructive postmodernism were said to be "what postmodernism in art is all about."

But the authors in this volume—Gablik, Beardslee, and Turner most explicitly—point to another form of postmodern art which is possible and, to a degree, already being actualized. This constructive or reconstructive art would help draw us toward a reenchanted world. This art would be deeply ecumenical, portraying those elements (stressed by Turner) that all cultures have in common, with which we can see through absolute relativism, while equally celebrating our diversities, with which we can enrich each other. It would recognize the creativity in us as awesome, having both divine and demonic potential, while recognizing it to be continuous with the creativity found throughout nature. And it would not focus solely on undifferentiated creativity; it would give equal attention to what Beardslee, following Whitehead, calls our intuitions of patterns of "rightness" inherent in reality. For a resource it would use precisely those overarching stories rejected by deconstructive postmodernists as "totalitarian," as Beardslee points out, as well as those moral and aesthetic "rules" which modernists (including deconstructive postmodernists) rejected as a "tyrannical imposition," as Turner points out. But it would not accept any of those traditional stories totally; it would use them instead as resources for a postmodern story that provides a bulwark against totalitarian policies.

The question for the art world of the coming generation is which of these paths it will take. Will it continue to acquiesce in its co-optation by the commodity system, using its irony to salve its conscience in the face of this massive acquiescence? Or will artists follow Gablik's call for art to be implicated "in the awakening sense of responsibility for the fate of the earth"? Will they follow Turner's call for an art that is genuinely postmodern, overcoming the illusion of alienation, the hatred of the past, and "the willful imposition of meaninglessness on a universe bursting with meaning"—an art that portrays life as miracle, magic, and enchantment, that "will once more seek after beauty, nobility, truth, and the sense of wonder," that is full of moral energy, public statement, and ideas, even theology? Will they participate in Fox's "rebirth of art, politics and spirituality that would constitute an authentic global renaissance"? Many of the religious communities of the world have joined this postmodern movement. One is tempted to say: "Artists of the world reconnect! You have nothing to lose but your narcissistic impotence." But the future of art depends less on volitional responses to ringing calls to moral duty than on whether artists of the coming generations become captivated by the reenchanting, reconnecting, recreating postmodern vision. In any case, I believe that the nature of the postmodern world will be significantly shaped by the emerging generation of artists.

A word about the order of the essays: Although each of the essays addresses two and often all three of the dimensions of life indicated by the book's subtitle, each essay has its dominant emphases. The essays placed first give primary attention to postmodern spirituality as such—its nature and grounds—while indicating its implications for social, political, economic, and cultural life only in quite general terms. The essays in the middle of the book become more explicit and detailed about social, political and economic issues. In the concluding essays, the relation between postmodern spirituality and art moves to center stage.

The fact that all these topics are covered, incidentally, is not unrelated to postmodernity and its perception of the interconnectedness of all things. Whereas modernity's belief in the essential separability of all things led to the compartmentalized approach to knowledge reflected in the departmental organization of the modern university, the postmodern perception of interconnectedness leads to the convinction, for example, that economic policy for a society cannot be discussed without consideration of the religious, aesthetic, moral, and political beliefs and aspirations of the members of that society.

I present this set of essays with great pride. Each is important in itself, and together they effectively portray several dimensions of what it would mean to move from modernity to postmodernity. All the contributors do not, to be sure, agree on all points. For example, although all the authors are critical of modernity in some respects and call for a recovery of premodern beliefs, values, and practices, some of the authors (with Frederick Turner as the clearest example) give more emphasis to the achievements of modernity and see the movement to postmodernity as flowing rather naturally out of these achievements, whereas other authors (with Matthew Fox as perhaps the strongest example) give more attention to the destructive aspects of the modern world and call for a more radical break with it, portraying the postmodern primarily as a recovery of certain premodern beliefs and practices. But these differences are matters of degree and emphasis; overall the reader will find a consensus that is remarkable, especially in the light of the vastly different backgrounds, personal and professional, of the various authors. This set of essays does seem to give voice to an emerging spirit of the times—a reconstructive postmodern spirit.

2

A MYSTICAL COSMOLOGY: TOWARD A POSTMODERN SPIRITUALITY

Matthew Fox

I. INTRODUCTION

From the point of view of spirituality the modern era has been devastating. It has tainted our souls to the point that we no longer even know what *soul* means; it has cut the most powerful instrument of humankind—our science—adrift from conscience, morality and wisdom; it has trivialized economics and politics; it has waged war on mother earth and her children with increasing vengeance and success—fulfilling Francis Bacon's command that we "torture mother earth for her secrets"; it has rendered our youth adrift without hope or vision; it has bored people in what ought to be the great communal celebration known as worship; it has legitimated human holocausts and genocides from that of the seventy million native people exterminated in the Americas between 1492 and 1550 to that of the six million Jews, as well as many Christians and homosexuals, in German death camps. Lacking a living cosmology, the modern era has sentimentalized religion and privatized it, locating it so thoroughly within the feelings of the individual that the dominant religious force of our civilization is that pseudo-religion known as fundamentalism.

In this essay I trace some elements of a postmodern spirituality that are possible and emerging already in practice as well as theory in this country and abroad. For fifteen years I have been involved in a postmodern spiritual practice and theory called "creation spirituality." Many of my observations will be gathered from my experience of that practice and theory. Our thinking about spirituality cannot take place from armchairs or academic towers but must include the dirtying of the hands, the stretching of the heart, the opening of the mystic inside, the practice of the "unselfconsciousness" (Eckhart's word) of the child or fool, the awakening of the right brain, the encountering of our greatest mystics of the past and present, the struggle for justice at many levels of society and its institutions and of our psyches, and the coming together of mystical traditions of East, West, North, and South. This inherently nondualistic methodology of *doing spirituality* is not unlike the call from Liberation Theologians of Latin America and the so-called Third World to combine *praxis* with reflection on that practice. If this is necessary for theology, it is even more necessary for spirituality.

Spirituality is about heart-knowledge and about awakening the being in us. We need to learn just to be. I have learned as much from sitting in sweat lodges, attending Sundances and Pow Wow dances, and attempting a practice of celibacy or of fasting as I have from reading histories of spirituality. No area of intellectual life suffers more from Cartesian educational one-sidedness—that is, from the modern world's definition of truth as "clear and distinct ideas" (Descartes)—than does spirituality. Experiences are seldom clear and distinct. They demand an exercise of our right brains. Here lies the authentic meaning of the word *asceticism:* to exercise our right brains.

Spirituality is not only about doing and exercising to be and become; it is also about power. During the modern era, there was an almost exclusive emphasis on spirtuality as "asceticism"—the term "ascetic theology" was first coined in 1655. Ascetic spirituality came to be understood as self-imposed deprivations that would bring about an altered state. This model of spirituality fit the Cartesian and Newtonian machine model of the universe very neatly and offered the added attraction of feeding the inherent need of an industrial society (society as machine) to be sadistic—that is, in control. Such a society needs masochists on which to run and over which to rule. Appeals to ascetic spirituality played this role very conveniently during the modern era. The result was that spirituality was not identified with power but with the relinquishing of power.

True spirituality, however, is about power. It is about developing the powers of creativity, justice, and compassion in all persons. It is about unleashing divine powers in us all. It is about grounding persons and communities in the powers that will enable them to survive and even flourish in the midst of adversity. Was Gandhi a powerful person? Or Martin Luther King, Jr.? Or Dorothy Day? Or Thomas Aquinas? Or Francis of Assisi? Or Hildegard of Bingen? Were Mozart, Marc Chagall, and Gustav Mahler powerful? Is the spirituality of nonviolence not a spirituality of a kind of power that is alternative to the ways of our modern civilization? "The prophet is the mystic in action," as William Hocking used to teach.[1] The mystic has somehow managed to imbibe the powers of the universe, the powers of the cosmos.[2] The power that the spiritual person imbibes is not human-made power; the mystic contributes to the redefinition of power in a culture—Jesus, for example, found power in compassion rather than in legalism and institutional sadism. He paid the price of a prophet for so doing. Jesus too was a person with power—the power to heal, to awaken, to excite, to transform. Such spiritual leaders are, of course, dangerous. In our day feminists are helping to redefine power.[3]

Where does the practice and the development of power in spiritual practice ultimately come from? It comes from one's cosmology, from the world in which one lives, from the universe itself. When Immanuel Kant separated the laws of the "starry heavens without" from the "moral law within," he was introducing a dualism into the religious consciousness of the West that would suck all power out of morality and render it passive *vis-à-vis* the true decision-makers of industrial civilization. Kant was depriving modern men and women of their cosmic power. He was rendering them sentimentalized, powerless regarding the powers of the world, leaving them only the power of their own inner feelings and of buying things. Not only Kant but the entire modern era did this to spirituality—it emasculated it and feminized it—in the pejorative use of that term employed by Anne Douglas in *The Feminization of American Culture*.[4] It rendered spirituality a "womanly thing," in the pejorative, dualistic, and patriarchal use of that term "womanly." That is, it rendered spirituality passive and inert. This was a very useful thing for a massively patriarchal society to accomplish—it allowed patriarchy to run wild with its militarism and war games; with its bloated left-brain definitions of schooling; with its rape of mother earth; with its disregard for youth; with its replacement of a mystical sexuality with its own industry of pornography; with its replacement of authentic worship—which is always a matter of relating microcosm to macrocosm—with words.[5]

A dualism that haunts spirituality to this day is that between individual and society, or the personal and the communitarian. A living spirituality, one built on experience, power, and cosmology, would never acquiesce to even the naming of such a dualism. In fact, spirituality is the naming and the living out of the vision of the people and the feeding of it—yes, it must be personally appropriated at a deep level of commitment; but no, it is never private or capable of being privatized. I would propose, along with historian M.D. Chenu, that a society's renaissance is by definition a spiritual event, a "rebirth based on a spiritual initiative."[6] Without a growing consensus as to what spiritual values a community shares and what spiritual practices it engages in, there can be no renaissance, no rebirth of the community.

In this introduction, I have tried to lay out some preliminary notes apropos of a critical look at the paradigm shift we are undergoing from the modern to the postmodern era of spirituality. I have written of spirituality as practice or experience and expression, not just as theory of values or morals; of spirituality as power, not the flight from power—but power as critically understood *vis-à-vis* a culture; of spirituality itself as the basis for a community's rebirth. These themes will reassert themselves as we look more directly at steps to a postmodern spirituality.

II. STEPS TO A POSTMODERN SPIRITUALITY

I would characterize a postmodern spirituality as occurring in five steps.

1. The most critical change between the modern and postmodern era in spirituality has to be the following: the emergence of a living cosmology on which to base a living spirituality. Newton's picture of the universe as a machine; Descartes' dualism between object and subject; Kant's insertion of moral law into our "souls" cut off from the universe; Bacon's dualistic ferocity against nature and women with the assumption that we are not nature—all this rendered authentic mysticism impossible during the modern era. What Max Weber called the "disenchantment of the world" which characterizes the modern era might also be called the death knell of mysticism. The Denial of the Mystic has followed right up to our own day and is evident in both cultural pathologies and in seminary classrooms—Catholic, Protestant and Jewish—where our next generation of presumed spiritual leaders learn next to nothing of their own mystical heritage: where, for example, courses on the Wisdom literature of the Bible, which is the cosmological and mystical literature of the Bible, are practically nonexistent, and where practices in spirituality such as art as meditation are next to invisible. Would-be scientists get academic credit for hours spent in laboratories, but would-be spiritual leaders get no credit for hours spent in art-as-meditation classes where

prayer and mysticism are learned, where the right brain is developed and the link between microcosm and macrocosm is experienced.

Just as it was scientists and their kept philosophers who got us into this antimystical bias, so, ironically, it is scientists who are leading us out of it. It was Einstein himself who said that "mysticism is the basis of all true science" and that "one who cannot stand rapt in awe is as good as dead."[7] Awe is what mysticism is all about—it begins with awe, as Rabbi Abraham Heschel makes clear ("Awe precedes faith" he writes),[8] and as Meister Eckhart declared in his sermon on "amazement."[9]

Cosmology reawakens our awe at being here. "Truly it is glorious, our being here," declares Rilke.[10] For cosmology gives us a story about how we came to be here—a story in the full context of the universe and its coming to be here—and how we fit into that story. Cosmology is thereby three things: it is the scientific story of our being here and our coming to be here (however one defines "scientific"—ancient peoples had their scientific story of how we came to be here); it is mysticism, or our psychic response to the awe of our being here; and it is art, that is, the expression of response to the amazing news that we are here.

Einstein, like Moses of old, has led us from the bondage of Newtonian mechanism to a certain wandering in the desert that may eventually result in a promised land, one flowing with the milk and honey of a living cosmology. In my opinion, it is no accident that Einstein was a Jew and thus had imbibed the Jewish spirituality from Wisdom literature which taught that the "spirit of the Lord fills the whole universe" (Wis. 1:7). Jewish cosmology teaches that the universe is one, and that we are part of it and can know our place in it. It is no secret that premier scientists, such as Nobel Prize winner Ilya Prigogine, Erich Jantsch, Brian Swimme, Fritjof Capra, Loren Eiseley, Alfred North Whitehead, Niels Bohr, and Lewis Thomas, are readmitting the essential mystery of the universe from microcosm (atomic levels) to macrocosm (galactic levels).[11] The fact that the scientific stories being told today are transcultural and that scientists are leading in the telling augurs well for the repollinization of the mystical brain of humanity, for a reenchantment of the universe. As more and more scientists come out of the closet as mystics, more and more other persons will be given the courage to do the same, persons from all professions and ways of life. Even, eventually, the ordained ones. Mysticism means, etymologically, "to enter the mysteries." Science, with the rediscovery of the mystery of nature which comes with it, is today inviting us all to enter the mysteries of our being here. This invitation represents the rebirth of a civilization, the lighting of the fire of a living cosmology.

2. How this translates theologically can be put in the following manner: We need to move from the Quest for the Historical Jesus to the

Quest for the Cosmic Christ. My book, *The Coming of the Cosmic Christ,* goes into considerable depth on this subject, but let me summarize a few salient points.[12] Yale church historian Jaroslav Pelikan, in a recent book, says that the "Enlightenment deposed the Cosmic Christ and made the Quest for the Historical Jesus inevitable."[13] Pelikan's observation stands as a landmark critique of the modern era of Biblical scholarship. All the weapons of theological scholarship during the modern era have been amassed around the quest for the historical Jesus. While this has not been an altogether fruitless task—the agreement on Jesus' words and on his identity as prophet has been useful—it is a task that is for the most part completed.

Were theology to redirect its immense energies around the Quest for the Cosmic Christ, new treasures would be unearthed that are exactly the mystical treasures that a new cosmology requires—treasures about the role of cosmology in the Gospels as well as the Cosmic hymns of the Christian Scriptures; treasures about "deep ecumenism" or the role of the Cosmic Christ in non-Christian spiritual traditions ranging from Israel to Goddess religions to Native American and Eastern religions; treasures about what true worship can and ought to accomplish when it is replaced in the proper setting for worship—namely, a living cosmology; treasures about re-doing relationships between puer and senex, between young and old; treasures about the awakening to folk art and about the awakening of eros, that is, of mystical sexuality, which needs to inspire creativity at all levels of culture and religion. (All these are treated in my book.)

Above all, treasures would be unearthed about the holiness of being, the holiness and theophany of Mother Earth and her amazing accomplishments. In the tradition of the Cosmic Christ—the tradition that every atom and every galaxy is a "glittering, glistening mirror" of Divinity (Hildegard's words)—we have a regrounding of a spirituality of reverence for all being, for all of Mother Earth. We relearn our own dignity and responsibility in the context of our own divinization. "Every creature is a word of God and a book about God," says Meister Eckhart. In this tradition we have the groundwork for an ecological spirituality that is truly transcultural as well. Who ever heard of a Buddhist ocean, a Lutheran sun, a Roman Catholic rainforest or an Islamic cornfield? The Cosmic Christ represents a deep archetype almost totally ignored in the modern era—one that can revitalize religion itself and biblical studies in particular. It once again puts scientist and theologian to work at a common—and worthwhile—task.

3. A third step is the rediscovery of the creation mystics of the Middle Ages. Thomas Kuhn points out that one of the characteristics of

a paradigm shift is that what was previously considered trivial now becomes central.[14] Just as the cosmological texts of the Bible—those of the Wisdom literature—have been considered trivial during the modern era, so too have the mystics of the Middle Ages. But, in fact, the period we call the Middle Ages was the last time the West had a living cosmology and the great mystics of that era therefore have much to teach us today. They all understood the Cosmic Christ theology of which I speak, and they lived it out in prophetic forms of social and institutional renewal. I speak of Hildegard of Bingen, Francis of Assisi, Thomas Aquinas, Mechtild of Magdeburg, Meister Eckhart, Julian of Norwich, and Nicolas of Cusa. The latter has been called by British physicist David Bohm a significant influence on his work. The ignoring in seminary training of Protestants and Catholics today of the living cosmology of which these mystic-prophets boast is a sign of the intellectual decadence bequeathed us by the modern era. Westerners cannot recover our spiritual roots without the gift of these great cosmological mystics of our past and the tradition they represent—a tradition that is thoroughly grounded in Scripture as well as in practice of a personal and a social-justice kind.

4. A fourth step is a deepening of our images of God and our imaging of our relationship with Divinity. One gift of any viable spirituality is to awaken us to living—and often forgotten—images of Divinity. When religion and society become tired, so do their images of God. A spiritual renaissance always involves an awakening to new, although often very ancient, Divine images. Following are a few that the modern era managed to bury for three hundred years.

God as Mother

This ancient image, celebrated in our Scriptures in Second Isaiah and in the Psalms, and deeply developed by the medieval mystics, is essential for a society that wishes to recover the sense of creativity as a Divine activity. "What does God do all day long?" Eckhart asks. He answers: "God gives birth. From all eternity God lies on a maternity bed giving birth."[15] And Julian of Norwich writes: "Just as God is truly our Father, so also is God truly our Mother." God "feels great delight to be our Mother," and "God is the true Father and Mother of Nature and all natures that are made to flow out of God to work the divine will."[16]

God as Below, Not Above

The dominant spiritual symbol during the patriarchal era and the modern era has been that of "climbing Jacob's ladder." Such symbolism reinforces hierarchical ladder-climbing and escape from the earth. I have criticized this symbolism elsewhere in writing of the need to move from "climbing Jacob's ladder to dancing Sarah's circle."[17] The sky god alone cannot awaken the deep levels of creativity and eros for which the modern era has left humanity starving. When Meister Eckhart says that "God is a great underground river that no one can dam up and no one can stop," he is reimaging Divinity for us. Hildegard does the same in painting the divine waters as an "abyss" from which Wisdom arises and the Christ arises, and in painting Sophia as a mermaid—that is, as the goddess Ea or the *magna mater,* the great mother of the sea. [18] To relocate Divinity in the depths of nature and of the self is again to reencourage an entire civilization to listen to its creative powers and to allow those powers to emerge once again. Divinity most emerges from the depths of human creativity. Not surprisingly, this is also the place from which the demonic most readily emerges. When ordinary persons are deprived of their creativity, the creativity of the Pentagon and of wasters of our forests and soil will take over.

Godhead, Not Just God

The tradition of the two sides of Divinity—that of God and that of Godhead—has been roundly ignored in mainline theologizing during the modern era for the same reason that mysticism has been ignored. Divinity is not just God; it is also Godhead. What is the difference? Meister Eckhart says that "God acts but the Godhead does not act."[19] Godhead represents the absolute mystery of Divinity, our deepest origins from which we came and to which we shall return. The Godhead is nonjudgmental; "no one missed me where God ceases to become," says Meister Eckhart.[20] In the Godhead there is total unity and utter silence. There, all things are one. God is that side of Divinity that engages itself in history, in creation, and in itself becomes as creatures themselves become and unfold. "Before creatures were, God was not yet 'God.' "[21] Humans are invited to experience and undergo both sides of the Divinity—God in history as well as the Godhead of mystery. It is more than coincidence, I believe, that the words for "God" in Latin and German are masculine (*Deus* and *Gott,* respectively), while the words for "Godhead" are feminine (*Deitas* and *Gottheit,* respectively). Godhead is a mystical term for Divinity and there is something cosmically maternal about it. "You are hugged by the arms of the mystery of God," declares Hildegard of Bingen.[22] The modern era of spirituality, so committed to patriarchy, lost a sense of the living Godhead.

God as Beauty

The modern era lost the sense of beauty as a theological category and a spiritual experience. Descartes actually developed a philosophy without an aesthetic anywhere to be found in it! Yet Thomas Aquinas and other creation mystics such as Francis of Assisi during the West's cosmological period talked of God as Beauty. "God is the most beautiful thing there is," Aquinas writes. "God is superabundant beauty." [23] Tellingly, Aquinas gets this imaging of Divinity from the Eastern Church, namely from the sixth-century Syrian, Denis the Areopagite. Eastern Orthodoxy never lost the Cosmic Christ and therefore never discounted the experience of Beauty as the experience of Divinity or, indeed, the naming of Beauty as God and God as Beauty.[24] It never succumbed to St. Augustine's ignoring of cosmology that set the West up for the split between science and mysticism which has characterized the modern era.

A Trinitarian Divinity

For all its call to orthodoxy around such doctrines as the Trinity, the modern era of spirituality, driven by and almost obsessed by the quest for the historical Jesus, has itself practically committed a heresy of Christolatry (or better, Jesusolatry). Where is the theological ink spent on God as Creator? Does it in any way balance out the emphasis given "my relationship with Jesus" or our redemption by Jesus? Traditionally, Christians considered three articles of faith as summarized by Luther: (1) Creation, (2) Redemption, and (3) Sanctification (which ought to be understood in the mystical or Cosmic Christ tradition as our divinization). Yet the modern era has so zeroed in on the second of these three that the first and third points are left hanging—and with them the spiritual experience and theological grounding for a God who is Creator and who is Spirit, Sanctifier, or Divinizer. No one could accuse Western Enlightenment theology of developing a theology of the Holy Spirit—which is one reason the West is so easily set up for pseudo-spiritualisms ranging from charismatic flight-from-justice spiritualities to fundamentalist Holy Roller spiritualities. The creation mystics bring a healthy, dialectical, Trinitarian Divinity back to our images and archetypes.

The Cosmic Christ

Perhaps the archetype that most summarizes the very ancient and premodern as well as postmodern images of Divinity is that of the Cosmic Christ. The Cosmic hymns celebrate this Christ as the one "who holds all things in unity" (Col. 1:17), who "sustains the universe by his powerful command" (Heb. 1:3), "in whom all things have their being" (Jn. 1:3), and "who all the living things in creation—everything that lives in the air, and on the ground, and under the ground, and in the sea" praise (Rev. 5:13). The tradition of the Cosmic Christ answers Gregory

Bateson's question, "What is the pattern that connects?"[25] The Cosmic Christ names the pattern that connects as justice, as loving, and as essentially friendly toward the universe and all things, humans included. The Cosmic Christ, then, being the Divine image in every atom and every galaxy, grounds a global morality in reverence for being. As Teilhard de Chardin put it, "Christ, through his Incarnation, is internal to the world, . . . rooted in the world, even the very heart of the tiniest atom."[26] The tradition of the Cosmic Christ also represents the Goddess and Gaia tradition in the West. The Goddess is about Divinity's immanence in all things and in the celebration of creation. So, too, is the tradition of the Cosmic Christ.[27]

Integral to the tradition of the Cosmic Christ has always been a development of the doctrine of sanctification, not in terms of Augustine's neurotic and egotistical question—"Am I saved?"—but in terms of the tradition of our being Cosmic Christs.[28] Are we Divinized and, if so, what is the evidence for it? Mechtild of Magdeburg and other mystics from the medieval era, when a Cosmic Christ theology thrived in the West, are blunt as to our Divinization: It means our being instruments of compassion understood as justice-making and celebration. Says Mechtild: "Who is the Holy Spirit? The Holy Spirit is a compassionate outpouring of the Creator and the Son. This is why when we on earth pour out compassion and mercy from the depths of our hearts and give to the poor and dedicate our bodies to the service of the broken, to that very extent do we resemble the Holy Spirit."[29]

Panentheism

The modern era, in its immense dualism and compulsion to control—even God, and certainly the Goddess—has left us with two options by which to envision humanity's relationship to Divinity. One of these is by way of *theism* (of which Deism is just a logical outcome). Theism teaches that we are here and God is out there somewhere. (Deists simply put God farther out.) One problem with this image of our relationshp with Divinity is that it literally kills the soul, as Jung warned when he said that one way to kill the soul is to "worship a God outside you." It also destroys any semblance of Jesus' teaching—a primary datum of the Quest for the Historical Jesus movement is that Jesus did indeed preach, and that his primary theme was: the "kingdom of God is *among you*."

The second option for imaging the human's relation to the Divine offered up by the modern era has been its widely heralded stance of *atheism*. In many respects, theism asks for atheism and invents it. If the only alternative I had was theism or atheism, I would be an atheist myself.

A God who has wound things up and does not care enough to be present to their unfolding invites not only neglect but denial. I am convinced that 99 percent of atheism in the modern era has in fact been antitheism, which, in my opinion, represents a wise rejection of the only God served up by the modern era.

Other images of our relationship with divinity do exist, however, if one goes back beyond the modern era. One is *pantheism,* which teaches that all is God and God is all. While at first blush this appears to be a Cosmic Christ doctrine, it falls short, because it too ends up controlling Divinity and eliminating Divine surprises and mystery, which carry us beyond what already is. In short, it denies the transcendence of the Divine. For that reason it has rightly been understood as heretical; it arrogates just too much to creation as it stands.

Still another image of our relationship to the Divine is that of *panentheism.* This is, in my opinion, the truly adult, truly mystical, truly appropriate imaging of the Divine/nature relationship (remembering—as the modern era did not—that humans *are* nature). I am not alone in this opinion; all my creation-centered mystical brothers and sisters of the Middle Ages concur. Mechtild of Magdeburg declares that "the day of my spiritual awakening was the day I saw and knew I saw all things in God and God in all things."[30] This is a precise naming of panentheism— "all things in God and God in all things." This perfectly orthodox naming of our relationship to Divinity is alluded to in the vine-and-the-branch imagery of John 15 as well as in Acts, which says "God is the one in whom we live, move and have our being" (Acts 17:28). Meister Eckhart is as strong as I am about the essential need to envision Divinity in panentheistic categories. "Ignorant people falsely imagine," he writes, "that God is outside of things. Everything that God does or creates he does or creates in himself, sees or knows in himself, loves in himself."[31] Hildegard of Bingen actually painted a picture of panentheism, that is, of all of creation existing in the belly of Divinity—a Divinity she called "Love" and a "Lady."[32]

Panentheism is one way of understanding the unfolding of God, for if creatures that exist within Divinity are being constantly created and recreated, then Divinity is also being affected. As Eckhart puts it, "God becomes where all creatures express God."[33] "What is creative," says Eckhart, "flows out but remains within." Creation is itself this way in relation to Divinity.[34] Thus panentheism, while being deeply curved and maternal in its imagery, also allows for the sense of the historical or undeveloped to happen as well. It combines elements of immanence and transcendence. The latter is understood as the "not yet"—not as what is above. Historical transcendence with spatial immanence, one might call this. Another name for it would be a prophetic mysticism or a mystical prophecy, where prophecy means a changing of history, a critique of history, and an interference with history. History and mystery come together in a panentheistic understanding of our relationship to Divinity. Its image is not one of linear "progress" (a heresy of modernistic thinking), nor is it an image of repetitive cycle (an image the East offers too blithely). Rather it is imaged as an ever-expanding spiral.

Panentheism destroys that dualism of dualisms which the modern era has bequeathed to us: The dualism of God/nature and God/us. "Everything that is in God is God," said Thomas Aquinas, citing a twelfth-century Synod.[35] Once again, the tradition of the Cosmic Christ emerges as a dominant archetype in a postmodern spirituality. Panentheism, by picturing our creative relationship to the Creator, also encourages creativity itself. Images of God do that for a civilization—or they do the opposite. Theism kills creativity as a spiritual imitation of Divinity. Panentheism demands it.

5. A fifth step to a postmodern spirituality is to name the mystical journey in Four Paths. It is curious how beholden the modern era's naming of the spiritual journey has been to Plotinus and Proclus, third- and fifth-century individuals who were neither Jewish nor Christian and who named the spiritual journey in the all-too-familiar fashion of the three ways of Purgation, Illumination, and Union. A postmodern spirituality must consciously reject this naming of the spiritual journey not only because it is utterly nonbiblical but also because it does not correspond to the depth-experience that mystics of our time are having. Awe, wonder, delight, creativity and justice are left out. This is a lot to leave out in a time of an awakened cosmology. Let us consider briefly the Four Paths of the Creation Mystical Journey, because they—and not the three ways—will constitute the naming of a postmodern spiritual journey.[36]

Path I: Via Positiva. Our first experience of the Divine is in terms of the delight, awe, and wonder of our being here. "Radical amazement," Rabbi Heschel calls it, and this experience is available to all of us on a daily basis, provided we are ready to undergo such ecstacies—be they in nature, in our work, in relationship, in silence, in art, in love-making, even in times of suffering.[37] "Just to be is a blessing, just to live is holy," says Rabbi Heschel. This intuition that creation is indeed a blessing, and the response of gratitude for it, constitute the experience of the *via positiva.* It is what drives so many scientists, working as they do with the wonders of nature, to mysticism, to what Einstein described as "standing rapt in awe." It is about seeing the Cosmic Christ in all things— including oneself. As Meister Eckhart put it: "When I flowed out of the Creator all creatures stood up and shouted and said 'Behold, here is God!' They were correct."[38]

Path II: Via Negativa. Our second journey into the mystery of Divinity and ourselves is that of experiencing the darkness—of letting go and letting be. In this movement, we "sink eternally from letting go to letting go into God," as Meister Eckhart puts it.[39] The sinking may be through meditation practices that allow us to let go of sensory input, such as fasting, Zen sitting, celibacy, or sweat lodges. Such letting-go leads to a return to our source, a return to our origins. A letting-go of words and images is essential to this journey; it is essential to a postmodern spiritual practice because so much of the modern era is wordy (part of the price we pay no doubt for an awakening of the left brain and for a patriarchal and "enlightenment" era that has been radically afraid of the dark, afraid of silence, afraid of what cannot be controlled).

Another way we undergo the *via negativa* is by way of suffering and pain. Letting pain be pain is an essential ingredient in learning from pain and in experiencing the dark. It is also essential for letting go of pain, as Mechtild of Magdeburg put it: "From suffering I have learned this: That whoever is sore wounded by love will never be made whole unless she embrace the very same love which wounded her."[40] The "dark night of the soul," the time when, in Mechtild's words, "the lantern burns out and we are reminded of our nothingness,"[41] can be a bottoming-out experience of immense spiritual depth and a source for new birth. God is not only a God of light (cataphatic Divinity of Path I) but also "superessential darkness," as Eckhart puts it (the apophatic Divinity). In many ways the Divinity we experience in Path I is God, while the Divinity of Path II is the Godhead, which is a "mystery within mystery who has no name and will never be given a name."[42]

Path III: Via Creativa. The modern era did not highlight creativity as a moral imperative, as the basic spiritual discipline, or as the most important ingredient of a living cosmology. Yet that is what is required in a postmodern era, one that carries us beyond the notion that the universe is already completed or is a machine in motion. In the creation mystical tradition the center of the spiritual journey is Creativity itself. Paths I and II—our experiences of Delight and of Darkness—culminate in Path III—Creativity. (And Path IV, as we shall see below, flows out from Path III.) From the point of view of Christian theology, the Incarnation and Creation, which constitute Path I, plus the Crucifixion and Kenosis (emptying), which constitute Path II, culminate in the Resurrection—the creative rebirth of Path III.

Creativity lies at the core of the creation journey because this is what it means to be Divinized or sanctified, namely to be *like God*. But who is God? God is Creator, God is constant birther of the universe and we are called to be co-creators with God. We birth, for example, the Cosmic Christ who is uniquely us when we birth ourselves. The primary spiritual practice in creation spirituality is that of art as meditation, wherein we come to grips with our images: trusting them, birthing them, accepting responsibility for them and taking the consequences of them.[44] Delight itself is one of the consequences of birthing our images. Meister Eckhart declares that it is good to be a virgin, namely one emptied of images (*via negativa*), but it is better to be a "fruitful wife."[44] For it is "by our fruits that they will know us," as Jesus warns about testing the spirits of mysticism.

When Meister Eckhart celebrates how we are "heirs of the fearful creative power of God,"[45] he is naming the *via creativa* for us. Our creativity is truly fearful, because it can lead to more weapons bent on destroying the earth, on the one hand, or on recreating jobs and society, on the other. Our Divine power—Creativity—is also our demonic power. Human choice is never of greater consequence than in the journey of the *via creativa*. It is in our creativity that we are called to choose between images. A fascist society would have us always choose *their* images—those of the ruling elite. But art as meditation grounds persons to listen to and then to choose their own deepest images; it grounds persons to know their treasure—which is hidden in the field of our psyches—and to cherish it, choose it, and put it out there. As Eckhart puts it, "what is true cannot come from the outside in but must come from the inside out and pass through an inner form."[46]

It is no small thing that contemporary science has reestablished creativity and generativity as being a basic law in the universe and that, at the same time, we rediscover the creation-centered mystical tradition that insists that our entire spiritual journey culminates in what we give birth to. Here we have a powerful instance of the rebirth of a cosmology: science and mysticism agreeing on the importance of creativity once again.

Path IV: Via Transformativa. While Creativity lies at the heart of the universe and at the heart of the human psyche and spiritual journey, it finds its fullest expression in the transformation of society itself. This transformation is an issue of *compassion,* the response to an interdependent universe in which "all beings love one another" (Eckhart).[47] Because of this fact, celebration and justice-making are meant to reign as the basis of all political action and structure. The spiritual journey culminates in compassion, as in Jesus' words, "be you compassionate as your Creator in heaven is compassionate" (Lk. 6:36). And compassion means both celebration and healing by way of justice-making. Path IV constitutes a Theology of the Holy Spirit, because the Holy Spirit is the Spirit who annoints all as prophets to "interfere" (Heschel's words) with the causes of injustice and its multiple expressions in racism, sexism, militarism, adultism, impersonal capitalism, and impersonal socialism. As the Holy Spirit worked to end the babbling symbolized by the Tower of Babel at the original Pentecost event, when persons of all races and countries and cultures understood the Good News, so too this same Spirit works to bring persons together today around Good News of humanity's power and responsibility to heal Mother Earth, to celebrate our shared existence, and to revere creation.

Justice-making lies so at the core of the creation journey that Meister Eckhart could declare, "the person who understands what I say about justice understands everything I have to say."[48] Justice, after all, is not an anthropocentric invention any more than is interdependence or compassion. Rather, in a living cosmology, justice as well as interdependence are laws of the universe and *therefore* (versus Kant) laws by which humanity ought to be living. A living cosmology regrounds humankind's politics in the laws of the universe. This is the primary gift that wisdom brings. The modern era has sought knowledge, not wisdom. A postmodern spirituality seeks wisdom along with its knowledge.

The four paths of the creation journey never end. They constitute the dynamic of the ever-expanding spiral journey on which we embark our whole life. As Eckhart says, "God is delighted to watch your soul enlarge."[49]

III. TOWARD A POSTMODERN SPIRITUALITY:
A SUMMARY

We can summarize the paradigm shift from modern to postmodern spirituality in terms of the following elements:

1. From anthropocentric to cosmological
2. From theistic (and deistic and atheistic) to panentheistic
3. From left brain (analytic) to both left brain *and* right brain (synthetic)
4. From rationalistic to mystical
5. From patriarchal to feminist
6. From the Quest for the Historical Jesus to the Quest for the Cosmic Christ
7. From knowledge to wisdom
8. From the three paths of Plotinus and Proclus to the four paths of Creation Spirituality

9. From linear to spiral
10. From a modern naming to an inclusion of premodern, modern, and postmodern spiraling
11. From climbing Jacob's ladder to dancing Sarah's circle
12. From obedience as the dominant virtue to creativity in birthing compassion as the dominant societal and personal virtue
13. From the sectarianism and piece-mealness of the Newtonian parts-mentality to the deep ecumenism of an era of the Cosmic Christ in all world religions
14. From dualism (either/or) to dialectic (both/and)
15. From sentimentalism to a passionate embrace of awe at our existence
16. From a flight from the world to a commitment to social and personal transformation
17. From Eurocentrism to a celebration of the wisdom of ancient and primordial peoples' spiritualities of micro/macrocosm
18. From worship as words—read, preached, and sung—to worship as a nonelitist celebration of our shared existence
19. From Divinity in the sky to Divinity of Mother Earth crucified.

Scientist Gregory Bateson asked in his last book the following question: "Is the human race rotting its mind from a slowly deteriorating religion and education?"[50] If our minds are being rotted by religion itself, it is because religion has lost its very core, which is the experience of a mystical cosmology. The same is true of education. Religion needs science and science needs religion, as Einstein insisted. The best hope for our planet is a recovery of a living, mystical cosmology. That can happen as we let the modern era recede, by incorporating a celebration of the mystical along with a celebration of the analytical. In this way we would be moving to a postmodern spirituality such as I have attempted to outline in this essay. And we as a species would experience a rebirth of art, politics and spirituality, which would constitute an authentic global renaissance.[51]

NOTES

1. See William Hocking, *The Meaning of God in Human Experience* (New Haven: Yale University Press, 1912).

2. Writes cosmologist/physicist Brian Swimme: "We sometimes fall into the delusion that power is elsewhere, that it belongs to a different group, that we are unable to find access to it. Nothing could be further from the truth. The universe oozes with power, waiting for anyone who wishes to embrace it. But because the powers of cosmic dynamics are invisible, we need to remind our-

selves of their universal presence. Who reminds us? The rivers, plains, galaxies, hurricanes, lightning branches, and all our living companions" (*The Universe is a Green Dragon* [Santa Fe, N.M.: Bear & Co., 1985], 151).

3. A fine example of a feminist critique of power is that of Adrienne Rich, *The Dream of a Common Language* (New York: W.W. Norton, 1978).

4. For critical studies of this sentimentalizing of mass culture in the modern era, see Anne Douglas, *The Feminization of American Culture* (New York: Alfred Knopf, 1977), and Matthew Fox, "On Desentimentalizing Spirituality," *Spirituality Today,* March 1978: 64-76.

5. On the vital role of worship in connecting micro- and macrocosm, see Otto Rank, *Art and Artist* (New York: Agathon Press, 1932), 113-15.

6. M.D. Chenu says that renaissance "literally involves new birth, new existence in all the changed conditions of times, places, and persons" (*Nature, Man and Society in the Twelfth Century* [Chicago: University of Chicago Press, 1968], 3).

7. Albert Einstein, *Ideas and Opinions* (New York: Crown Publishers, 1982), 39, 11.

8. Abraham Heschel, *God in Search of Man* (New York: Farrar, Straus, and Cudahy, 1955), 77. See the excellent study of "Wonder and Awe" in Heschel's thought in John C. Merkle, *The Genesis of Faith: The Depth Theology of Abraham Joshua Heschel* (New York: Macmillan, 1985), 153-72.

9. See Meister Eckhart, Sermon Two, in Matthew Fox, ed., *Breakthrough: Meister Eckhart's Creation Spirituality in New Translation* (Garden City, N.Y.: Doubleday, 1980), 65-67 (henceforth abbreviated *BR*).

10. Stephen Mitchell, trans., *The Selected Poetry of Rainer Maria Rilke* (New York: Vintage, 1984), 189.

11. Isabelle Stengers and Nobel Prize winner Ilya Prigogine say: "Today the balance is strongly shifting toward a revival of mysticism, be it in the press media or even in science itself, especially among cosmologists" (Ilya Prigogine and Isabelle Stengers, *Order Out of Chaos* [New York: Bantam Books, 1984], 34).

12. See Matthew Fox, *The Coming of the Cosmic Christ* (San Francisco: Harper & Row, 1988).

13. Jaroslav Pelikan, *Jesus through the Centuries* (New Haven: Yale University Press, 1985), 182.

14. Thomas S. Kuhn, *The Structure of Scientific Revolutions* (Chicago: University of Chicago Press, 1970), 103.

15. Matthew Fox, *Meditations with Meister Eckhart* (Santa Fe, N.M.: Bear & Co., 1982), 88.

16. Brendan Doyle, *Meditations with Julian of Norwich* (Santa Fe, N.M.: Bear & Co., 1983), 71, 75.

17. For a fuller discussion of this basic mystical symbol change, see Matthew Fox, *A Spirituality Named Compassion* (San Francisco: Harper & Row, 1979), 36-67.

18. See Matthew Fox, *Illuminations of Hildegard of Bingen* (Santa Fe, N.M.; Bear & Co., 1985), 70-73.

19. See *BR*, 78.

20. *Ibid.*, 77.

21. *Ibid.*, 215.

22. Gabrielle Uhlein, *Meditations with Hildegard of Bingen* (Santa Fe, N.M.: Bear & Co., 1982), 90.

23. Thomas Aquinas, *De divinis nominibus,* c. IV, 1.v, nn. 343-56.

24. Nicholas Berdyaev, writing from the Russian Orthodox tradition, declares that "the beauty of a dance, a poem, a symphony or a picture enters into eternal life. Art is not passive, but active, and in a sense theurgic [i.e., a work of co-creation with God]" (*Slavery and Freedom* [New York: Charles Scribner's Sons, 1939], 171-72).

25. See Gregory Bateson, *Mind and Nature: A Necessary Unity* (New York: Bantam Books, 1979), 8-10.

26. See the excellent study by J.A. Lyons, *The Cosmic Christ in Origen and Teilhard de Chardin* (Oxford: Oxford University Press, 1982).

27. See Charlene Spretnak, *Lost Goddesses of Early Greece* (Boston: Beacon Press, 1978), 42-47.

28. Krister Stendahl says that Augustine "was the first person in Antiquity or in Christianity to write something so self-centered as his own spiritual autobiography. . . . With Augustine, Western Christianity with its stress on introspective achievements started. . . . The introspective conscience is a Western development and a Western plague" (*Paul among Jews and Gentiles* [Philadelphia: Fortress Press, 1976], 16-17).

29. Sue Woodruff, *Meditations with Mechtild of Magdeburg* (Santa Fe, N.M.: Bear & Co., 1982), 117 (henceforth abbreviated *Mechtild*). Compassion is also the ultimate Divine attribute for Meister Eckhart and the culmination of the spiritual journey, because "whatever God does the first outburst is always compassion" (see *BR* 417-546).

30. *Mechtild,* 42.

31. *BR,* 73.

32. *Illuminations of Hildegard of Bingen,* 38-41.

33. *BR,* 77.

34. *Ibid.,* 65.

35. Thomas Aquinas, *Compendium theologiae,* 37, 41. The synod referred to is the Synod of Rheims, held in 1148.

36. I elaborate at length on the Four Paths and Twenty-Six Themes of creation spirituality in my *Original Blessing* (Santa Fe, N.M.: Bear & Co., 1983). On Eckhart's outlining of the Four Paths, see my "Meister Eckhart on the Fourfold Path of a Creation-Centered Spiritual Journey," in Matthew Fox, ed., *Western Spirituality: Historical Roots, Ecumenical Routes* (Santa Fe, N.M.: Bear & Co., 1981), 215-48.

37. For a fuller elaboration of natural ecstacies, see Matthew Fox, *Whee! We, wee All the Way Home: A Guide to a Sensual, Prophetic Spirituality* (Santa Fe, N.M.: Bear & Co., 1981), 43-54.

38. *BR,* 302.

39. *Ibid.,* 174.

40. *Mechtild,* 69.

41. *Ibid.,* 61.

42. *BR,* 175.

43. See Matthew Fox, "The Case for Extrovert Meditation," in *Spirituality Today,* June, 1978: 164-77, and Mary Richards, *Centering* (Middletown, Conn.: Wesleyan University Press, 1964).

44. *BR,* 274.

45. *Ibid.,* 405.

46. *Ibid.,* 399.

47. Matthew Fox, *Meditations with Meister Eckhart,* 26.

48. *Ibid.,* 5.

49. *BR,* 146.

50. Bateson, *Mind and Nature,* 109.

51. For more on this global renaissance, see my *The Coming of the Cosmic Christ.*

3

THE ECOLOGICAL SELF: POSTMODERN GROUND FOR RIGHT ACTION

Joanna Macy

In a recent lecture on a college campus, I gave examples of actions being undertaken in defense of life on Earth—actions in which people risk their comfort and even their lives to protect other species. The examples included the Chipko, or "tree-hugging," movement among North Indian villagers to fight the lumbering of their remaining wood-lands, and the Greenpeace organization's intervention on the open seas to protect marine mammals from slaughter. A student, Michael, wrote me afterwards:

> I think of the tree-huggers hugging my trunk, blocking the chainsaws with their bodies, I feel their fingers digging into my bark to stop the steel and let me breathe.
> I hear the bodhisattvas[1] in their rubber boats as they put them-selves between the harpoons and me, so I can escape to the depths of the sea. . . .

Members of the Chipko Movement in Indian Himalayas. (Photo courtesy of Rainforest Action Network, San Francisco.)

I give thanks for your life and mine ... and for life itself. I give thanks for realizing that I, too, have the powers of the tree-huggers and the bodhisattvas.

What strikes me in his words is the shift in identification. Michael is able to extend his sense of self to encompass the self of tree, of whale. Tree and whale are no longer removed, separate, disposable objects pertaining to a world "out there" but intrinsic parts of his own vitality. Through the power of his caring, his experience of self is expanded far beyond what Alan Watts termed the "skin-encapsulated ego."

I quote Michael's words not because they are unusual. On the contrary, they express a desire and a capacity arising in many people today as, out of deep concern over what is happening to our world, they begin to speak and act on its behalf.

Among those who are moving beyond conventional notions of self and self-interest, shedding them like an old skin or confining shell, is John Seed, director of the Rainforest Information Center in Australia. I asked him one day how he managed to overcome despair and sustain the struggle against the giant lumber interests. He said, "I try to remember that it's not me, John Seed, trying to protect the rainforest. Rather, I am part of the rainforest protecting myself, I am that part of the rainforest recently emerged into human thinking."

This ecological sense of selfhood combines the mystical and the pragmatic. Transcending separateness and fragmentation, in a shift that Seed calls a "spiritual change," it generates an experience of profound interconnectedness with all life. This has in the past been largely relegated to the domain of mystics and poets. Now it is, at the same time, a motivation to action. The shift in identity serves as ground and resource for effective engagement with the forces and pathologies that imperil planetary survival.

A variety of factors converge in our time to promote such a shift in the sense of self and self-interest. Among the most significant are 1) the psychological and spiritual pressures exerted by current dangers of mass annihilation, 2) the emergence from science of the systems view of the world, and 3) a renaissance of nondualistic forms of spirituality.

This essay explores the role of these three factors—planetary peril, systems thinking, and nondualistic religion, specifically Buddhist teachings and practice—in promoting this shift. It is written from a conviction that a larger, ecological sense of self will characterize the postmodern world, and that without it there simply may *be* no postmodern world.

I. PERSONAL RESPONSE TO PLANETARY CRISIS

The shift toward a wider, ecological sense of self is in large part a function of the dangers that threaten to overwhelm us. Given accelerating environmental destruction and massive deployment of nuclear weapons, people today are aware that they live in a world that can end. For example, public opinion polls indicate that over half the population expects nuclear weapons to be used, and two thirds believe that once they are used, the resultant nuclear war cannot be limited, won, or survived.[2] The loss of certainty that there will be a future is, I believe, the pivotal psychological reality of our time.

Over the past ten years my colleagues and I have worked with tens of thousands of people in North America, Europe, Asia, and Australia, helping them confront and explore what they know and feel about what is happening to their world. The purpose of this work, known as Despair and Empowerment Work, is to overcome the numbing and powerlessness that result from suppression of painful responses to massively painful realities.[3]

As their grief and fear for the world is allowed to be expressed without apology or argument and validated as a wholesome, life-preserving response, people break through their avoidance mechanisms, break through their sense of futility and isolation. And generally what they break through *into* is a larger sense of identity. It is as if the pressure of their acknowledged awareness of the suffering of our world stretches, or collapses, the culturally defined boundaries of the self.

It becomes clear, for example, that the grief and fear experienced for our world and our common future are categorically different from similar sentiments relating to one's personal welfare. This pain cannot be equated with dread of one's own individual demise. Its source lies less in concerns for personal survival than in apprehensions of collective suffering—of what looms for human life and other species and unborn generations to come. Its nature is akin to the original meaning of compassion—"suffering with." It is the distress we feel on behalf of the larger whole of which we are a part. And, when it is so defined, it serves as trigger or gateway to a more encompassing sense of identity, inseparable from the web of life in which we are as intricately interconnected as cells in a larger body.

This shift is an appropriate, adaptive response. For the crisis that threatens our planet, be it seen in its military, ecological, or social aspects, derives from a dysfunctional and pathogenic notion of the self. It is a mistake about our place in the order of things. It is the delusion that the self is so separate and fragile that we must delineate and defend its boundaries, that it is so small and needy that we must endlessly acquire and endlessly consume, that it is so aloof that we can—as individuals, corporations, nation-states or as a species—be immune to what we do to other beings.

Such a view of the human condition is not new, nor is the felt imperative to extend self-interest to embrace the whole in any way novel to our history as a species. It has been enjoined by many a teacher and saint. What is notable in our present situation, and in the Despair and Empowerment Work we have done, is that the extension of identity can come directly, not through exhortations to nobility or altruism, but through the owning of pain. That is why the shift in the sense of self is credible to those experiencing it. As poet Theodore Roethke said, "I believe my pain."

Despair and Empowerment Work draws on both General Systems Theory and Buddhist teachings and practice. Both of these approaches inform our methods and offer explanatory principles in the move beyond ego-based identifications. Let us look at them in turn to see how they serve the shift to the ecological self.

II. CYBERNETICS OF THE SELF

The findings of twentieth-century science undermine the notion of a separate self, distinct from the world it observes and acts upon. As Einstein showed, the self's perceptions are shaped by its changing position in relation to other phenomena. And these phenomena are affected not only by location but, as Heisenberg demonstrated, by the very act of observation. Now contemporary systems science and systems cybernetics go yet further in challenging old assumptions about a distinct, separate, continuous self, showing that there is no logical or scientific basis for construing one part of the experienced world as "me" and the rest as "other."

As open, self-organizing systems, our very breathing, acting, and thinking arise in interaction with our shared world through the currents of matter, energy, and information that flow through us. In the web of relationships that sustain these activities, there are no clear lines demarcating a separate, continuous self. As postmodern systems theorists aver, there is no categorical "I" set over against a categorical "you" or "it."

Systems philosopher Ervin Laszlo argues,

> We must do away with the subject-object distinction in analyzing experience. This does not mean that we reject the concepts

of organism and environment, as handed down to us by natural science. It only means that we conceive of experience as linking organism and environment in a continuous chain of events, from which we cannot, without arbitrariness, abstract an entity called organism and another called environment.[4]

The abstraction of a separate "I" is what Gregory Bateson calls the "epistemological fallacy of Occidental civilization." He asserts that the larger system of which we are a part defies any definitive localization of the self. That which decides and does can no longer be neatly identified with the isolated subjectivity of the individual or located within the confines of his or her skin. "The total self-corrective unit which processes information, or, as I say, 'thinks' and 'acts' and 'decides,' is a *system* whose boundaries do not at all coincide with the boundaries either of the body or of what is popularly called the 'self' or 'consciousness'."[5]

"The self as ordinarily understood," Bateson goes on to say,

is only a small part of a much larger trial-and-error system which does the thinking, acting and deciding. This system includes all the informational pathways which are relevant at any given moment to any given decision. The 'self' is a false reification of an improperly delimited part of this much larger field of interlocking processes.[6]

The false reification of the self is basic to the planetary ecological crisis in which we now find ourselves. We have imagined that the "unit of survival," as Bateson puts it, is the separate individual or the separate species. In reality, as throughout the history of evolution, it is the individual *plus* environment, the species *plus* environment, for they are essentially symbiotic. Bateson continues:

When you narrow down your epistemology and act on the premise "What interests me is me, or my organization, or my species," you chop off consideration of other loops of the loop structure. You decide you want to get rid of the by-products of human life and that Lake Erie will be a good place to put them. You forget that the eco-mental system called Lake Erie is a part of *your* wider eco-mental system—and that if Lake Erie is driven insane, its insanity is incorporated in the larger system of *your* thought and experience.[7]

Although we consist of and are sustained by the currents of information, matter, and energy that flow through us, we are accustomed to identifying ourselves with only that small arc of the flow-through that is lit, like the narrow beam of a flashlight, by our individual perceptions. But we do not *have* to so limit our self-perceptions. It is as logical, Bateson contends, to conceive of mind as the entire "pattern that connects." It is as plausible to align our identity with that larger pattern and conceive of ourselves as interexistent with all beings, as it is to break off one segment of the process and build our borders there.

Systems Theory helps us see that the larger identification of which we speak does not involve an eclipse of the distinctiveness of one's individual experience. The "pattern that connects" is not an ocean of Brahman where separate drops merge and our diversities dissolve. Natural and cognitive systems self-organize and interact to create larger wholes precisely through their heterogeneity. By the same token, through the dance of deviation-amplifying feedback loops, the respective particularities of the interactive systems can increase. Integration and differentiation go hand in hand. Uniformity, by contrast, is entropic, the kiss of death.

The systems view of the world, unfortunately, has not characterized or informed the uses our society has made of systems science. The advances permitted by its perceptions of pattern and its models of circuitry have been mainly employed to further values and goals inherited from a mechanistic, reductionistic interpretation of reality. Systems thinker Milady Cardamone hypothesizes that it is the feminine-like quality of the systems approach that has kept our society from fully grasping this wholistic style of perceiving the universe.[8]

Molecular biologist and Nobel Prize winner Barbara McClintock reveals, however, how practical and revolutionary the results can be when science is done from the perspective of the ecological self. Her discovery of the interactive nature of the cell, as opposed to the previously accepted master control theory, came out of her ability to see the cell and feel herself as part of the system. "I actually felt as if I were down there and these [internal parts of the chromosomes] were my friends."[9]

III. THE BOUNDLESS HEART OF THE BODHISATTVA

In the resurgence of nondualistic spiritualities in our postmodern world, Buddhism in its historic coming to the West is distinctive in the clarity and sophistication it offers in understanding the dynamics of the self. In much the same way as General Systems Theory does, its ontology and epistemology undermine any categorical distinctions definitive of a self-existent identity. And it goes further than systems cybernetics, both in revealing the pathogenic character of any reifications of the self and in offering methods for transcending them.

Bronze Buddha from Tibet, making the gesture of "Calling the Earth to Witness." (Photo courtesy of Hilary F. Marckx, ©1988.)

Dependent co-arising (*pratitya samutpada*), the core teaching of the Buddha on the nature of causality, presents a phenomenal reality so dynamic and interrelated that categorical subject-object distinctions dissolve. This is driven home in the doctrine of *anatman* or "no-self," where one's sense of identity is understood as an ephemeral product of perceptual transactions, and where the experiencer is inseparable from his or her experience. The notion of an abiding individual self—whether saintly or sinful, whether it is to be protected, promoted or punished—is seen as the foundational delusion of human life. It is the motive force behind our attachments and aversions, and these in turn exacerbate it. As portrayed symbolically in the center of the Buddhist Wheel of Life, where pig, cock, and snake pursue each other endlessly, these three—greed, hatred, and the delusion of ego—sustain and aggravate each other in a continuous vicious circle, or positive feedback loop.

We are not doomed to a perpetual rat-race; the vicious circle can be broken, its energies liberated to more satisfying uses by the threefold interplay of wisdom, meditative practice, and moral action. Wisdom (*prajna*) arises, reflected and generated by the teachings about self and reality. Practice (*dhyana*) liberates through precise attention to the elements and flow of one's existential experience—an experience which reveals no separate experience, no permanent self. And moral behavior (*sila*), according to precepts of nonviolence, truthfulness, and generosity, helps free one from the dictates of greed, aversion, and other reactions which reinforce the delusion of separate selfhood.

Far from the nihilism and escapism often attributed to Buddhism, the path it offers can bring the world into sharper focus and liberate one into lively, effective action. What emerges, when free from the prison cell of the separate, competitive ego, is a vision of radical and sustaining interdependence. In Hua Yen Buddhism it is imaged as the Jeweled Net of Indra: a cosmic canopy where each of us—each jewel at each node of the net—reflects all the others and reflects the others reflecting back. As in the holographic view in contemporary science, each part *contains* the whole.

Each one of us who perceives that, or is capable of perceiving it, is a *bodhisattva*—an "awakening being"—the hero model of the Buddhist tradition. We are all *bodhisattvas*, able to recognize and act upon our profound interexistence with all beings. That true nature is already evident in our pain for the world, which is a function of the *mahakaruna,* great compassion. And it flowers through the *bodhisattva's* "boundless heart" in active identification with all beings.

Christina Feldman, like many other women Buddhist teachers today, points out that this bodhisattva heart is absolutely central to spiritual

practice. It is more transformative of ego and more generative of connection than the desire to be perfect, pure, or aloof from suffering. It is
already within us, like a larger self awaiting discovery.

> We find ourselves forsaking the pursuit of personal perfec-
> tion and also the denial of imperfection. To become someone dif-
> ferent, to pursue a model of personal perfection is no longer the
> goal. . . . Learning to listen inwardly, we learn to listen to our world
> and to each other. We hear the pain of the alienated, the sick, the
> lonely, the angry, and we rejoice in the happiness, the fulfillment,
> the peace of others. We are touched deeply by the pain of our
> planet, equally touched by the perfection of a bud unfolding. . . .
> We learn to respect the heart for its power to connect us on a
> fundamental level with each other, with nature and with all life.[10]

The experience of interconnection with all life can sustain our social
change work far better than righteous partisanship; that is the teaching
of Vietnamese Zen monk Thich Nhat Hanh. In Vietnam during the 1960s,
he founded Youth for Social Service, whose members rescued and aided
homeless, hungry, and wounded villagers on both sides of the war. From
their ranks he created a nonmonastic Order called Tiep Hien, now
gradually spreading in the West under the name Interbeing.

I take his poem "Call Me by My True Names" as an expression of
the ecological self. To quote a few lines:

> Do not say that I'll depart tomorrow
> because even today I still arrive.

> Look at me: I arrive in every second
> to be a bud on a spring branch,
> to be a tiny bird. . . in my new nest,
> to be a caterpillar in the heart of a flower,
> to be a jewel hiding itself in a stone.

> The rhythm of my heart is the birth and death
> of all that are alive. . . .

> I am the frog swimming happily
> in the clear water of a pond,
> and I am also the grass snake who,
> approaching in silence, feeds itself on the frog. . . .

I am the 12-year-old girl, refugee on a small boat,
who throws herself into the ocean
after being raped by a sea pirate.
I am also the pirate,
my heart not yet capable of seeing and loving. . . .

Please call me by my true names
so that I can hear all my cries and my laughs at once
so that I can see that my joy and my pain are one. . . .

Please call me by my true names
so that I can wake up. . . .[11]

IV. BEYOND ALTRUISM

What Bateson called "the pattern that connects" and Buddhists image as
the Jeweled Net of Indra can be construed in lay, secular terms as our
deep ecology. "Deep ecology" is a term coined by Norwegian philosopher Arne Naess to connote a basic shift in ways of seeing and valuing.
It represents an apprehension of reality that he contrasts with "shallow
environmentalism"—the band-aid approach applying technological fixes
for short-term human goals.

The perspective of deep ecology helps us to recognize our embeddedness in nature, overcoming our alienation from the rest of creation and
regaining an attitude of reverence for all life forms. It can change the way
that the self is experienced through a spontaneous process of ever-widen-
ing identification. It launches one on a process of self-realization, where
the self-to-be-realized extends further and further beyond the separate
ego and includes more and more of the phenomenal world. In this process, notions like altruism and moral duty are left behind. Naess explains:

Altruism implies that ego sacrifices its interests in favor of
the other, the *alter*. . . . The motivation is primarily that of duty. . . .
What humankind is capable of loving from mere duty or more
generally from moral exhortation is unfortunately very limited. . . .
Unhappily the extensive moralizing within the environmental movement has given the public the false impression that we primarily
ask them to sacrifice, to show more responsibility, more concern,
and better morals. . . . The requisite care flows naturally if the self
is widened and deepened so that protection of free nature is felt
and conceived of as protection of ourselves.[12]

Please note: Virtue is not required for the emergence of the ecological self! This shift in identification is essential to our survival at this point in our history precisely because it can serve in lieu of ethics and morality. Moralizing is ineffective; sermons seldom hinder us from pursuing our self-interest as we construe it. Hence the need to be more enlightened about what our real self-interest is. It would not occur to me, for example, to exhort you to refrain from sawing off your leg. That would not occur to me or to you, because your leg is part of you. Well, so are the trees in the Amazon Basin; they are our external lungs. We are just beginning to wake up to that, gradually discovering that the world *is* our body.

Economist Hazel Henderson sees our survival dependent on a shift in consciousness from "phenotype" to "genotype." The former, she says, springs from fear of the death of the ego and the consequent conflict between the perceived individual will and the requirements of society or biosphere.

We may be emerging from the "age of the phenotype," of separated ego awareness, which has now become amplified into untenable forms of dualism. ... The emerging view is rebalancing toward concern for the genotype, protection of species and gene pools and for the mutagenic dangers of nuclear radiation, chemical wastes and the new intergenerational risks being transferred to our progeny, about which economics says little.[13]

V. Grace and Power

The ecological self, like any notion of selfhood, is a metaphoric construct, and a dynamic one. It involves choice. Choices can be made to identify at different moments with different dimensions or aspects of our systemically interconnected existence—be they hunted whales or homeless humans or the planet itself. In so doing, this extended self brings into play wider resources—resources, say, of courage, wisdom, endurance—like a nerve cell opening to the charge of fellow neurons in the neural net. For example, in his work on behalf of the rainforest, John Seed felt empowered *by* the rainforest.

There is the experience then of being acted "through" and sustained "by" something greater than oneself. It is close to the religious concept of grace, but, as distinct from the traditional Western understanding of grace, it does not require belief in God or supernatural agency. One simply finds oneself empowered to act on behalf of other beings—or on behalf of the larger whole—and the empowerment itself seems to come "through" that or those for whose sake one acts.

This phenomenon, when approached from the perspective of Systems Theory, is understandable in terms of synergy. It springs from the self-organizing nature of life. It stems from the fact that living systems evolve in complexity and intelligence through their interactions. These interactions, which can be mental or physical, and which can operate at a distance through transmission of information, require openness and sensitivity on the part of the system in order to process the flow-through of energy and information. The interactions bring into play new responses and new possibilities. This interdependent release of fresh potential is called "synergy." And it is like grace, because it brings an increase of power beyond one's own capacity as a separate entity.

As we awaken, then, to our larger, ecological self, we find new powers. We find possibilities of vast efficacy, undreamed of in our squirrel cage of separate ego. Because these potentialities are interactive in nature, they are the preserve and property of no one, and they manifest only to the extent that we recognize and act upon our interexistence, our deep ecology.

As David Griffin wrote of the emerging postmodern world in his introduction to an earlier volume in this series, "the modern desire to master and possess is replaced in postmodern spirituality with a joy in communion."[14] That joy in communion is, I believe, a homecoming to our natural interexistence with all life forms, home to our deep ecology, home to the world as Dharmabody of the Buddha. And it brings with it the capacity to act with courage and resilience.

NOTES

1. A term in Buddhism for a compassionate being.

2. See *Voter Options on Nuclear Arms Policy* (Public Agenda Foundation, 1984).

3. See my *Despairwork* (Philadelphia: New Society Publishers, 1982) and *Despair and Personal Power in the Nuclear Age* (Philadelphia: New Society Publishers, 1983, 1988).

4. Ervin Laszlo, *Introduction to Systems Philosophy* (New York: Harper & Row Torchbook, 1973), 21.

5. Gregory Bateson, *Steps to an Ecology of Mind* (New York: Ballantine Books, 1972), 319.

6. *Ibid.,* 331.

7. *Ibid.,* 484.

8. Milady Cardamone, "The Feminine Aspect of the Systems Approach," *Proceedings of the Annual Meeting of the Society of General Systems Research* (Louisville, Ky.: Society for General Systems Research, 1987), F-44.

9. Evelyn Fox Keller, "Women, Science and Popular Mythology," in Joan Rothschild, ed., *Machina Ex Dea* (London: Pergamon Press, 1983), 143.

10. Christina Feldman, "Nurturing Compassion," in Fred Eppsteiner, ed., *The Path of Compassion* (Berkeley, Calif.: Parallax Press, 1988), 20-21.

11. Fred Eppsteiner, ed., *The Path of Compassion* (Berkeley, Calif.: Parallax Press, 1988), 31.

12. From an unpublished brochure by John Seed. See also Arne Naess, "Identification as a Source of Deep Ecological Attitudes," and "Self Realization: An Ecological Approach to Being in the World," in John Seed, Joanna Macy, Arne Naess, and Pat Fleming, ed., *Thinking Like A Mountain: Toward A Council of All Beings* (Philadelphia: New Society Publishers, 1988).

13. See Hazel Henderson, "Beyond the Information Age," *Creation,* March/April 1988: 34-35.

14. "Introduction: Postmodern Spirituality and Society," David Ray Griffin, ed., *Spirituality and Society: Postmodern Visions* (Albany: State University of New York Press, 1988), 1-31, esp. 15.

4

THE ONLY SURVIVABLE WORLD: A POSTMODERN SYSTEMS APPROACH TO A RELIGIOUS INTUITION

Bernard J. Lee

I. INTRODUCTION

Jesus seems to have sensed with pressing perspicacity the interconnected-ness of all human lives as a necessary result of who God is for us. The intuition was not without cost for him both internally and externally as he tried to respond with his life. Internally, he had to confront his sense of a vocation solely to the House of Israel with stunning faith that he found outside of Israel. Externally, he was welcomed to table fellowship with the Pharisees, who in turn could not understand Jesus' inclusion at his own table fellowship of those they excluded: sinners and other undesirables. I believe that a systems interpretation of Jesus' religious intuition can help deliver his narrative to a postmodern world that can surely bear to hear it.

Postmodern is in danger of becoming a new fad word. Words become faddish because they name something so insightfully that they get popularized. So if *postmodern* is becoming a fad, it is because it is naming an experience of great cultural change that many people are beginning to sense. These are seismic shifts in many of the meaning structures we used to accept. But when we get down to the details of what *postmodern* connotes, there are many meanings afloat. I shall therefore indicate one particular postmodern concern that belongs to the context of these reflections.

With the rise of historical consciousness has come an awareness of the perspectival character of all of our perceiving, knowing, and speaking. There is no such thing as a metahistorical or metacultural position from which all historical positions can be adjudicated. The situation of multiple positions and multiple narratives is normative. After citing Jean-François Lyotard's caricature of postmodernism "as incredulity to metanarratives," Calvin Schrag offers the following summary:

> If you are postmodern you will resist the urge to tell big stories (or tall tales!). You will consolidate your discourse into local rather than grand narratives. You will steer clear of unifying principles and overarching designs that purport to tell the whole truth and nothing but the truth about all time and existence.[1]

While I am willing to give up metastories, I hold strongly to the possibility of megastories which historical persons can choose to live. I am not alone in suggesting that we had better find a very different megastory to live out of than we have chosen thus far if there is to be a twenty-first century.

I was brought up in a Christian faith that never questioned whether there would be a next century. Our hope image was that God's reign on Earth would inevitably come. In my honest moments today I know that the reign of God may not occur, and that we human beings, as necessary agents in the co-creation of history, may terminate rather than propagate human life if we do not with God protect the preciousness of our shared existence on this planet. But merely local stories about local ownership of the world are insufficient. This is the aspect of postmodernity that I have in mind through the reflections that follow.

II. THE DARKSIDE OF HUMAN HISTORY

Carl Jung was asked whether he thought there would be a nuclear holocaust. He said it all depends on how we human beings come to terms with our own darkness.[2] The only survivable world is one in which we have come to terms with our darkness—not conquering it, but coming to terms with it, because you cannot be a finite being and not have darkness.

I want to focus upon a particular aspect of our darkness, to which I shall propose a religious intuition from my Christian tradition, and offer a systems framework for its context. But I must add two notes about what the word "Christian" means for me in this context.

First, ever since I recognized that Jesus never stepped outside of his Jewish faith to be who he was and to do what he did, I have been bent upon the retrieval of Jewishness for Christian selfhood today.[3] The religious experience and the religious intuition to which I shall be referring are unthinkable apart from the Jewish heritage which constituted the assumptive world of Jesus. Greek interpretations of the Jesus event have obscured the intuition that I find so vigorous and vital. I believe that my work in Judaism (which involves Judaism's work in me!) has helped me to make a recovery.

Second, my instincts have been disciplined for some time now in the methods and persuasions of process-relational modes of thought. I have come to my more recent perceptions of the Christian scriptures with process-relational eyes and ears. And those presuppositions that I have brought with me have shaped what I found. In the context of this essay, I would stress especially my profound conviction that we have no merely private destinies as persons or nations, but that the destiny of the world is of a piece—not because we have a necessary metastory, but because we are interconnected. We live in a system in which whatever happens to any part of the system reverberates in small or large ways throughout the whole system.

I take up the human experience of darkness to which Carl Jung referred. When theologians grapple with human darkness, they often pitch their discussion in terms of Sin. Not "sins," like "how many times did I do such and such a thing?," but Sin in the singular with a capital "S"—as in "Original Sin." The question being asked, really, is "in what fundamental orientations of the human heart does our darkness—personal and communal—originate?"

III. A BIBLICAL NARRATIVE OF DARKNESS

Our first family—Adam and Eve and their two oldest sons—is a compelling typology of Original Darkness. Let us look first at the parents, then at the sons.

Adam and Eve could not tolerate the limitations of their creatureliness. And here we have a first source of darkness. The snake said, "You are ignorant like a creature. If you eat the apple, you will be smart like God. Eat the apple and you will have transcended your finitude." And they bit. Among contemporary writers, probably no one has better described this side of darkness than Ernest Becker in *The Denial of Death:*

> The prison of one's character is painstakingly built to deny one thing and one thing alone: one's creatureliness. The creatureliness is the terror. Once admit that you are a defecating creature and you invite the primeval ocean of creature anxiety to flood over you. . . . To see the world as it really is . . . makes thoughtless living in the world of men an impossibility. It places a trembling animal at the mercy of the entire cosmos and the problem of meaning in it.[4]

Finitude does not seem to rest easily upon us reflective finite ones!

In the United States experience today, we seem—as a piece of national creature anxiety—unable to admit our limited role among the nations of the world, our inability to control destiny. In short, like J. Alfred Prufrock, we see the moment of our greatness flicker, and we are afraid. Nations do come and go. Only a snake says, "Well maybe not. Perhaps you can be eternal like God." Today that temptation has become a terrible, terrible danger—an incredible recess of darkness.

And now to Adam and Eve's children. Cain and Abel competed for God's affection. One got a bigger share. The other killed for it. This is a second source of our darkness. We are individual subjectivities competing for the same affection, the same goods, the same power, the same control, the same honors—and let us admit it, the same oil in the Mideast. Cain killed Abel. It is a hard fact, but we have been killing ever since Eden. Yet, we still celebrate and promote competition that maims.

What makes the world different today from anything before is our maiming weapons. There would be nothing left. We know that this is not idle doomsday talk. One Trident I submarine carries four times as much destructive power as was unleashed in all of World War II (Nagasaki and Hiroshima included). The newer Trident II carries twenty-eight times as much. That is only one submarine.

Can we make it go another way? Are there better ways to be together upon this earth? Sociologists and anthropologists are nearly of one voice in telling us that human nature does not have a given meaning. It is the human task to create its meaning. Beavers know what dam to build. But, as Clifford Geertz reminds us, *our* genes are silent on the building trades, and that includes building human nature.[5] Similarly, Peter Berger observes that "it is the 'nature of man' to produce a world. What appears at any particular historical moment as 'human nature' is itself a product of man's world building activity."[6] Berger also understands that one of the principal functions of religion is to engage in "world building," that is, in constituting the meanings out of which we live. It is both a secular and religious function of religion to do that.

I believe that there is a religious intuition in the experience and teaching of Jesus that offers a mode of world construction, a version of human nature, that counters the darkness of Cain and Abel. It is this I wish to address. The Adam and Eve syndrome mentioned above—the creaturely urge to be "cured" of finitude—is equally crucial, but not my primary concern in this essay.

IV. A SYSTEMS INTERPRETATION: THE RELATIONAL WEB

I want to address issues of large-scale creative transformation. In Christian terms, I mean the evangelization of culture. There are two ways of questioning the character of "transformation." The first asks, "What kind of individuals must you have in order to have a community that is strong and healthy?" The second asks, "What kind of community must you have in order to make it probable that strong, healthy individuals will emerge?" The first asks, "How must individuals be transformed to have good community?" The second asks, "How must the relational web, which is what a community is, be transformed if strong, interesting, healthy individuals are to come from its womb?"

Both questions are useful and both are right. But I want to suggest that the second is more useful and, as it were, more right. That is what a systems perspective teaches us. Our identity emerges out of our relationships. To shape identity most profoundly, we must shape the relationships out of which identity is forged. But the relationships constitute a system. The crucial object of transformation, then, is the system, the relational web.

Christianity has spent most of its time in history calling on individual persons to be converted, to have (in biblical terms) a *metanoia*. But increasingly I understand that, in Jesus, God calls the *relational web* to submit to transformation so that history will be safe and there will be a twenty-first century.

"Relational Web" is an image used frequently by two process theologians, Bernard Meland and Bernard Loomer. It is an image for the intricate intercrossing, interlacing strands that web us into a corporate destiny. Let me name what I presume to be the principal relationships that do the webbing—these are the relational structures in which we find ourselves day to day, moment to moment:

1. There are the relational structures between parents and children, brothers and sisters, in short, those constituted through procreation. Notice that I am saying "relational structures" and not "relationships." What I am naming are the patterned ways in which we interact, the narrative structures of our lives together.
2. There are relational structures between the leader and those led, between the "boss" and the "worker."
3. There are relational structures between adversaries, patterned responses to enemies.
4. There are relational structures between friends.
5. There are relational structures between neighbors, those who are geographically close enough to interact and make claims by their proximate presences.
6. There are relational structures between nations: economic, political, military.
7. There are relational structures between men and women that are poignantly shaped by the sexual identity and sexual needs of both.
8. There are relational structures between religions.
9. There are relational structures between social and economic classes.

Put all of these together and you have a relational web.

V. JESUS' RELIGIOUS INTUITION

The relational web is that immensely complex texture of patterns of relationships crisscrossing each other and together forming the web that forms us. I suggest that the religious intuition of Jesus addresses the texture of the relational web in profound and specific ways.

Let us begin with the biological family (Mk. 3:31-35). Jesus is at home. When Jesus's mother and brothers get home, they cannot even get close to him because of the crowd. So they pass a message up to him. Upon receiving the message he asks, "Who are my mother and my brothers?" Looking at those sitting in a circle around him, he says, "Here are my mother and my brothers. Whoever does the will of God is my brother and sister and mother."

In Luke 11:19-21 a woman, awed by Jesus, shouts above the crowd, "Happy is the womb that bore you and the breasts that nursed you." Jesus admits the blessedness of a mother-son relationship (implied in the comparative form of the adjective he uses), but insists that "more blessed are those who hear the Word of God and keep it."

Neither of these stories is a "put down" for the mother, brothers, and sisters of Jesus. Rather, through our shared response to God we are brought into a relationship with each other that is more ultimate than roles that are biologically constituted. The roles do not disappear— mother still remains mother, son still remains son. But when who I am as a child of God meets who my mother is as another child of God, we have an equality and a commonality that transforms for the better who we are as mother and son. Any family systems analyst can testify to the importance of meeting a parent or a child beyond the role. Something more ultimate than the role catches us up in a relational web that is stronger than a role.

Let us take another role. We ordinarily think of the leader as one who directs others in what to do or where to go. In most cultures, power means the ability to prevail in relational situations, often the ability to impose. In Luke's Gospel (22:24-27) there is a dispute among the disciples about who is the greatest. Jesus intervenes. He points out that the model of power they are discussing is the same as that of pagan kings who lord it over their subjects. Jesus says that in the community that follows him, the leader behaves as the one who serves the others in community.

It is interesting that in Mark's Gospel the scene takes place while they are on the road (10: 32-45). This is the proto-version of the incident. Matthew adds to the drama on the road by having the mother of James and John ask for the highest place for her sons. Luke takes the story off the road and places it at the Last Supper. In so doing, he places the discussion within the context of the eucharistic community and its leadership structure. The message is about the exercise of power in community. The same point is made at the Last Supper in John's Gospel (13: 2-16). After washing the feet of his community, Jesus "put on his clothes again and went back to the table. 'Do you understand,' he said, 'what I have done to you? You call me Master and Lord, and rightly; I am. If I then, the Lord and Master, have washed your feet, you should wash each other's feet.' "

Now that is a reversal! In our world, success tends to be measured (by individuals and nations) by how much control one has over others, by how much one can affect any course of events while remaining minimally affected. When we speak of the corridors of power, that is what we mean. I am afraid the program suggested by Jesus would sound like a "Handbook for Wimps" in the corridors of power. But we know, do we not, what a strong person it takes to be vulnerable to the lives of others, to be willing to be shaped by the experience of others. How much love-

lier and safer our world will be when the relational webs of power structures come close to what Jesus proposes, when those who lead listen
first and listen continually to the needs of the community. The same is
true for power structures between friends; power structures within every
family; power structures between teachers and students, between pas-
tors and parishes, between presidents and citizens; in power structures
everywhere in the relational web (and they *are* everywhere).

The relational structure between foes is perhaps the most highly
charged of all (Lk. 6:27-35). Everyone loves those who love them back.
And we should certainly do that. But the real trick is to do good to those
who are bent upon our undoing—to pray (honestly!) for those who treat
us badly, to bless those who shout us down with curses, that is, to love
our enemies. In other words, all the behaviors we use in our best relationships with our friends, we must use in relationships that we experience as hostile. Isaiah got at the same thing when he said that, because
all people have the same God, they should hammer their swords into
ploughshares. If there is but one God for all, then it is stupid, wrong-
headed, and full of Sin to relate as if we are two or three or four peoples.
We are one people.

There is a difference of only one letter between friend and fiend.
In the relational web transformed by the religious intuition of Jesus, the
letter "r" goes back into every "f-iend." Adversary language is obsolete;
it is wrong; it is the basis for unpeace.

I am deeply concerned about the amount of adversary language
that has been reintroduced into the daily vocabulary of the American
experience in the recent past (not that it ever disappeared). "Empire of
evil" is not helpful. What sane human being could kill another human
person whom he or she did not even know? Yet in war we do it. As
Gabriel Marcel long ago pointed out, we disguise the precious person-
hood of the other by epithets to be able to kill: stop the krauts; get the
niggers; waste the gooks. What different behaviors would be elicited if
we called Soviets, Cubans, and Sandanistas our brothers and our sisters!
I do not mean that we should naively ignore critical and potentially
destructive differences. But we have the power so to construct the meaning of human existence that the one who differs most critically and even
dangerously does not thereby cease being a brother or a sister.

Let me give an example. Commander John Williams described a
program conducted at the U.S. Navy Base in Newport, Rhode Island.
The purpose of the program is to teach officers and enlisted men about
their "adversaries" in the Soviet Union, presuming I suppose that they
are themselves totally different in character (that is, that they themselves do no have the character of being an adversary). Williams said that

the program was "designed to be as objective as possible." One of the lecturers in the program "couldn't resist comparing a somewhat hefty Soviet woman with Miss Piggy." This language is not engaged in the social construction of sisterhood and brotherhood. It constructs adversarihood.

I do not pretend that calling conventional enemies brothers and sisters is without risk. It is full of risk. It has never been tried by more than a few individuals and groups. Its outcome is unknown. But, to quote John Cobb, "To name the *Logos* Christ is to express and elicit trust. It is to promise that the unknown into which we are called is life rather than death. In short, it is to call for and make possible conversion from bondage to the past to openness to the future."[8]

Because Plan A, the adversary approach to the relational web, has never worked—because never in history has it brought peace, because so often it has spilled blood upon the earth—Plan B seems worth a try: everywhere and always to put the "r" back in "f-iend." As Dostoevsky observed, "The earth is soaked with the tears of humanity from its crust to its core." Surely this tale that might be told about the world is worth a try.

Albert Camus once said that what the world expects of Christians is that they voice their condemnation of war in such a way that no doubt could arise in the heart of the simplest person. They should get away from abstractions and confront the blood-stained face of history. Rather than mere condemnation, perhaps we Christians can change our war-based language about each other, and soon change the meanings out of which we live.

Now I turn to another role that structures the relational web, that of neighbor (Lk. 10:29-37). Love God totally. Love your neighbor as yourself. That is the whole Law. The young lawyer answered correctly. Then he asked Jesus to elaborate further on who the neighbor is that must be loved as oneself. Jesus told the story of a man beat up by robbers and left bloody and half dead in the ditch on the dangerous road to Jericho. A Jewish priest passed that way, and crossed to the other side of the road. And a Levite likewise. Then a Samaritan stopped—someone who in that relational web would have been a bitter and detested enemy. He bandaged and medicated the man, took him to an inn for care, and paid the bills.

Who was the neighbor? The one who saw deep need in a human being and, transcending any social or tribal distinction, met the need. It is human need that puts someone in my backyard, or my need that puts me in his or her backyard. "Neighbor" is not next-doorness. It is need, human need. That counts for nations too. The tribalism that ever allows anyone "to fight for God and country" is a deep violation of the relational web that an early first-century Jewish man was summoning into existence. He was engaged in the art of world construction.

There is perhaps no more trenchant need incumbent upon churches today than to free religion from all cultural tribalism, thereby enabling it to serve as a foundational experience for world community. What if nations called other nations in need their neighbors, and then loved their neighbors as themselves?

The provocative intuition of Jesus at work here is a recognition that the Fatherhood of God makes all men and women brothers and sisters to each other, and this condition is intended to be the ultimate thing about us. It constitutes a new structure, and all other structures—however necessary they be—are subordinate to that one. In her book, *In Memory of Her,* Elisabeth Schussler-Fiorenza notes Jesus' realization that this condition brings all patriarchy to an end. "You must call no one on earth your father, since you have only one father, and he is in heaven" (Matt. 23:9).

Even as we recognize that perhaps the sexually unbiased word "parent" may better catch culturally what "Father" named for Jesus, the consequences of this language are the same. We are sisters and brothers because we are children of the same parent who is God, and we must never attempt to be God the Father or God the Parent in God's stead. Schussler-Fiorenza writes that "Jesus uses the 'Father' name of God not as a legitimization for existing patriarchal power structures in society or church but as a critical subversion of all structures of domination. The 'Father' God of Jesus makes possible 'the sisterhood of men' (in the phrase of Mary Daly) by denying any father, and all patriarchy, its right to exist."[9]

Having invoked the teaching of Jesus addressed to multiple aspects of the relational web, I turn to two other figures: Charlotte Bronte (she knew something important) and Paul of Tarsus (so did he).

Jane Eyre, a young country girl, goes to the Thornfield Estate to become a governess for the young charge of Mr. Rochester, Master of Thornfield. Jane is very much attracted to him. However, she reminds herself:

> You have nothing to do with the master of Thornfield, further than to receive the salary he gives you for teaching his protegee, and be grateful for such respectful and kind treatment as, if you do your duty you have a right to expect at his hands. Be sure that this is the only tie he seriously acknowledges between you and him; so don't make him the object of your fine feelings, your raptures, agonies, and so forth. He is not of your order: keep to your caste, and be too self-respecting to lavish the love of the whole heart, soul and strength where such a gift is not wanted, and would be despised.

In spite of these words of warning to herself, Jane does fall in love with him. And his affection for her is genuine. But he decides to marry some-

ONLY SURVIVABLE WORLD   59

one of his caste, Miss Ingram, "a beautiful and noble woman." He even hopes Jane will remain at Thornfield as governess because he wants her near. What anguish that would be for Jane! She knows this relational web is rotten, and she addresses the master of Thornfield:

> Do you think I can stay and become nothing to you? Do you think I am an automaton?—a machine without feelings? And can bear to have my morsel of bread snatched from my lips?—and my drop of living water dashed from my cup? Do you think, because I am poor, obscure, plain and little, I am soulless and heartless? You think wrong!—I have as much soul as you—and full as much heart! And if God had gifted me with some beauty and much wealth, I should have made it as hard for you to leave me as it is now for me to leave you. I am not talking to you now through the medium of custom, conventionalities, nor even of mortal flesh. It is my spirit that addresses your spirit, just as if both had passed through the grave, and we stood at God's feet equal—as we are!

This is a profound insight for Jane. Charlotte Bronte may not have been a theologian, but she knew something critical about human relationality. The way we are with each other before God puts us on an equal footing that transcends the medium of custom, convention, and even mortal flesh. We speak, spirit to spirit, the core of who I am to the core of who you are—what is ultimate in me addresses what is ultimate in you. That makes all the difference. That redeems the relational web, and redeems us who are incubated in its nurturing matrix.

Finally, let us return to Paul whose words to the Galatians (3:27-28) are a splendid summary: "You are, all of you, sons [children] of God through faith in Christ Jesus. All baptized in Christ, you have all clothed yourselves in Christ; and there is no more Jew or Greek, slave or free, male and female, but you are all one in Christ." Note first that the racial and social equality of all human persons is an immediate effect of our being children of one and the same Divine Parent. Paul is responding to one of the profoundest intuitions of Jesus about the consequences of having God for our ultimate Parent.

Paul knows, of course, that even when we are one and equal, we do not lose our national identity. My grandmother was baptized and did not lose her Spanish accent. Paul understands also that we do not change our social or fiscal condition at baptism. These identities, these roles, are necessary to life. The point is that they may be semi-final but never final. There is a deeper relational base than these. When race, sex, nationality, and economic status are functioning in a relational web that respects our equality as God's children as primordial, the relational web is safe from dividing us or destroying us. This is the only survivable world.

Most English translations do not pay attention to a Pauline shift in language in the text cited above. Baptism puts an end to the distinction of Greek *or* Jew, slave *or* free. Both pairs are separated by *or*. But then Paul says that baptism puts an end to male *and* female. The difference is with meaning. The expression "male and female" is very familiar language from Gen. 1:27. It would have invoked the moment of creation and the marriage relationship familar to Jews, namely, a very patriarchal structure. Elisabeth Schussler-Fiorenza says that Paul understands baptism to put an end to the inequality that exists in patriarchal marriage.[10] Marriage partners are children of the same God and therefore equal. Gender carries no privilege.

In a stunning metaphor (whose familiarity has made it lose much of its incredibility), Paul recognizes that the religious intuition of Jesus is that the world could become a single Body (I Cor. 12:12-27). In each person's body, if one part is hurt, all parts hurt with it. That is because the body is an organized system. No part is self-sufficient; all parts need the other parts. If we create the meaning of reality as the Greeks did, with the autonomous individual as the foundational unit, the most we can say about Paul's sense of the Body of Christ is that it is a magnificent poetic image. But if we begin with the relational web as foundational—if we are convinced that being is irreducibly social—then the organicness of our togetherness is *concretely real,* and "Body of Christ" becomes a particular way in which its meaning can be construed. As Bernard Loomer has pointed out, we do not become related because we love. We are already related. Love is what redeems our relatedness.

For his bodily understanding of human reality, Paul must surely be having recourse to Hebrew instincts fashioned out of the corporate personality of Israel. The conception of the community as a person is genuinely Semitic (and I roundly disagree with the value judgment of this sense of things as "primitive"). H. Wheeler Robinson, in his essay on "The Group and the Individual in Israel," remarks how often the psychology of an age shapes its sociology.[11] To survive, our world needs a Body psychology, a sense of ourselves as a single Body, so that each part feels what other parts feel, so that no one—individual or nation—can be sick or healthy alone. Robinson says that in this passage in Paul "we see the new synthesis in its clearest form, especially if we interpret the metaphor, as we should, by Hebrew and not by Greek psychology. . . . It implies a new kind of individual, but one who, like the true Israelites of old, could never be divorced from his social relationship."[12] Nothing less than a new meaning of human nature is proposed as a basis for making history.

Jesus did not discover the Parenthood of God. But his own identity was so immersed in it that he was able to explore, through his own reality, its effects throughout the relational web. The genius of Jesus, if one may put it that way, was to have recognized the consequences of God's Parenthood as a mode of world construction. The Kingdom. Salvation history. The Only Survivable World. Pick your nomenclature.

VI. CONCLUSION

So we are back to where we started. It is true that the transformation of individual lives alters the relational web. But it seems a larger truth that the transformation of the relational web is a transformation of the womb that begets us, and thus becomes our own profoundest means of transformation.

This religious intuition is not just a message that transforms relationships. It calls for a transformation of the very basis of all human relationality — not just of relationships one by one, but of the very texture of relationality. What is at stake is a structural alteration of relational patterns, a rewriting of the narrative structure of human experience.

And this transformation is not just between individuals on the scale of our gentlest intimacies, but between nations and civilizations on the scale of a world — a world that may thereby survive and be resplendent.

I believe deeply in this religious intuition and want for all the world to admit it seriously into our world construction. Many aspects of it must be translated into social, political, and economic theory in order to go to work on the world. It must be available through secular sacrament as well as religious ritual. I am painfully aware that time may indeed be short.

NOTES

1. Calvin D. Schrag, "Liberal Learning in the Postmodern World," *The Key Reporter* [Phi Beta Kappa] 54/1 (1988).

2. Cited in Barbara Hannah, *Active Imagination* (Santa Monica, Calif.: Sigo, 1981), 8-9.

3. Bernard J. Lee, *The Galilean Jewishness of Jesus* (New York: Stimulus/Paulist, 1988).

4. Ernest Becker, *The Denial of Death* (New York: Free Press, 1973), 87, 60.

5. Clifford Geertz, *The Interpretation of Cultures* (New York: Harper Colophon, 1973), 93.

6. Peter L. Berger, *The Sacred Canopy* (Garden City: Doubleday Anchor, 1969), 7.

7. Tim Murphy, "U.S. Sailors Get Peek Inside Soviet Navy," *Los Angeles Times,* Nov. 30, 1984, Part I-A: 8.

8. John B. Cobb, Jr., *Christ in a Pluralistic Age* (Philadelphia: Westminster, 1975), 85.

9. Elisabeth Schussler-Fiorenza, *In Memory of Her* (New York: Crossroads, 1983), 151.

10. *Ibid.,* 211.

11. H. Wheeler Robinson, *Corporate Personality in Israel* (Philadelphia: Fortress, 1964), 22.

12. *Ibid., 33.*

5

WARRIORS, WOMEN, AND THE NUCLEAR COMPLEX: TOWARD A POSTNUCLEAR POSTMODERNITY

Catherine Keller

I. EGO BOUNDARIES AND APOCALYPSE

Judy Grahn, in *The Queen of Wands,* has the old crone Spider Webster declare: "He is singing the end of the world again, he has sung it before. ... He dwells in threats of fire, Armageddon, Hiroshima, Saigon, and Tyre, Berlin, Gomorrah, Hell itself, the story of fire, his theft of it."[1] The day Ronald Reagan was re-elected (a greater shock, somehow, than the recent election of George Bush), the wail of sirens offered an eerie accompaniment to the song of victory on the campus where I then taught. First, the fire alarms went off, and fire engines came screaming onto campus while we all stood out in the cold, never knowing whether the alarm was false. When we were finally back in the classroom, the Cin-

cinnati emergency sirens, those which would be sounded if any were to be sounded for a nuclear attack, suddenly pulsed their deafening alarm. (Just a test, as it turned out.) While they were wailing, we sat there, silent, the students strangely uncool, momentarily held in the grip of the portentous. "Portend," as in a good or ill omen, comes from the Latin *monstrum*, "monster," from *monere*, "to warn" (the root of de-monstration). And with the warning songs of certain she-monsters we will finally have to do, most reverently, in this examination of the nuclear complex and its threatened monstrosity.

Later that day, I wandered aimlessly into a bookstore, staring at the news stand, when suddenly the cover of *Esquire* magazine leapt into focus: "The Secret Love of a Man's Life," announced the cover, next to a beautiful woman, in combat helmet and sexily torn army-green T-shirt, gazing with insouciant allure at the male readership. "Why Men Love War," the lead article's title, accounted for the iconography: presumably the woman symbolized war itself. The cover seemed to promise the sinister answer to a question become, amidst the portents of the day, inevitable. I needed to hear from a man openly rhapsodizing this necrophilic passion, this doomsday song. I bought my first *Esquire* magazine.

The author, William Broyles, Jr., a Vietnam veteran, makes an intelligent, confessional attempt to come to terms with this secret lust, presenting his arguments with the disarming honesty of someone "man enough" to tell the truth, no matter how embarrassing, how unpretty. But how unconventional is this truth after all? Its aim is by no means to disarm: "war *is* beautiful," he claims, while not denying its ugliness. Describing a "beastly scene" in which dozens of dead North Vietnamese soldiers are being loaded (the morning after) onto mechanical mules, he describes a colonel's and his own exchange of smiles of mystical "ecstasy," of "bliss." "That was another of the times I stood on the edge of my humanity, looked into the pit, and loved what I saw there. I had surrendered to an aesthetic that was divorced from that crucial quality of empathy that lets us feel the sufferings of others. And I saw a terrible beauty there."[2] In this confession of a disempathic aesthetic lies, perversely, an important omen for feminist spirituality in its revisioning of the self. Recall Nancy Chodorow's psychoanalytic account of how little girls emerge from the preoedipal period "with a basis for 'empathy' built into their primary definition of self in a way that boys do not."[3] To this analysis we will return, if we are to understand the "nuclear complex."

In Broyles' analysis of the disempathetic bliss, the love of war derives not from any lust for killing, but from a two-fold limit experience: the transcendence of individuality in "comradeship" and the transcendence of the mundane life in an experience of "initiation." The soldier's experience of the *rite de passage* belongs, we may presume, to what Eliade calls the "initiatory ordeal of the heroic type," surviving here in modern warfare in profane, "degenerate form." "What made this love [of your comrades] so intense was that it had no limits, not even death," continues Broyles. Furthermore, "The only men who kept their heads felt connected to other men, a part of something, as if comradeship were a collective life-force, the power to face death and stay conscious."[4] There is nothing new in this glorification of the buddy system, this male-to-male intimacy which is "the enduring emotion of war." Yet we must ask: what is it about male experience that renders intimacy with each other possible only under the desperate circumstances of war? Why is the grandiosity of destruction, the life-or-death limit-situation of war, required in order for men to feel "connected"? Recall here Nancy Chodorow's analysis of the resolution by little boys (within Patriarchal Western modernity) of the oedipal conflict: "Boys come to define themselves as more separate and distinct, with a greater sense of rigid ego boundaries and differentiation."[5]

As to the second mode of transcendence, Broyles offers the following, quite extraordinary, analysis:

> War may be the only way in which most men touch the mythic domains in our soul. It is, for men, at some terrible level the closest thing to what childbirth is for women: the initiation into the power of life and death. It is like lifting off the corner of the universe and looking at what's underneath. To see war is to see into the dark heart of things, that no-man's-land between life and death, or even beyond.[6]

In this unabashed psalmody, we receive a contemporary text of warrior-mysticism. Indeed, male initiation symbolism in religious cultures around the world, as well as in archaic civilizations, does evoke either the atmosphere or the threat of death, often through the most gruesome tortures, as the means of rebirth through the Father—dying, according to the history of religions, to the "profane," natural, mother-born self. For women, on the other hand, the periods of symbolically charged transition have been life-centered, so that our rituals of initiation, at least within the patriarchies, have been associated with the natural processes of menarche, childbirth, and menopause.

Transposed into the scene of war, this means: what life-creation is for women, life-destruction is for men. Why is this? Broyles surely helps Mary Daly's case for a woman-centered "biophilia" opposed by patriarchal "necrophilia."[7] Is there a lack of satisfactory peace-time peak experiences for many or most men? Do their self-definitions as "separate and distinct" selves render a limit-experience something attainable only by sheer destruction? Are the "rigid ego boundaries" perhaps so taut as to block transformative permeations and permutations in the normal course of living? Is a man's experience trapped inside such dense walls as to require an explosive shattering before the individual locked inside can break free, into both his soul's "mythic domains" and the life-force of live connection? If war is "a sexual turn-on that conceals inadequacies," why is sexual vulnerability in males so (literally) *mortifying*? And what is this "dark heart of things," this "no-man's-land" underneath the universe? Have the soul's "mythic domains" become appallingly, and now apocalyptically, dark, precisely because the collective warrior has failed to face them?

Still these aesthetic-erotic domains of horror mesmerize him, attract him, in their hellish authenticity, and the more he cannot normally break through his boundaries to *face them* and to explore these domains, the more he craves the explosion of all boundaries in war. And the more he can project and act out his "initiation" in wars and rumors of wars, the less he needs to face this "no-man's-land."

Taking our clue from Broyles' language, we may wonder if the absence of "man" in this war-zone of transcendence is the heart of the matter. Is it God encountered here, unrecognized but sublimely experienced (hence the language of religious bliss)? Or is the no-man Woman, unrecognized but ecstatically *known* (hence war as cover girl, as "sexual turn-on," and as analogue to child-birth)?

Let me propose that both are true, and that recognizing this metaphoric morass of hideously beautiful Divinity and Femininity will help to solve a seemingly unrelated paradox of the nuclear age: that nuclear war supersedes the warrior. The warrior-ethos with its aesthetics of disempathy has produced weapons that would in fact deny the warrior the limit-experiences, the glory, the spiritual satisfaction he derives from war. It not only changes the rules of the game—a game which according to Broyles is "a brutal, deadly game but the best game there is"—but ends all games. The ecstasy of war horror, in which in some perverse way the suppressed woman and the hidden deity are anonymously experienced, will help us to trace a continuum extending from warrior to warhead. This continuum unfolds from a core complex, a way of being, feeling, and acting, which I call, for reasons that will become evident, the "nuclear complex." And face it we must, if "he is singing the end of the world," using the strongman arguments and cadences of the warrior to mount the crescendos of his ultimate song of war—the war indeed to end all wars, the war to end the world.

The project of feminist spirituality, in which woman's self-image and the *imago dei* converge, may provide a critical twist of perspective in the matter—or rather antimatter—of nuclear terror. Whatever helps us to *face* the warrior and his warheads not only lends courage and energy to the disarmament struggle. *Facing,* we shall see, turns out to be just what the warrior does not do, never did, and seeks with his apocalypse to avoid eternally. Thus, by facing him—by, for instance, diagnosing his nuclear complex—a realistically possible alternative to the warrior-ethos and its doomsday consequence may be encouraged. And as feminist peace activists report, the sense of an alternative rises from women in the movement much more powerfully than from men, among whom one often senses a despairing fatalism, a sense of the inevitability of nuclear exchange. This despair on the part of some of the most committed male peace activists might suggest a sense in which they too—unconsciously, unintentionally, indeed against their best intentions—partake of this nuclear complex.

II. On Defense: Oedipus and the Nuke

What *is* the nuclear complex?

The phrase itself comes from Freud, who was hardly thinking of nuclear arms when in *Totem and Taboo* he first called the Oedipal complex the nucleus of the neuroses, and indeed the fundamental challenge to the maturing ego. Nonetheless, more than "semantic mirage" (Derrida) can be detected in the correlation of the Oedipal complex and the global pathology of nuclear proliferation. The Oedipal complex represents that phase of continued intimacy with the mother, in which the boy wishes his father, the admired but dreaded rival, dead, giving rise to the universal neurosis:

> In addition to the hate which seeks to get rid of the father as a rival, a measure of tenderness for him is also habitually present. The two attitudes of mind combine to produce identification with the father; the boy wants to be in his father's place because he admires him and wants to be like him, and also because he wants to put him out of the way.[8]

Inasmuch as the complex is not resolved effectively, there will be a guilty, lingering readiness to be punished for the patricidal wish, combined with a continuing fear of paternal authority. The obstacle to the son's complex, bringing him in "normal" cases to give up both his desire to possess his mother and to kill his father, is the *fear of castration.* Through the fear that his father will castrate him, in other words, the male child conforms to the demands of society and in effect internalizes, as his superego, the castrating patriarch. The cycle is therefore assured of continuance in the ensuing generations.

Suspending the literalism of the biological and sexual framework of psychoanalytic theory (as do many neo- and post-Freudians), we cannot help but enjoy the pellucid power of Freud's infra-patriarchal hypothesis to explain the interaction of enemy males which provides the contents and discontents of our "civilization": the deadly drone of the war songs of written history. Within the Judeo-Christian civilization, with its father-fixation, men must, in Freud's view, reserve not only a murderous hostility and competitiveness, but also a neurotic guilt complex which leads them to acquiesce in and even to seek "punishment." Fear of castration promotes desire for castigation. One suspects a relation to the population's massive acquiescence in the nuclear threat today in this light.

By contrast, if it is "healthy," men's very ego-structure is in these terms a direct product of defense—a defense against "castration" by the rival male. Here we note the "dream of a perfect defense," to cite former Secretary of Defense Harold Brown's phrase for the Strategic Defense Initiative,[9] otherwise known as Star Wars. If, to attain normative manhood, the resolution of the psychological nuclear complex indeed *depends* upon the fear of castration, the "civilized" (that is, patriarchal) male would subsist on fantasies of defense.

Let us explore for a moment (which as far as I know Freud did not) the root metaphor of "castration." While the Latin noun *castrare* means "to remove the testicles," the noun form, *castrum,* refers to "a fortified place, a camp," and forms the root of "castle." The American Heritage Dictionary suggests that the common denominator is the idea of separation. Hence, a well-defended place, a fortification, is a place cut off from its surroundings. This suggests the irony that to be defended against being 'cut off' is to be *already cut off.* Thus an ego shaped in defense against (symbolic) castration is *ipso facto* castrated. Stemming from the same root (*kes*) is *castus,* "chaste," meaning "cut off from," which is related to ancient definitions of "holiness" or "purity" as a state of separation *from*, and is also the basis for "caste" and "castigation" and the very meaning "to cut off from"; also from the same root is *kasso,* meaning "empty, void; quash." We have in this sense an etymological omen of the relation between masculine castration anxiety and the militarization of culture in the ancient construction of fortified camps, always justified by the needs of "defense" ("*civi*-lization," as we know it, does arise from the structure of the Bronze Age walled city). We also have an omen of the expected status of women within the warrior's world, as "chaste" possessions sexually and socially cut off from the surrounding public world; of woman's chastity symbolizing the patriarchal caste system; and of the ultimate *telos* of the death-driving system of separation, the annihilation which seeks to replicate globally that emptiness, that void, in which his cut-off condition traps the warrior-ego, the "normal" male. Castigating and being castigated, does the warrior now seek to quash life itself?

We begin to see the relevance here of Nancy Chodorow's revised standard version of psychoanalysis for diagnosing "why women mother," why women and not men continue from one generation to the next to provide the primary childcare. She is able to demonstrate from an expanded view of the Oedipal drama how the Western "nuclear family" functions *increasingly* in this century as a sociological breeder of the Oedipus complex. On this basis she analyzes the types of self-structure that emerge for boys and girls within the implosive nuclear family relations. The gender differences result not merely from role-conditioning imposed from the larger society, but from the subtle intrafamilial relations of the nuclear family, which itself functions as the socioeconomic microcosm of society (Aristotle's *oikos*).

Because women within a patriarchal society function as the primary caretakers of young children, their bond with both boys and girls in the early years represents a highly charged, symbiotic intimacy. When the father begins to penetrate the emotional scene during the so-called Oedipal period, the effects, as even Freud finally acknowledged, admit of no neat symmetries between the sexes. To cite Freud here, the Oedipal complex in boys—their state of intimate connection with the mother, and aroused competitiveness with the father—"is literally smashed to pieces by the shock of threatened castration." (If this is true of androcentric culture, what spirit, what potentiality, is *here* quashed in the boy?) In his later, highly defensive and overtly antifeminist essay "On Femininity," Freud admits:

> We have to reckon with the possiblity that a number of women remain arrested in their original attachment to their mother and never achieve a true change-over towards men. This being so, the pre-Oedipal phase in women gains an importance which we have not attributed to it hitherto.[10]

The "true change-over towards men" as objects of primary love, which, as he acknowledges, happens only with tragic consequences in women, represents the basis not only of the socially requisite heterosexuality but of the subordination of women to men, for women accept in the change-over the "inferiority of their equipment." Yet the perplexed discovery of the extended preoedipal phase of woman-identification in girls leads him to an interesting concession: "it would seem as though we must retract the universality of the thesis that the Oedipus complex is the nucleus of the neuroses."

In other words, those conditions of fear and defense obtaining in the early childhood of males, which we have linked with the warrior-ego, do not obtain with girls and therefore do *not* obtain universally. One can at least begin to ask whether these conditions must universally hold good even for men. If the Freudian "nuclear complex" in fact psychologically parallels the nuclear obsession of the superpowers, this question has more than merely psychoanalytic importance.

Chodorow capitalizes on Freud's late and uneasy discovery of the "dark world" of women's enduring, repressed, highly troubled but never "smashed" bond with their mothers. Her description of postoedipal gender personality (upon which Carol Gilligan relies for her hypothesis concerning gender difference) elaborates on the character of the mother-daughter bond while theoretically undermining the psychoanalytic misogyny by placing it in sociological context. She shows how the traditional family format leads to a dangerous overload of the preoedipal bond and so results in later ambivalence toward the mother, and so toward all women, on the part of both male and female. Moreover women will grow up seeking to reconstitute the triangular intimacy of the Oedipal phase, in which they had included the father while sustaining intimacy with the mother. Women will end up mothering to gain with a child the intimacy they lack with a husband and once experienced with the mother.

Men will both need and flee women: thus war is the man's game, the great escape from Mother ("It was Florence Nightingale who ruined wars").[11] And because of the early fear of the father, men will resist intimacy with other males. No wonder, then, the comradeship of war comes as such a boundless revelation, a true limit-experience.

Even within the sociology of patriarchy, something of importance is left to women, something I believe we must not disdain but *strengthen*. It is left to us because it is exactly what is denied and disvalued by the culture. As Chodorow epitomizes her analysis of gender difference:

> From the retention of preoedipal attachments to their mother, growing girls come to define and experience themselves as continuous with others; their experience of self contains more flexible or permeable ego boundaries. Boys come to define themselves as more separate and distinct, with a greater sense of rigid ego boundaries and differentiation. The basic feminine sense of self is connected to the world, the basic masculine sense of self is separate.[12]

As Gilligan has shown, this masculine sense of an independent self has been in psychological theory universalized, so that the process of separation becomes identical with that of maturation; if women are recognized as more empathetic and less "cut-off," they are also marked as morally inferior. Such a judgment expresses not only the bias of the normative psychologies but the basis of the nuclear complex itself.

III. NUTS

Let me begin to redefine the nuclear complex in a way that takes into account the results of the Oedipal neurosis of patriarchal civilization, but that stands outside the Freudian perspective. Consider the definition of "nuclear": "a central thing, or part, around which other things are grouped; core." Is not this precisely the self-concept of a separate self? It is an atomic entity whose experiences and relations are arranged around a central core: the Freudian ego, the Aristotelian individual, the Jungian Self, the Cartesian soul-substance. It provides the basis for dualism of self/other, mind/body, spirit/flesh. The etymology of "nuclear" is revealing: it stems from the Latin *nux,* meaning "nut." (The reader may recall here precisely which part of the anatomy is subject to castration.) It relates to the Germanic word meaning a "sharp projection." Thus we see phallocentric weaponry arising as the self-projection of selves like hard nuts. Such a self becomes separate, hardened, precisely by virtue of its metaphoric castration-anxiety: defense precedes offense. Selves who grow hard shells "go nuts," and as a culture, nuclear madness and our collective ability to repress our knowledge of the threat testify to nothing else.

The nuclear ego, then, is the normative idea of a self as clearly delimited, separate, and independent from its relations. It takes shape as the standard male ego within the patriarchal pressure cooker of the traditional nuclear family, which itself functions as the microcosm of the socio-economic system now arming itself to the teeth in the name of defense. A series of nuts within nuts—an image to be contrasted to the web with its nodes of interconnection.

The nuclear ego, itself the integer of disintegration, fragmentation, and separation, requires an unfragmented perspective for diagnosis. It can no more be understood apart from the larger political situation than can global conditions be diagnosed apart from the psychological. Indeed, holism methodologically requires, as does feminism, that the personal and the political become describable as dimensions of a complex and interdependent continuum of relations, because the defensive dynamics of the nuclear ego, separating itself off from everything else and in the process breaking everything from everything, generates an entire worldview based on dichotomy, cutting off, cosmic castration.

No wonder the nuclear ego sings in apocalyptic overtones: in the weapons madness echoes a collective desperation to be "saved" at any cost—saved less from the enemy than from the ever-tightening constrictions of a fragmented, atomized life. And so the experience of war, which functions as a rite of passage moving the warrior beyond the limits of normal experience, escalates to the Infinite Power its capacity for sheerly negative transcendence—liberation from self and (m)other. No wonder the hope expressed by the apocalyptic eschatology of the Western patriarchal religion for the first time becomes capable of literalization. The biblically based desire for the End of the World now *contributes* to the nuclear threat, whatever its original salutary expression of solidarity with those oppressed by "the world." (Women working within biblical traditions cannot simply point the finger at extremists like Jerry Falwell, who can hardly wait for the "rapture" of nuclear apocalypse, but must realize the death-wish implicit in the yearning. It is from the outset associated with the biblical version of the Divine Warrior.) I would suggest that the old imagery of apocalyptic eschatology at work in the Christian West may be what unconsciously bridges the plausibility gap between warrior and warhead.

The patriarchal image of God (which is not to say all past or possible male or biblical metaphors for the Divine) reflects and indeed engenders the ideology of separation—for His own transcendence is "ab-solute": cut off from the world. The atomic ego is created in the image of a separate God.

Inasmuch as God remains a patriarch, albeit a victim of the same old chain of patricides—this is the one said to have died—his ghost is now incarnate in the lifeless hosts of anti-life, the missiles in which this culture has placed its faith and trust. Nuclear weaponry inspires the "fear of God" in us all, even children—and a sense of security, awe, and strength in many. Godhead has become Warhead: the ultimate incarnation of what Mary Daly exposes as "necrophilic phallic lust." A profane androcentrism now finds its hope for self-transcendence in the nuclear image of the fail-proof phallus, the steel missile carrying the *nux* which cannot be castrated.

A massive repression like the nuclear complex casts—to switch to a Jungian symbol—a massive shadow. Not only do the superpowers project the shadow of their own internalized fear of the godly father onto each other. In an eerie sense, nuclear terror projects the *shadow of connectivity.* For nothing in history manifests more assuredly the truth of global interdependence than the Mutually Assured Destruction promised by a nuclear exchange. MAD indeed, the continued repression of this shadow, by which it builds—at the rate of three U.S. warheads a day—its demonic capacities. Its power derives from the denied energies of life's unlimited interconnection. Is this the length to which the collective Warrior is finally driven by his berserk unconsciousness to burst the boundaries of his fortified ego? We begin to sense here a craving to break out of the nuclear boundaries, a perversely mystical yearning which reflects the technological ability to burst the atomic nucleus. But the craving is unconscious, massively defended against, and therefore inconceivably dangerous. If, then, the shadowy, repressed reality of connection is not consciously claimed, acclaimed, explored, suffered, and realized, we remain in danger of making the ultimate sacrifice in the cult of the warhead—the surrender of all life in an initiation ritual of endless death.

I suggested at the outset, however, that in some sense the warrior in his ecstasy seems to merge with something otherwise lost to himself, something breaking him momentarily out of the limits of his fortified ego, something suggestive at once of the Divine and of the female. At this point in history, the repressed side of the Divine must be largely experienced in female metaphors—dark and furious metaphors, because revelations do not appreciate being stifled. But further: if connectivity itself is experienced (in a culture beset by the nuclear complex) as shadowy, frightening, threatening to annihilate individuality and to asphyxiate freedom, we must recall the conditions for the appearance of connectivity in human experience.

Chodorow characterizes the woman's sense of self, in contrast to that of the male, as "connected to the world." Only through female socialization to dependency does connectivity come to suggest self-loss. But because initially children of *both sexes* take part in the same empathetic continuum of relations, a continuum in a culture where women function as the nurturers, this continuum will massively and inevitably symbolize itself, for good and ill, as female. All experience of connectedness *per se* will be mysteriously, threateningly, luringly tinged by the primordial relation to the mother—precisely that relation which the male child had violently to rupture in order to "be a man." But the connectedness violated and quashed in patriarchal society extends from the interpersonal to include our intertwining relations with body, with earth, with other societies, with cosmos.

Thus the interconnection of life at all levels endures, with women, a coprimordiality of oppression. When the warrior now prepares not the intimate glories and initiatory ordeals of the battlefield, but the final Big Bang, one senses the icy void within him driving us blindly toward fiery holocaust, the vengeance upon all the connected life from which he feels excluded in one ejaculatory ecstasy of interdependent doom. The paradox of the hard nuts which find defense *from* castration only in an *a priori* self-castration comes to a head. No *petit mort* here: if warriors find beauty in horror, here would be the ultimate aesthetic blow-out. The deadly parody of connection in the paroxysm of man-made apocalypse would be the final outcome of the nuclear complex, in which it resolves itself by death rather than healing.

What of healing? I have stressed the metaphor of the complex, suggesting a mental illness capable in principle of being healed, rather than the metaphor of death-drive or necrophilia which, combined with our technological capacity, might suggest the inevitability of doom.

IV. THE WARRIOR'S CRINGE

It is not inevitable.

Healing, however, requires *facing.* Drawing on the mythic dimension, we will see that facing is precisely what the warrior does not do, never did do, and will try at any cost to avoid. This avoidance mechanism seeps into all of us who live in his culture and threatens to void life itself. Grant me first the following axiom: that myths of the Divine hero and later the legendary hero, pervasive through the ancient world, express and inspire the development of what I have here called the nuclear ego. That is, the archetype of the warrior—not "eternally true" but certainly cross-cultural and cross-temporal in its collective appeal—provides the metaphoric matter for the separative and defensive-hostile self. (This is true whether or not individual specimens actually become soldiers.) Myths of the Divine Warrior predate and preform the biblical tradition, and indeed come to a new fruition in the imagery of apocalyptic battle and triumph. But I just want to draw out two pagan examples of the very limited but very telling motif of *facing.*

In the *Enuma Elish,* the Babylonian creation epic which depicts the rise of the warrior-god Marduk to preeminent power and which influenced many cosmogonic biblical themes, there is a critical scene of transition before Marduk is called forth as hero of his generation to slaughter the Tiamat, "the Old Hag, the first mother."[13] Tiamat, the primordial waters, the preformative chaos, has been breeding monsters in her fury and grief. The young gods have murdered her spouse, Apsu, a patricide motivated by the father's own infanticidal attempts (the Freudian scenario exactly). Tiamat had defended the children against him, but cannot tolerate their killing her primordial lover. The strategy does not begin with the familiar heroic slaughter of her, but rather as follows: the "sagacious counsellor" Ea says, "I will meet Tiamat and calm her spirit, when her heart brims over she will hear my words, and if not mine then yours may appease the waters." This is a courageous intent: to speak heart-to-heart (*coeur*-age) in appeal to her attested warm-heartedness, to pursue peace negotiations (here in the heavens and not in Geneva). It is repeated twice, and twice this is the result: "Nudimmud took the short road, went the direct way to Tiamat; but when he saw her whole strategy he could not face her, but he came back cringing."

Fascinating: an open admission of cowardice. Only after two gods fail to risk facing her anger is "the hero Marduk" prevailed upon as one courageous enough—not to face her, but to slaughter her. The courage of confrontation and appeal to heart, to hearing, is circumvented, and the courage of the new patriarchal order of warrior-gods, who need not face the anger of the displaced goddess, finds theological glorification. (Is this the hidden model for the frequent resumption of arms reductions talks? It does seem to serve as model in many heterosexual relationships.)

Another mythologem even more familiar attests to the same heroic failure to face: recall Perseus, who believes that if he looks at Medusa's face he will be turned to stone. Again, rather than face the Other, kill her! But does not the myth itself again attest to an implicit cowardice? If he faces her, he will be *petrified*—and so, he confronts neither the reality of this monster nor his own *fear*. The warrior's courage to kill without human confrontation, always justified in the name of defense, allows him to avoid his own fear, his anger, the unknown powers, the strangeness of the Other. In the psychology of the nuclear complex, is it not precisely the Other who is kept out—excluded by the very self-definition of a separate self? In matters of intimacy as in matters of international policy, the Other is the Alien, unfaced, and faceless.

But two morals especially may be drawn from these myths. First, they divulge how in our subliminal sensibilities we are taught that the monster is female, or rather that the female, if powerful, is monstrous. In a culture based, as is modernity preeminently, upon the Oedipal (patricidal) competition between murderous males, the primordial matricide nonetheless takes on a much greater emotional, political, and theological importance. The Babylonian patricide precedes the primordial combat with Tiamat, but occupies only a few verses; her defeat, the matricide, constitutes the true triumph, and almost half the epic. Out of her body, Marduk's world is created. This is the myth of creation as destruction; in its grip we create the means of cosmic destruction.

In what sense, in an age of nuclear terrorism led by male heroes, against the alien male heroes, does the true enemy turn out to be *female*?

The defeat of female "monsters" symbolizes the defeat of prepatriarchal modes of being, culturally, bodily and spiritually; and Medusa turns out to have been not unlike Tiamat, a prepatriarchal figure of female power: a gorgeous Gorgon. Her beauty, however, appears hideous in the perspective of the aesthetics of disempathy. The warrior heroes, with their separate selfhood, seem not only to defeat some prior, matricentric form of power, but also *to emerge by means of this defeat:* the shattering of the preoedipal bond, not only in the life of the individual but in the life of the culture. Do these women, these goddesses, these metaphors of female energy, become monstrous because they threaten the masculinist separatism, threaten to prevent its coming to be in the first place? Remembering that "monster" means "portent," are these monsters now rearising ragingly, portentously, whimsically, most evidently in the rearising of women? Are they the true enemy of the ruling powers of the nuclear age, in which no longer is combat man-to-man, but man-to-life? Do these shadowy women—monsters because they have been suppressed in the world, repressed in the experience of the warrior and in themselves— arise as metaphors of the lost side of the deity, the demonized "dark feminine" who cannot be faced on pain of reconnection? If the hero would face her with her anger—in himself, in his abruptly wounded relation to his mother, in his women friends, in his theology without goddess— would something *positively* apocalyptic begin to reverse the course of faceless destruction?

This brings us to the second matter to be "faced." The continuum extending from the first (the Divine) warrior to the warhead is continuous after all at the level of myth and metaphor. The warrior at first seems to be one whose courage is proved in his ability to "face" his opponent; thus the original images of heroes, such as the Greek iconography of war, show a vividly homoerotic interchange between warriors deadlocked in the embrace of battle, their weapons posed in deliberately phallic positions. But from arrows, through bullets, to the bomb, technology amplifies the power of the weapon in such a way as to render the foe increasingly distant, increasingly disconnected—finally, indeed, capable of being killed with no lingering drag of human empathy. With the machinery of nuclear war, the enemy Other remains absolutely without a face, absolutely undifferentiated. Through the perverse interdependence of mutual destruction, the enemy is finally so little an Other as to have become Oneself: the killer becomes the killed. Both sides die. But when we learn that in the most primordial imagery of the warrior there is already the failure to face, the cowardice which avoids confrontation in favor of annihilation, we see that the primordial warrior always symbolized the pseudo-courage of nonfacing, no matter what the choreography of battle. And we learn that what primordially is not faced is the petrifying female.

Now, however, she must be faced. Let me share a concluding portion of the "Song of Marduk." A bit nervous even in his gloating, the poet here speaks of the defeated Tiamat:

> Let her life be narrow and short,
> let her recede into the future
> far-off from man-kind,
> until time is old, keep her
> for ever absent.[14]

That future into which she receded against her will is surely upon us. She has been there all along—what but her cosmogonic corpse does the warrior glimpse, to cite Broyles, in "lifting the corner of the universe and looking at what is underneath"? After all, according to the *Enuma Elish,* the universe is made not only out of her body but *within* it. Time— the time, that is, of the warrior-deity and his secular substitutes—is "old." The nuclear complex must be faced and healed if it is not to bring on the end of time. How do we accomplish this facing in the face of the inexorable political odds of terminal modernity?

V. THE COURAGE OF OUR CONNECTIONS

Tiamat certainly can return as the primordial chaos, in an apocalyptic discreation of sheer regressive annihilation. Then the repressed will return as a shadowmode of vengeance wreaked by the repressors upon their own world. Alternatively? We may take heart from the knowledge that a deep cowardice is at work in the nuclear complex. We may face its many faces with a bold peacefulness—whether as they occur in men we know in the male-identified personnae we have inevitably donned to function in the world, in the institutions of the male-defined world, or in the economic and political institutions of nuclear holocaust most particularly. *If interconnection is the cosmic case, then work on each face of the complex affects the whole.* Women have been doing these things massively, and the effect has not been trivial. Thus the peace actions of the women's antinuclear movement have been powerful confrontations, expressing wholehearted anger at the terrifying destructiveness of our nuclear policy, and, at one and the same time, creatively ritualistic affirmations of interconnection. From the weaving of the wool web to obstruct the Pentagon (1980, 1981), to women dancing hand in hand on missile silos in the moonlight at Greenham Common (1983), to "the Ribbon" sewn across the country to be tied together around the Pentagon (1985), the ritual symbolism of connection confounds the nuclear complex angrily, healingly, religiously.[15] The web of life, woven of all sentient beings, has arisen with the spontaneous force of a new collective metaphor. In the women's peace encampment and actions such as Seneca Falls, web-imagery is everywhere, encompassing all other images. In the antinuclear movement, the web of life functions both to summon the power of our connections and to entangle the missiles of anti-life. In this way we connect also with the enemies of connection—the Pentagon and its products must also be woven in.

Now we must cultivate a new courage: the courage of our connections. And this "we" must include men, and not those merely incapable of the Marduk or Perseus personality, but those willing to face their fear, their fallibility, their cowardice, their anger, including the anger of the darkly divined—indeed darkly divine—woman. Anger inevitably allows facing: but only if anger itself is faced.

Not to neglect Medusa here, as we name our songs, that most petrifying face of all time, who when left as enemy even to women must be that petrifying paralysis in ourselves that we know so well, especially, perhaps, vis-à-vis the monstrum, the omen, of the nuclear age: Here are excerpts from a poem by a major feminist voice for peace, activist Barbara Deming, called "A Song for Gorgons":

> Gorgons, unruly gorgons,
> With eyes that start, with curls that hiss—
> Once I listened to the father's lies,
> Took their false advice:
> I mustn't look at you, I'd turn to
> Stone.

> But now I meet your clear furious stare and
> It is my natural self that I become.
> Yes, as I dare to name your fury,
> Mine.
> Long asleep,
> It writhes awake.

> . . . .

> This is a song for gorgons—
> Whose dreaded glances in fact can bless.
> The men who would be gods we turn
> Not to stone but to mortal flesh and blood and bone.
> If we could stare them into accepting this,
> The world could live at peace.[16]

The peacemaking anger here invoked receives further elaboration in her essay "On Anger," where she distinguishes from it the intrinsically violent and unhealthy anger:

> This anger asserts to another not: "you must change and you can change"—but: "your very existence is a threat to my very existence." It speaks not hope but fear. The fear is: you can't change—and I can't change if you are still there. It asserts not: change! but: drop dead!
> The one anger is healthy, concentrates all one's energies; the other leaves one trembling, because it is murderous. . . . Our task, of course, is to transmute the anger that is affliction into the anger that is determination to bring about change. I think, in fact, that one could give that as a definition of revolution.[17]

Feminist spirituality is all about this transmutation of affliction into the energy of self- and world-transformation. To claim the courage of our connections requires facing up to the otherness, often the murderously angry otherness, of both our selves and of those others with whom we claim connection. Facing transforms. Deming cites a song from the women's movement in the sixties: "Our anger is changing our faces, Our anger is changing our lives."[18] But before connecting with the enemies, we must be aware that connection with each other has barely begun, and so has barely begun to generate its revolutionary force field. Deming again: "Surely all of us are nerved by one another, catch courage from one another"—this in an essay aptly titled "We Are All Part of One Another."[19]

But if we are thinking of people shaped by the nuclear complex to experience themselves as separate, it is hard to discern the connecting links between us. Nonetheless the hopeful "you can change" anger remains appropriate. Although the early fortification of the psyche creates a hard nut of a self, a dense wall of defenses, Chodorow's analysis shows how it is created and therefore *that* it is created— and so, not inevitable, not essential to maleness, not natural. Neither, however, does the nuclear threat allow us simply to wait for a few generations to see whether, through the development of new forms of childcare, parenting, and options for sexual intimacy, there will be an evolution of more assertive, differentiated women and more permeable, connected men. What we must grasp *now* is the truth that separation is the illusion, indeed the delusion of Defense. No one and no thing is *really* separate from anything else. That is why the build-up of fortifications, in the soul and now in the skies, remains crucial to the survival of the nuclear illusion. In the continuing insistence on an alternative based on the intertwining energies of

all life within each individual, accordingly, there is the power of reality—
or, more modestly, the power of livelier and more fitting metaphors.

Goddesses, webs, and ribbons dance this alternative, as well-faced
monsters croon the songs of inseparability. In fact, the atom with its
nucleus has joined the round, its power threatening thermonuclear blow-
out only because the fallacy of the hard nuts has not been relinquished,
and the very power that belies the boundaries of these so-called building
blocks of reality has therefore turned against us. As Einstein said, "the
unleashed power of the atom bomb has changed everything except our
way of thinking." And this way of thinking, feeling, acting, and being has
become, therefore, apocalyptically self-contradictory. Men seek to control (by containment within their power generators, their defensive mechanisms) what can *be* neither controlled nor contained. In protest against
a "fragmentary self-world view" (in which even physicists continue to
view the universe in terms of traditional atomism, in spite of aspects of
relativity and quantum theory which point beyond "the analysis of the
world into separate parts"), physicist David Bohm writes:

> Each relatively autonomous and stable structure (e.g. an atomic
> particle) is to be understood not as something independently and
> permanently existent but rather as a product that has been formed
> in the whole flowing movement and that will ultimately dissolve
> back into this movement. How it forms and maintains itself, then,
> depends upon its place and functions in the whole.[20]

In fact, the atom itself seems to want to sing from the heart, or rather
the nucleus, of a reality in which "we are all part of one another." Modern civilization need not seek universal destruction in order to find transcendence of itself: in the infinite richness of connectivity itself, its deaths
part of the flowing movement from life to life, is rooted the courage to
face one another undefended. This is the courage out of which we may
be already creating a postmodern, postnuclear culture.

I conclude by quoting the same poem by Judy Grahn (who earlier
warned us that "he is singing the end of the world again") that I quoted
at the close of an essay in a previous volume in this series:[21]

> They say she is veiled
> and a mystery. That is
> one way of looking.
> Another
> is that she is where
> she always has been, exactly in place,

and it is we,
we who are mystified,
we who are veiled
and without faces.

"Apocalypse," we recall, means "to remove the veil"—supposedly of the unknown virgin bride at the moment of consummation. Thus the warrior's initiation by destruction, "lifting the corner of the universe and looking at what is underneath," rips the veil off of a mystery that never was hidden. The veil was the separation imposed by the fathers and the father of the fathers. Another aesthetic, one not freed from human empathy to the horrors of transcendent destruction, invites us to its beauty. *Aesthesis* is all about feeling, *em-pathos,* feeling what is *in* us, feeling our way *into* the other. When we have faces, *an aesthetic of the panempathic field* comes painfully and joyously into focus. An integrity twining—portentously—around the metaphor of the missing "she" weaves itself of our mutually indivisible individualities. Then we feel each other, every other, webbily, songfully, facing our endless differences with a delicate courage. The postmodern age is then dawning.

NOTES

1. Judy Grahn, "Spider Webster's Declaration: He is Singing the End of the World Again," *The Queen of Wands* (Trumansburg, N.Y.: The Crossing Press, 1982), 54.

2. William Broyles, Jr., "Why Men Love War," *Esquire,* December, 1984: 62. Also found in *Brothers in Arms* (New York: Knopf, 1986).

3. Nancy Chodorow, *The Reproduction of Mothering* (Berkeley: University of California Press, 1978), 167.

4. Broyles, "Why Men Love War," 58.

5. Chodorow, *The Reproduction of Mothering,* 169.

6. Broyles, "Why Men Love War," 61.

7. Mary Daly, in *Gyn/Ecology: The Metaethics of Radical Feminism* (Boston: Beacon Press, 1978), and *Pure Lust: Elemental Feminist Philosophy* (Boston: Beacon Press, 1984).

8. Sigmund Freud, "Dostoevsky and Parricide," *The Complete Works of Sigmund Freud,* Vol. XXI (London: The Hogarth Press, 1961), 183.

9. Harold Brown, *New York Times,* March 10, 1985.

10. Freud, "On Femininity," *op. cit.,* 126.

11. Actually, the correct quote is: "It was Florence Nightingale ruined wars" (the character Chuck, in Katharine Anne Porter's *Pale Horse, Pale Rider).*

12. Chodorow, *The Reproduction of Mothering,* 169.

13. The *Enuma Elish,* in *Primal Myths,* ed. Barbara Sproul (San Francisco: Harper & Row, 1979), 94.

14. *Ibid.,* 113.

15. See Alice Cook & Gwyn Kirk, *Greenham Women Everywhere* (Boston: South End Press, 1983); Susan Koen, Nina Swaim and Friends, *Ain't No Where We Can Run: Handbook for Women of the Nuclear Mentality* (Norwich, Vt.: WAND, 1980); Lynne Jones, ed., *Keeping the Peace* (London: The Women's Press, 1983); *Piecing it Together: Feminism and Nonviolence* (Devon, England: Feminism and Nonviolence Study Group, 1982); Pam McAllister, ed., *Reweaving the Web of Life: Feminism and Nonviolence* (Philadelphia: New Society Publishers, 1982).

16. *We Are All Part of One Another: A Barbara Deming Reader,* ed. Jane Meyerding (New Haven: New Society Publishers, 1984), 219.

17. "On Anger," *ibid.,* 213.

18. *Ibid.,* 212.

19. "We Are All Part of One Another," *ibid.,* 164-65.

20. David Bohm, *Wholeness and the Implicate Order* (1980; London: Ark Paperbacks, 1983), 14.

21. Catherine Keller, "Toward a Postpatriarchal Postmodernity," David Ray Griffin, ed., *Spirituality and Society: Postmodern Visions* (Albany: State University of New York Press, 1988), 63-80.

22. Grahn, "Spider Webster's Declaration," 12.

6

RELIGION AND POLITICS: VERGING ON THE POSTMODERN

Richard Falk

Future historians will certainly notice that ours has been a period of unexpected, varied, and multiple resurgence of religion as a political force. This resurgence is not a universal phenomenon, but it is widespread and, in certain parts of the world, it has become a dominant preoccupation of power-wielders, as a rationale for or a threat to politics. Whatever else is occurring, despite the continued ascendancy of science and technology, we are witnessing an extraordinary recovery of religious ways of understanding human experience.

To explore these developments, I propose to rely upon the following distinct, yet interpenetrated, designations of societal identity: premodern, modern, and postmodern. Such categorization is sweeping in its generalizing claims and can only be used in conjunction with an array of caveats and qualifications. Within the premodern are often pockets of modernist, and even postmodernist, anticipation. As well, the modern and postmodern contain remnants of the premodern. Premodern indigenous peoples, modern secular societies, and postmodern gropings coexist. There is, in other words, extraordinary unevenness of cultural circumstance throughout time and across space. Beyond this, the core perceptions of what such designations entail are bound to range widely.

Despite these difficulties, this categorization seems useful, even necessary, to gain insight into certain crucial macrohistorical tendencies that condition contemporary flows of events. The essential argument is that modernism is associated with the ascendancy of reason, science, and statist forms of political organization as they emerged in Europe during the thirteenth through the seventeenth centuries, culminating in the triumph of industrial capitalism in the nineteenth century and, finally, complemented by the October Revolution in Russia that brought state socialism into the world. Implicit in the dynamic of modernism was its globalization by way of colonialist extension and capitalist expansion. A strong feature of modernism was its basic secularism, a worldview that found meaning in the combination of materialistic and scientific developments, rendering knowledge the equivalent of what an earlier age had regarded as salvation.

The premodern, by contrast, was the condition of societies and consciousness prior to the conjoined predominance of reason, scientific technology, and state power. There were, of course, many variations on the premodern motif, including several that stressed community, hierarchy, tradition, and human dependence on higher forces of nature that were linked to the gods. For premodern societies, religion was indispensable to avoid a sense of arbitrary dependence on the caprice of nature. The political leadership could sustain its legitimacy mainly by upholding a claim to sustain sacred tradition. Except under conditions of imperial rule, the separation of religion and politics was almost inconceivable in premodern experience. The struggle to achieve religious tolerance was an early feature of that experience and the relative attainment of such tolerance was a justification for modernism. When Jesus said "Render unto Caesar that which belongs to Caesar," the basic claim was one of religious autonomy purchased by way of secular deference. In an important respect, the Spanish Inquisition represented the death rattle of premodern dispositions toward a state religion in the face of modernist impulses toward diversity and freedom.

As modernism took hold, the place of religion tended to become marginalized. Religion remained useful for political leaders in certain modernist settings, but it was no longer at the heart of power or human fulfillment. At the core of modernism was the capacity to mobilize economic forces and to wield destructive capabilities for security purposes.

In the late twentieth century, modernism retains control over political life, with a few relatively minor exceptions. But there is something new unfolding that challenges modernism from without and within, what we will call "postmodern" as a way of describing some new orientations toward the nature of politics that are arising to overcome the felt inadequacies of modernism. These postmodern moves are connected with the feeling that modernism no longer provides the basis for human meaning and species survival. One type of postmodernism is zealously antimodernist in sentiment, reasserting the centrality of literal readings of religious interpretations of human experience. The theocratic regime in Khomeini's Iran is a prime example. Another type of postmodernism is convinced that modernist dynamics are disastrously self-destructive and seeks to recreate a human future by introducing considerations of ecology and spirituality. Such postmodern emphases are often anti-ecclesiastical and nontheistic in their expression and belief, while tapping into religious feeling by confirming the sacred and viewing human destiny in its nonmaterialistic spiritual aspects. The Green movement, with its various embodiments, seems to be postmodernist in this specific respect.

The contemporary situation is confused by these cultural happenings. Some sectors of world society remain resolutely modernist. A few islands of fundamentalist success disclose the religious revisioning of modernism, and not necessarily in a liberating direction. Especially in the non-Western societies of Asia and Africa, the role of religious influence remains overwhelmingly reactionary, often being allied with operative centers of repressive state power and validating unjust and exploitative societal arrangements, although on occasion providing a potent vehicle of purifying nationalism in relation to alien rule. Only in Europe and parts of Latin America does one discern a consistent pattern of antimodernist religious outlooks opposing the normative deficiencies of modernism. This antimodernism can take many forms, but two stand out: The main religious tradition can be reinterpreted to emphasize the mandate to liberate individuals and groups from exploitative arrangements (for instance, as manifest in liberation theology); or, outside of formal religious traditions there can be a new overall interpretation of what life is about that goes beyond rationalist inquiry and derives significance from workings of, and connections with, nature (for instance, as expressed in "deep ecology").

The rise of postmodern religion as a challenge to modernism is, thus, not necessarily positive from a normative outlook. It may induce a postmodern "solution" that is fundamentalist or cultist in character and destructive of human potential. Or, it may merely allow premodernist perspectives to be used repressively by those in control of the state and market.

But what is indisputable, and of great significance, is the loosening of the modernist grip on the political imagination. This loosening alters our sense that history moves all in one way, creating cultural space for a variety of new forms of politics that share the urge to counter the destructiveness and spiritual dryness of modernism and works to provide human society with more satisfactory accounts of the proper end of history.

I. THE CHANGING ROLES OF POLITICS AND RELIGION

Many of the confusions of the present age arise out of the reversal of roles associated with politics and religion:[1] from politics we had come to expect radical challenges and a capacity for far-reaching societal innovation; from religion we had expected consolation and community but no tangible contribution to the public good.

In Western liberal democracies, in fact, the separation of church and state has been largely celebrated for its contribution to the making of the modern world. This separation formalized the confinement of religion to the sphere of purely private concerns. Such constraint was intended to facilitate governmental efficiency as well as to provide the basis for a unified politics of the state in the face of religious pluralism, with its background of devastating sectarian warfare. In the modern world, religious identity was declared irrelevant to the rational enterprise of administering the political life of society.

In Marxist-Leninist societies this process had gone even further as the state had sought to dominate the private sphere as well—an approach aptly called "totalitarian." It had relegated religion to the domain of "superstition," a premodern impediment to the true basis for hope: material progress, the dictatorship of the proletariat, the elimination of class conflict, and public ownership of the means of production.

East and West, despite their continuing genuine differences concerning the role of private property and the market, as well as their contrasting views on the proper scope for individual conscience and political dissent, were in truth not far apart with regard to the status of religion. Although the West has taunted the East for its atheism, the West has itself "killed" God by denying the relevance of spiritual perspectives to the conduct of public affairs. The consumerist spirit of the West has been at least as materialistic in its way as the insistence in the East on deifying the state as the only legitimate object of worship. Both East and West are expressions of the modern project: to rest human prospects upon the expansion of productive efforts, relying on a continuous flow of technological innovations to make life better for a higher and higher proportion of humanity. In this regard, the ideological debate between state planning and market allocation of resources is a tactical, intramural controversy carried on within the framework of modernist assumptions.

By and large, organized religion, with notable exceptions, rather timidly adjusted to its diminished influence, especially in the West, where its institutional prerogatives were largely respected in the private sphere. In the East, organized religion either acquiesced and became an enfeebled servant of state power, or did its best to survive extreme coercive pressure reflecting the Marxist-Leninist dogma that religion is "the opiate of the people" and has no place in a revolutionary socialist society, especially given the relentless secularism of the modern project. Religion is an intrusion of the premodern, no longer needed as comforter for those exploited by capitalist class domination. The momentum was behind industrialism and the general conviction that modernization provided a universally valid solution to human torments connected with hardship and poverty. An extreme version of this view extended the hostile assessment of modernism to politics as well. In the society of tomorrow, it was hoped on some fronts, the issues for the leaders to decide would become exclusively technical in character, matters of allocating resources for purposes of efficient use, leaving all decisions in the hands (or heads) of technical experts, or better, computerized procedures.

The disappearance of politics (and politicians) in the wake of the disappearance of religion (and religious divines) was premised on the acceptance of efficiency and instrumental rationality as sufficient to minister to the totality of needs in organized societal life. This technocratic optimism about human capacities to eliminate problems of scarcity and the resistance of nature assumed extreme forms that now seem ludicrous. Herman Kahn, now dead, but earlier a respected futurist (besides being a notorious nuclearist), turned his formidable intellectual powers to what he conceived to be one of the greatest challenges likely to emerge from this triumphal scientism in the next century: the menace of boredom arising from an abundance of leisure time! In other words, this ultra-materialistic vision of the future envisaged abundance replacing scarcity as the main challenge to societal leadership.

In the course of the last twenty years, these circumstances have changed in a number of crucial respects. The inevitability of modernization has been openly opposed from diverse directions. Such opposition has had the common feature of reviving a sense that religion (along with politics) is somehow relevant to the core issues of the current human situation. I will discuss two radically different forms of this change.

From one direction there has been a series of shifts within the religious domain calling for active participation by devout Christians in struggles for liberation from oppressive economic, political, and cultural conditions. Especially in Latin America, priests and theologians have broken out of their roles as upholders of the established societal order and have increasingly associated the mission of the church with an active involvement in overcoming the suffering of the poor. The liberationist perspective insists that the essence of religiosity is solidarity with the poor rather than attendance at church or the display of religious devotion through financial contributions. Even a nonprofessing Christian is given a better purchase on salvation than a professing Christian who devotes his muscle or resources to an oppressive political order. Such an ecclesiastically shocking claim was bound to stir things up in the Vatican, as indeed it has. "Liberation theology" is the name that has been given to these tendencies, especially prominent in Latin America, to emphasize the role of religion-in-the-world, a role that has drawn directly upon the main nonreligious source of social and political radicalism—namely, Marxism—for its sense of direction appropriate to the practice of revolutionary politics. The sublime and surprising realization that religion, to rediscover its ground of vitality, needed to enter into coalition with its most determined ideological adversary has yet to be widely acknowledged, much less appreciated, in the North. What is more, the receptivity of radicals to the participation of priests and theologians in their shared political enterprise represents a drastic reformulation by secular revolutionaries and radical reformers of the nature of struggle, as well as an altered vision of justice. Remember, religion had previously been an enemy and obstacle for revolutionary socialism, as well as a source of resistance to it. Now, all at once, Christianity has emerged as a revered ally of transformative politics.

The triumph of the Sandinistas in Nicaragua involved the most significant fusion of Marxism and Christianity yet to achieve an embodiment in history. It is such a troublesome phenomenon for conventional Western thought that its reality has been largely ignored, if not denied. American mainstream commentary on the Nicaraguan political system has largely explained developments since Somoza by reference to familiar East-West categories: the government in Managua has been labeled Marxist-Leninist and it has been largely portrayed as a Central American replica of Fidel Castro's Cuba. For pragmatic reasons, liberals in this country have not contested these assessments; even those ardently opposed to helping the *contras* were eager to insulate themselves from accusations of Marxist sympathies or insufficient concern about Soviet strategic penetration in Central American affairs. Yet, dispassionate witnesses and commentators have consistently noticed the real and persisting importance of religious convictions and vocation to the new leadership in Nicaragua. The Nicaraguan Foreign Minister, Miguel

D'Escoto, one of four ordained priests among the nine top Sandinistas, requested a leave of absence a few years ago so that he might fast in protest against the extension by Congress of further aid to the *contras*.[2]

Even if such an act is discounted as a gesture, it is a symbolically significant expression by a supposedly radical, Marxist-oriented political movement of its renewed willingness to join hands with those who find religion at the center of their personal and revolutionary being. Such a premodern form of political expression by a high government official alters the public understanding of political language, creatively implying the potency of nonviolent and religiously sanctified instruments of protest and resistance. One could hardly imagine a comparable American official making a response that so engaged his personal being and body, and included a comparable expression of religious conviction.

The United States Government has refused to acknowledge this religious component of the Nicaraguan experience, stressing instead the anti-Sandinista strain evident in the clerical hierarchy, especially evident in Miguel Obando y Bravo, one of the few Central American churchmen ever elevated to cardinal. Apparently the Vatican was recognizing his role in stemming the tide toward a reconciliation between Marxism and Christianity, and was giving ecclesiastical encouragement to prelates to take active, partisan roles in opposition to radical politics. In effect, the United States, for ideological reasons, does not wish to cope with a world in which Marxism and Christianity are allied in form and substance, preferring good-evil polarizations as a way of rationalizing intervention against the Sandinistas in the familiar currency of the Cold War. If our adversary is no longer godless, the United States government cannot so easily continue to vindicate its resort to force through rationalization of itself as representing a fair and generous people who gained their own political independence after a harrowing armed struggle against a colonial adversary.

Whatever we may wish, a Christian presence has emerged at the center of radical opposition politics in many countries of the Third World. In South African townships it has generally been religious leaders who have given direction and transcendent passion to the anti-apartheid movement. In South Korea it has been, along with students and workers, the Christian churches that have joined ranks with democratic forces and opposed a militantly anti-Communist governing coalition. And in the Philippines, many believe that it was the tilt in an anti-Marcos direction at the critical moment by Cardinal Sin, the highest figure of the Catholic Church, despite warnings from the Malacanang Palace that the Communists carrying on an armed struggle would benefit, that facilitated the triumph of the moderate, yet intensely democratic, movement led by

Corazon Aquino. Significantly, ideological affinities have given way to normative affinities: the Christian commitment, with exceptions, has increasingly sided with the poor, almost regardless of ideological implications. And political radicals have reciprocated, welcoming and revering Christian leaders who join their struggle, feeling validated by such an affirmation, and seeking to bridge from their side the gap between their political vision and the progressive side of the religious tradition. Religious and political perspectives have converged spontaneously to accord priority to a nationalist creed that seeks above all to wrest control over resources, culture, and the state from foreign hands, and to transfer that control to authentic representatives of the people.

It is not only in the Third World that such a constructive pattern of religion and political interpenetration has occurred. In Poland, the Solidarity Movement, although initiated by workers, has been consistently inspired and protected by priests and officials belonging to the Catholic Church. The main Solidarity figures, including Lech Walesa, have presented themselves all along as devout Catholics. Of course, the Polish Church has quite a conservative background; its stance is part of a long battle against Soviet influence. Yet, the church has been, possibly unwittingly, swept along in a political movement that is anti-authoritarian and motivated by a democratic ethos that itself seems quite at variance with hierarchical and anti-democratic notions of authority long associated with the history of Catholic tradition and practice in Poland. In Afghanistan, too, religious traditions and leaders have been a prominent aspect of nationalist resistance to Soviet encroachment.

Extending this survey to Western Europe and the United States, one finds less focus, yet a definite reassertion of religious presence on many political battlefields. In the peace movement, religious personalities have been at the forefront. In the United States, the Sanctuary Movement has enlisted several hundred churches of all denominations in a stand that has challenged the primacy of state power in a crucial realm of public policy: control over the dynamics of immigration, especially deportation. The willingness of religious communities to extend protection in the form of "sanctuary" to "illegal" refugees from Central America, especially El Salvador, is impressive, given prospects for prosecution and even imprisonment. A surprising number of Americans recently engaged in nuclear resistance have been involving Nuremberg notions of personal accountability to confirm and validate their duty to disobey illegal state policy in war and peace, although the probable consequence is a criminal indictment. The main justification for such a stand rests on an altered sense of citizenship and patriotism, but its underlying motivation is generally a manifestation of a religious conviction, often arising in the setting of a communal or semicommunal circle of believers who profess a radical version of Christian faith that seeks, above all, to be attuned and responsive to actual and potential suffering in the world. In this critical respect, religion and radical politics converge on the idea of taking suffering seriously.[3]

It would be a grave error to assume that all religious ventures in the political domain are motivated by progressive purposes or imagery. Quite the contrary. From the other direction there has been a remarkable surge of fundamentalist religion in the last few decades. The most vivid instance is undoubtedly the Islamic Revolution led by Ayatollah Ruhullah Khomeini in Iran. The Iranian undertaking to banish alien modernism in favor of a restored, rigorous, theocratic polity has shocked the Western secular sensibility while mobilizing many of its own poor and stimulating many in the Islamic world, especially among the youth. The fundamentalist appeal has demonstrated its capacity to exact sustained and extreme sacrifice for an indefinite period, while offering no materialist inducements. When Iraq attacked Iran in 1980, a consensus among smart modernist analysts anticipated a rapid and decisive Iraqi victory, underestimating the capacities of fundamentalist Iran to resist the superior forces of Iraq, especially in the face of the substantial collapse of its military capabilities under the Shah as a result of the Islamic Revolution. The fundamentalist tidal wave generated by the Islamic revolution has already been responsible for adding an unpredictable element to the political life of several Islamic countries.

But, again, the fundamentalist resurgence is not confined to Islam, or to the Shi'ites in Iran. In Central America, for instance, evangelical and fundamentalist Christianity has flourished alongside liberation theology and has promoted a politics of deference to reactionary interests, including an acceptance of foreign economic and military claims on national independence. In Afghanistan, and arguably in Poland as well, the positive role of religion in nationalist resistance must be balanced against reactionary attitudes toward social and economic issues of reform. And, in many parts of Asia and Africa, religious institutions have backed repressive governing structures, often giving a religious sanction to cruel practices of law enforcement. Such tendencies are evident in several Islamic countries, but also seem prominent in Buddhist Sri Lanka, where the religious establishment has goaded the government to adopt the most uncompromising policies on matters involving the rights of Tamils.

The appearance of American fundamentalists in the form of "the moral majority" and evangelical Christianity has represented a determined assault on the lifestyle of secular modernity, especially as embodied in big cities. This sort of fundamentalism reconciles many Americans to their pessimistic expectation of nuclear doom by converting this dread of catastrophe into the realization of a divine plan. The result is a "blessed assurance" of salvation, to quote one writer who was astonished by the widespread yearning for the rapture of Armageddon that she found in Amarillo, Texas, where the Pantex facility produces America's entire arsenal of nuclear bombs.[4] The AIDS epidemic has acted as a kind of objective confirmation of the fundamentalist critique of modernism, with its permissive ethos of private relations, especially sexual relations, and has induced a repressive backlash of great potential fury. The reality of this backlash is now manifest in the sudden rise of unprovoked street violence against gays in America that is often quietly tolerated, if not encouraged, by local police.

While awaiting the end of time, fundamentalists are preoccupied with punishing the infidels—those who refuse to heed the true faith. Their harsh exclusivity fits well with ideological stereotypes of the enemy in Moscow embodying an evil that contrasts with the essential goodness and innocence of Americans. Of course, such a moral dichotomy revives the Manichean heresy that had envisioned the climax of history to be a war between forces of light and darkness, with victory going to the former. The rejection of Manicheanism by the early church was a consequence of its tendency to banish evil from the self and, hence, effectively to deny the basic doctrine of original sin with its indwelling notion of evil. The Manichean claim was a manifestation of deadly pride, a fundamental vice since Medieval times. It is ironic that the Cold War hardliners have brought Manicheanism back into the churches in the guise of unremitting anti-Communism. Along with that shift, there has been a religious assertiveness on matters formerly assigned to secular control—for instance, the determined efforts to make prayer part of public education. After the Congressional rejection of Robert Bork, President Reagan's candidate to the United States Supreme Court, J. Clifford Wallace, a Mormon with lower court experience, was supposedly attracting positive attention in the White House because he did not believe in the separation of church and state.

How are we to interpret this tendency toward religious self-assertion, whether in a liberating or fundamentalist mode? Is it coincidentally associated with various local circumstances of conflict and tension in the world? Or is a wider pattern of secular and modernist discontent inducing a variegated religious revival?

My hypothesis is this: the complex modern project to apply science and technology to human problems has encountered several severe challenges that are undermining both its legitimacy as a creed and its coherence as a basis for action. Simplistically put, modernism as practiced has given us nuclearism, an overwrought encounter between human activity and ecological viability, as well as an atomized social fabric whose members suffer from acute forms of alienation. Normative and spiritual blinders have not well served the human species, at least not in this country. Of course, the modernist logic continues to lure many of us with its promises to overcome *with* technology the difficulties that technology has created: more modernization for the Third World; computerized democracy; and the strategic defensive initiative (SDI) for a superpower. But the crisis of modernism is generating nonmodernist responses as well. To cope successfully, we are urged by some to look backward (a heroic premodern antecedent) and by others to strive for a far greener future (a heroic postmodern prospect). Both nostalgia and aspiration are emotive expressions of discontent with the instrumental modes of fulfillment associated with modernist solutions.

Religion provides the materials out of which to fashion either type of response, and thereby to recast politics. Marxism—as a radical politics attractive to the oppressed—often fails to mobilize mass support in the cultural circumstances of Third World and non-Western societies and is substantially discredited in many societies. Liberalism—as a moderate politics attractive to those with humane values and middle-class interests—cannot ground its convictions (which are generally little more than calculations) on terrain that is firm enough to support radical societal restructuring or normative risk-taking of any consequence. A religious radicalism has far greater mass appeal, especially given an overall disenchantment with the Soviet model and with the dismal experience of revolutionary guidance issued from Moscow. A religious grounding deepens and extends struggle, enabling mass forms of resistance that incur risks and accept sacrifice, insists upon an agenda of radical restructuring, and yet does not abandon normative discipline.[5] The secular mentality tends to depersonalize suffering, whereas the religious mentality generally regards seriousness about suffering as central to its undertaking. Of course, religious fundamentalism drives out modernists, but in a bloody manner.

II. INTERPRETING THE RELIGIOUS AWAKENING

But the religious awakening has another dimension. There is a reinterpretation of what religion is about, and a basic, if rarely articulated, insistence that true religion is antithetical to institutionalization and hierarchy. In this respect, modernism is associated with the institutionalization of authentic religious experience transmitted from various premodern traditions and

bureaucratic stifling through the growth of formalized religious establish-
ments. Postmodern religiosity is associated with liberating spiritual interpretation of the human situation from all aspects of church dogmatics.
It may operate in a reformist mode by seeking to work within the ecclesiastical framework, or it may insist that appropriate religious activity
can only flourish in deinstitutionalized settings that repudiate "structure."

Manifest in these postmodern strivings is an exciting new energy
intent on remaking religion, and, with it, politics and culture. Such remaking can either breathe life into inherited symbol systems by invoking a
counter-tradition long marginalized by the mainstream, or by going back
to a moment in the past prior to passage across some Rubicon of ecclesiastical and doctrinal decay. In Christianity, reference can be made to the
Franciscan understanding of the sacred web of life, or to the glorious
era of Christianity, prevalent during the centuries before the conversion
of Constantine, which was pacifist and associated with the spirituality of
the poor. This remaking can also occur by weaving a new relational web
of symbolic significance: by celebrating the arrival of a new goddess
religion, or a religion that is animistic without being pagan. The eventual doctrinal and institutional form of this religious remaking remains
uncertain and inchoate, but there is undeniably present a widespread
drive to recover an unmediated religious understanding of life-forces
and a renewed sense of human purpose.

This new religion seems grounded in the earth (as distinct from
descending out of the sky), and is richly relational. An influential passage from the inspirational anthropologist and neuro-ecologist Gregory
Bateson captures the ethos that lies at the center of this new spirituality:

> What pattern connects the crab to the lobster and the orchid to
> the primrose and all four of them to me? And me to you? And all
> six of us to the amoeba in one direction and to the back-ward
> schizophrenic in another? What is the pattern which connects all
> the living creatures?[6]

Another scriptural text of postmodernist religion (and politics) is contained in a poem by Gary Snyder entitled "Revolution in the Revolution
in the Revolution." Cleverly parodying Marxist-Maoist rhetoric about the
drift of revolutionary energy, Snyder turns the secular rhetoric and sensibility of Communist ideologies in an unexpectedly ecological direction:

> Revolutionary consciousness is to be found
> Among the most ruthlessly exploited classes:
> Animals, trees, water, air, grasses.

Snyder can be read as saying that the Marxists cut off their analysis too soon, and did not push their revolutionary fervor deep enough, into the earth itself. Or Snyder can be heard more cynically as dismissing Marxist materialism for the true revolution, that of the spirit, which includes giving our blessings to the whole of nature and finding power not from the barrel of a gun but, as he reveals later in the poem, from Buddhist meditation. In his words,

> & POWER
> comes out of the seed-syllables of mantras.[7]

The new religious sensibility endows all of nature with a sacred, privileged status. The political implications are acknowledged and lead to new forms of struggle in which modernist centralism and violence are under assault from a variety of postmodernist sources. It becomes worth dying for the sake of dolphins, whales, perhaps even on behalf of rivers, mountains, and forests.[8]

Illustrative is the *Rainbow Warrior* incident in which French intelligence agents exploded two bombs on a Greenpeace ship while it was docked in Auckland, New Zealand, on July 10, 1985, killing a member of the crew. The ship and its multinational crew were seeking, on behalf of the earth and all its inhabitants, to protest and disrupt French nuclear testing in the Pacific. Recourse to political violence by France represented a modernist effort to destroy the postmodernist kind of challenge being mounted by Greenpeace. It was clearly an act of war by modernism (as represented by the militarized state) against postmodernism (as represented by an unarmed voluntary association of green-oriented individuals). There was a silence of most governments about such a terrorist tactic. The explosions on the *Rainbow Warrior* released a swirl of statist emotions. After all, France was upholding the primacy of the state in external relations, but it was doing so by an illicit and terroristic violation of the sovereign rights of a white, predominantly Western country (the violent deed being done in New Zealand without permission and in defiance of the country's antinuclear stance). Even governments hostile to France were discreet, possibly giving subconscious expression to a growing anxiety about the statist framework as the basis of international problem-solving. The interplay of forces released by the *Rainbow Warrior* affair suggests the persistence of the modernist framework of state power, but also the vitality and legitimacy of the postmodernist impulse, which was eventually validated by an $8.1 million damage award issued after hearings under United Nations auspices before a panel of international law specialists.[9]

The results of this process were ambiguous, and not satisfying over-all. If the government of New Zealand had not been on record itself as antinuclear, and had not felt itself as partly the object of the French attack, it is not clear that France would have acknowledged formally its liability for the damage caused. Even as it was, the damages awarded were offset to a certain extent by the agreement of the New Zealand government to release the French agents in its custody and allow France to administer a brief period of nominal confinement. France may have been induced to pay ransom for its intelligence agents and, in this cir-cumstance, to admit its own wrongdoing, but, in effect, the implication of this penalty is that the wronged party was a state (the modernist adver-sary) rather than a social movement (the postmodernist adversary).

The postmodern religious revisioning may assume shaky forms, for instance, by placing stress on the "harmonic convergence" of August, 1987, which enabled the earth to obtain a "cleansing energy" from a rare alignment of planets. This alignment was supposedly of sufficient mag-nitude to overcome a period of catastrophic events otherwise predicted to transpire on earth by several ancient calendars. Such "readings" of the cosmos are assuredly a kind of antimodernist backlash which do not lead us to enter the process of transformation in any serious or sustaina-ble way. Gathering at sacred sites around the world at a given time may be exhilarating for the participants, and it is possessed of an irresistible potential for media hype, but it does not address the real issues of power, depravity, danger, and destruction in our world. Nor, I might add, do most of the New Age expressions of religious sentiment that promise their adherents growth and tenderness *in vacuo,* or, what amounts to the same thing, on sunny beaches and breathtaking mountain heights. It is not sensible to place our trust in any appeal that does not concretely and courageously respond to the actuality of suffering (past, present, and future) in our world. It is certainly a sign of ethical sensitivity or, more astutely, of political cynicism (the legacy of Bitburg) for American lead-ers to visit the charnal houses of the Holocaust, as George Bush did in 1987, perceptively writing in the Visitors' Book at Birkenau: "In remem-brance lies redemption." But, truly, to remember the atrocities of others is not in itself redemptive. To visit the diseased survivors of Hiroshima might be redemptive for American politicians *if* the occasion of the first atomic attack on a human settlement was then and there acknowledged without qualifications as a crime against humanity. In fact, American political figures have mostly stayed away from Hiroshima, probably not daring to look back, or not being willing to dedicate themselves to the pursuit of a nuclear-free world, or not even being willing to confront the human consequences of an atomic attack.

The path from a religious renewal to a political renewal is complicated, controverted, and still quite difficult to discern. As I have suggested, several assured features are present: (1) an ecological feeling for the wholeness of experience as primary; (2) a decentering of anthropocentric presuppositions about the divine plan and the locus of the sacred; (3) a grounding of religious and political life in the challenge of suffering, not only of humans, but of other animals and even the rest of nature as well; (4) a conviction that the creative and imaginative locus of energies is passing from those who currently preside over established hierarchies of state and church; (5) a trust in the cooperative potential implicit in human nature, as well as a distrust in a variety of "realisms" and "rationalisms" that claim human nature to be ineradicably aggressive and entrapped within current behavioral and organizational enclosures; and (6) closely related, a disenchantment with violence as the means to security, justice, revolution, and transformation.

Among the controversies are those about whether to connect the politics of postmodern thought with left or progressive modernist causes— to have associations with established political parties, with organized labor, and with the extension of rights in relation to current structures of governance. Is the postmodern a continuation in a different direction, or a new start?[10] A specific cluster of disputes concerns the degree to which the postmodern ethos accepts the outlook of the egalitarian "deep ecologists," those who would altogether withdraw any privileged status from human strivings and aspirations, sharing resources on the basis of some sort of parity with animals, plants, and even rocks and mountains. Some of them fall into the trap of encouraging an exquisite sensitivity to the feelings of the nonhuman and even inanimate world while turning away from the correctable torments of human society. But not all postmodernists go this far as they recoil from modernist rifts with nature.

Neither religion nor politics has, as yet, crystallized around a definitive embodiment of the postmodern. Fascinating explorations are, to be sure, being undertaken in response to particular felt urgencies of time and space. I would encourage careful scrutiny of the Green party movements in various countries—perceived both as the emergent postmodern and as the waning, yet still formidable, modern.[11] The inner tensions of Green politics represent different ways of deconstructing the modern at a given historical moment and in a particular place. There are closely related instances of grassroots activism in Asia, especially India, which are intent in a Third World circumstance on revitalizing democracy by reversing the flow of energy from periphery to center, by stressing the primacy of the local and concrete.[12] In a more explicitly postmodernist religious frame are the *communidades de base* throughout Latin America, which were initially the seedlings of liberation theology but more recently persist as exploratory frameworks for testing and evolving new styles and formats for politics.[13]

Similarly, the new social movements associated with feminism, peace, and the environment that have ebbed and flowed since the 1960s — with their distinctly transnational reach — are better understood as the quest for comprehensive renewal and societal transformation than as issue-specific and programmatic.[14] In contrast, those formations seeking reforms, such as International Physicians for Social Responsibility and Amnesty International (both certified by the receipt of Nobel Peace Prizes), are quintessentially modernist, seeking to nudge existing institutional frameworks into minimal decency without posing the slightest transformative challenge.

The postmodern can be identified by its necessarily challenging character. The otherness it seeks can be grasped by a crude contrast with the modern: the postmodern reveres nature and the cosmos and finds sacred and mysterious energy embedded in life itself.[15] From this embeddedness a new religiosity is beginning to take specific shape, but its distinct form and credo are not yet quite discernible. Only glimpses appear on still distant horizons. Enough is happening so that Bethlehem is once again on alert!

III. POSTMODERN RELIGIOUS REVISIONING

The argument of this essay can be summarized as follows.[16] The secularism of modernist civilization does not inspire confidence in its capacity to respond to fundamental challenges in the contemporary world: nuclearism, ecological decay, mass misery. Indeed, these challenges are severe as a consequence of the modernist experience with technology, war, and indifference to nature. As a result of this situation, modernism is losing its hold over the cultural imagination. In reaction, a dynamic of cross-penetration is underway between politics and religion, producing a series of developments that can be either constructive (liberationist) or destructive (fundamentalist). Politics is being reinfused with religious symbols and claims, whereas religion is being summoned to the trenches of popular struggle, including even recourse to violent tactics.

This breakdown of the modernist separation and antagonism between politics and religion represents a series of societal efforts to handle a new agenda of human demands. Perhaps most striking in this regard is the reconciliation of Marxism and Christianity in several Third World settings, a process that is one of mutual enrichment without any apparent effort to subordinate one to the other. This process is also extremely threatening to established hierarchies. This is evident in Rome's defense of clerical privilege and its insistence on retaining fully centralized ecclesiastical control over matters of ritual and creed. Also the United States government with its ideological fervor against Marxist tendencies in the Third World has refused to admit the evidence of this reconciliation, and continues to attack left governments that are religiously conditioned on the premise of their godlessness. In actuality, a modernist secular state may be far less religious than a state that is governed by a revolutionary movement influenced by the new Christianity of base communities.

These concerns at the core of current world conflict and ideology remain entrapped within an essentially modernist framework for the conduct of international relations: distinct territorial states looking forward to an expansion of their productive capacities as the primary means by which to relieve the misery of their peoples. To find more effective and humane means to mobilize peoples to pursue these ends is a challenging, hopeful development, the full potential of which remains untested.

At the same time, there is emerging a postmodern political sensibility that is animated by an entirely different worldview. It, too, is a kind of religious politics or political religion, though it does not grow out of the hitherto dominant interpretation of established world religions, especially those of a monotheistic character in which the divine reality has been imagined to be above and external to nature, or those that emphasize ecclesiastical structure. The postmodern orientation is ecological at its foundation, finding spiritual coherence in the processes of nature itself. Safeguarding the miracles of creation, including the habitat for human and animal life, against violence, destructiveness, and pollution becomes the most critical religious undertaking, especially given our growing realization that natural life-support systems are under severe and growing strain.

The human species has a special coevolutionary capacity and responsibility. Unlike other species, we are aware of our roles in the world, and bear the burdens of awareness for disrupting the ecological order to such a dangerous and unnecessary degree. As such, we can respond to the pain of the world by devoting our energies and resources to various forms of restorative action and creating the institutional forms and public understanding that are needed for such a dramatic reorientation of behavior. This "conversion" from secularism is underway in various enclaves of human existence, but to an uneven degree, and virtually not at all if influence is assessed by reference to powerfully entrenched governmental and market structures associated with administering the modernist enterprise.

The premodern anticipates the postmodern, although historically it gave way to the modern. The postmodern draws on the distant past, but it cannot reproduce it, although it can relearn ancient wisdom and adapt it to current world conditions. The acute sense of jeopardy, complexity, and technological unfolding, and the sheer density and interpenetration of peoples and cultures in the contemporary world, provide an assurance that the postmodern is a way forward, not a repetition. To succeed, the postmodern unfolding needs to be both a political way (to deal adequately with resources, relations among societies, group identity, human and nonhuman needs and aspirations) and a religious reawakening (the release of spiritual energy associated with this readjustment of role and mission).[17] To what extent Green politics, new social movements, reemergent indigenous peoples, or small communities of faith and resistance are vehicles of this postmodern possibility remains to be seen. Assuredly, each of these tendencies is expressive of a reaction against modernist encroachment and a partial revelation of what a fused religious and political postmodern consciousness imagines an alternative, preferred world might be. Such imaginings are being given a preliminary concreteness in the form of many discrete explorations. There is a common thread: the sense that the whole and the part are united in reality, not alternatives, and that problem-solving and value-realization require both attentiveness to wholes (shared participation in species, life, planet) and greater fulfillment for distinct parts (ethnic, gender, cultural specificities).[18] Nothing, as yet, has gelled into a pattern that can claim for itself the definitive *imprimatur* of postmodernism, or that can monitor initiatives to decide whether or not their contribution is genuinely postmodern, rather than merely antimodern.

NOTES

1. This essay was originally presented as a keynote address for a conference on "Revolution, Religion, and World Politics" at the College of St. Thomas in St. Paul, Minnesota, October 5, 1987.

2. For a general assessment, see Andrew Reding, "Seed of a New and Renewed Church: The 'Ecclesiastical Insurrection' in Nicaragua," *Monthly Review,* July/August 1987: 24-55; also Reding, ed., *Christianity and Revolution: Tomas Borge's Theology of Life* (Maryknoll, N.Y.: Orbis Books, 1987). See also the statement by the National Directorate of the FSCN of October 7, 1980, "The Role of Religion in the New Nicaragua," in Tomas Borge et al., *Sandinistas Speak* (New York: Pathfinder Press, 1982). A useful firsthand account is Joll Millman, "Nicaragua's Social Revolution Rests Largely on Scripture and Christian Base Communities," *In These Times,* February 24-March 8, 1988: 12-13, 22.

3. This focus is developed powerfully by Upendra Baxi in "Taking Suffering Seriously: Social Action Litigation Before the Supreme Court of India," *Delhi Law Review* 91 (1979-80), 8-9. See also Baxi's *Courage, Craft and Contention: The Indian Supreme Court in the Eighties* (Bombay, India: N. M. Tripath, 1985).

4. Cf. A. G. Mojtabai, *Blessed Assurance: At Home with the Bomb in Amarillo, Texas* (Boston: Houghton Mifflin, 1986).

5. Sharon D. Welch, *Communities of Resistance and Solidarity: A Feminist Theology of Liberation* (Maryknoll, N.Y.: Orbis Books, 1985).

6. Gregory Bateson, *Mind and Nature: A Necessary Unity* (New York: Bantam, 1979), 8-10.

7. Both quotations from "Revolution in the Revolution in the Revolution" are in *Regarding Wave* (New York: New Direction Books, 1970), 39.

8. For ethical and legal rationales, see Christopher Stone, *Earth and Other Ethics: The Case of Moral Pluralism* (New York: Harper and Row, 1987).

9. *The New York Times,* Oct. 3, 1987: A2.

10. See Petra Kelly, *Fighting for Hope* (Boston: South End Press, 1984) and, with Rudolf Bahro, *Building the Green Movement* (Philadelphia: New Society, 1986); see also the report of tension among the German Greens, *The New York Times,* Oct. 11, 1987: 22.

11. For a convenient summary of the Green perspective, see Charlene Spretnak, *The Spiritual Dimension of Green Politics* (Santa Fe, N.M.: Bear and Co., 1986), 78-82.

12. For excellent information on India, see the regularly published issues of the *Lokoyan Bulletin* published in Delhi, India under the editorship of Smitu Kothari and Harsh Sethi.

13. See Richard Shaull, *Naming the Idols: Biblical Alternatives for U.S. Foreign Policy* (Oak Park, Ill.: Meyer-Stone Books, 1988).

14. See Zsuzsa Hegedus, "The Challenge of the Peace Movement: Civilian Security and Civilian Emancipation," in Saul H. Mendlovitz and R. B. J. Walker, eds., *Towards a Just World Order* (London: Butterworths, 1987), 191-210.

15. For intriguing speculations along these lines with some scientific foundations, see J. E. Lovelock, *Gaia: A New Look at Life on Earth* (New York: Oxford University Press, 1979).

16. See my earlier essay, "In Pursuit of the Postmodern," in David Ray Griffin, ed., *Spirituality and Society: Postmodern Visions* (Albany: State University of New York Press, 1988), 81-98.

17. The fundamentalist option can be considered an *inappropriate* religious awakening that is quite likely to present a major challenge in the years ahead, especially given the uncertainties associated with this multifaceted process of transition from modernism to postmodernism.

18. The practical and theoretical implications of this conjoined vision are explored in R. B. J. Walker's *One World/Many Worlds* (Boulder, Colo.: Lynne Reinner, 1988).

7

FAMILY, WORK, AND CULTURE: A POSTMODERN RECOVERY OF HOLINESS

Joe Holland

What is the relationship of family to work, and of both to culture? This is an ancient question at the heart of human spirituality. This is why one of the deepest spiritual conflicts in late modern society is over the cultural meaning of work and family.

In this essay about the relationship of family, work, and culture, I propose that our modern culture is now entering a fundamental crisis. The essence of this crisis is that *the foundational cultural vision of the modern world—the mechanistic dream of autonomous freedom and progress—is failing to regenerate our ecological, social, and spiritual life. Within this crisis, the basic contradiction is revealed in modernity's fundamental degradation of work, linked to an expanding attack on the family. Further, this cultural attack on the family and work is reinforced by certain strains of Western spirituality that have played a strategically central role in both classical and modern Christianity.*

103

In addressing this proposal I first analyze how late modern culture simultaneously undermines family and degrades work. Second, I sketch the resulting cultural debate over family and work now emerging within liberalism. Third, I probe how the modern crisis of family and work flows in part from roots in classical Western spirituality. Finally, I conclude with a brief reflection on a healing postmodern path through this crisis of late modern culture.

This essay is part of a series of intellectual explorations which I have been undertaking into the crisis of modern culture and the search for a healing postmodern spirituality. As an exploratory reflection on broad generalities, it is full of statements that may warrant greater nuancing, qualification, and illustration, that may appear gratuitous or remain undocumented, and/or that may even seem ill-founded. I ask the reader to take the study according to its genre—a tentative and generalizing exploration.

I. THE BREAKDOWN OF MODERN CULTURE

Both the liberal (or capitalist) and the Marxian (or socialist) cultural ideologies of modernity are producing the opposite of what they intended. Instead of their promised "freedom and progress," they are producing an increasingly enslaved and destructive world—ecologically, socially, and spiritually.

The late modern battle over family and work becomes a highly personal and rooted way of entering the late modern battle over culture and its embodiment. The contemporary experience of family and work is both a window into the crisis of late modern culture and a seed for its creative transformation. It is our way of immediately participating in the battle between the destructive idolatries of late modern culture and the creative and healing re-spiritualization of a holistic postmodern culture.

The Modernization Process

I begin with a few words about modern ideologies in relation to modern culture.

In modernity, rationalist ideologies are the form of culture. For modernity, such ideologies attempt to provide a total explanation of reality by a mechanistic understanding of science that considers itself autonomous from spiritual and ecological values and from human community. In its depth, the crisis of modern culture is the crisis of modern rationality, that is, of the mechanistic understanding of science.

On the more hopeful side, as many social interpreters, including Pope John Paul II, have suggested, a new and healing postmodern form of culture is being born.[1] This form of culture is arising from a postmodern holistic vision of science understanding itself as profoundly "value-laden" and called to deepen the conscious communal creativity of ecological, social, and spiritual life. This postmodern form of culture, with its scientific vision, provides the basis for a postmodern vision of society and, within that, a postmodern vision of family and work.

This postmodern culture being born will attempt to embody itself in a postmodern form of political economy. For this reason, the debate over the form of the political economy becomes central to the creative unfolding of the new culture. The debate over the political economy is in turn a debate over the present cultural form of family and work.

A central cultural issue under debate in the late modern crisis is the public/private dichotomy. *The separation of the "private" from the "public" enabled the modern form of science and technology to develop its genius unfettered, but also to emerge as autonomous from ecological, social, and spiritual communion.*

Modern liberalism's expansion of the public/private dichotomy rendered the cultural realm of religion a "private" affair. This privatization brought gains in religious freedom, but at the price of religion's public role of supplying cultural guidance for the political economy. The classical transcendent orientation of religion had undervalued economic life as part of the worldly "lower" way, but it nonetheless provided a cultural framework for ordering the economy. The modern bourgeois consciousness, however, created a still deeper dualism which severed all connections between the political economy and religion.

In the modern liberal thrust to free the market, the economy was also "privatized," but this meant something entirely different from the liberal privatization of religion. While the privatization of religion was aimed at weakening it, the privatization of the economy was aimed at expanding its power by weakening state access to it. An autonomous economy would paradoxically function as the structural center of modern liberal society with little religous or political accountability.

The most powerful sector of modern society, its techno-scientific economy, was defined as outside state and religious control. The absurdity of applying the term "private" to the modern capitalist economy becomes clear today when "private" multinational corporations, whose gross annual product is greater than that of many nation-states, may determine the fate of the ecosystem.

At the same time, the family also came to be viewed as "private" in the same sense as religion and thereby weakened in power. The family was no longer seen as the first and fundamental cell of society, but as something outside society's public sphere. The foundation of society came to be seen instead as the autonomous individual, making voluntary contracts with other autonomous individuals. No doubt this shift has had a good side—for example, the modern expansion of romantic love, curtailment of the social power of the aristocracy (which ruled through family), and a deepening of individual subjective depth and creativity. But these changes also meant that the society would less and less base itself on the familial value of creative communion across time and space.

The Separation of Family and Work

The privatization of religion, the economy, and family enabled the industrial revolution to undertake a twofold but intimately related process of eroding family and degrading work. This simultaneous erosion of family and degradation of work began with the modern separation of work and family.

As modernity deepened, economic activity was progressively uprooted from the family farm, the family workshop, and the family store, and simultaneously divorced from the religious meaning embedded in those communal forms. These family-centered work arrangements were replaced by mass economic bureaucracies of factory, office, and sales chain, as well as by mass organizations of workers in the industrial unions. The whole process was guided by an autonomous and secularized understanding of technology, mediated through the market-led expansion of production for the sake of maximization of profit (or, in the communist case, power).

The resulting eroding of family and degrading of work happened in several ways. First, as Paul Shervish has shown,[2] the industrial factory system uprooted production from family life and reduced the family's economic function to the circular external processes of selling labor and purchasing finished goods, leaving the reproduction of labor and the consumption of goods as the only remaining internal economic acts of family life. Family was no longer a source of productive creativity. In short, human production was uprooted from human reproduction.

Second, based on the modern mechanistic paradigm of science, the uprooted industrial production system in turn developed a technological style yielding fragmented individualism coupled with massified conformism. In this individualizing/massifying process, the cellular root of family began to erode: first, with forgetfulness of the ancestors; second, with weakening of the extended family; third, with a destabilizing of the nuclear family; and finally, with a social attack on the unborn, the handicapped, and the elderly.

With the industrial production system uprooted from the reproduction system, the reproduction system itself was being undermined. A technological style based on the mechanistic model of industrial production isolated from reproduction inevitably produced social structures that turned against reproduction.

Third, work itself was stripped of creativity, at least for the working classes. As developing industrial technologies expressed ever more powerfully the mechanistic vision of production, human labor was progressively deskilled.[3] Economic creativity became the function not of labor but of the technologies and of the elites who controlled them. Labor was seen only objectively as a "factor of production," as a "labor force" to be exploited, or a "labor market" to be externally and mechanistically managed, along with natural resources and capital.

Accordingly, when production was uprooted from reproduction, not only was the reproduction system threatened by the erosion of family; the production system itself was degraded by the mechanistic denial of labor's creativity.

This dual modern attack on the production/reproduction system was not only social in character but also ecological and spiritual. Modern mechanistic culture simultaneously began to uproot itself from its ecological matrix by denying nature's underlying creativity and treating it only as an inert object to be exploited and managed. Similarly, life's spiritual depth was flattened under the impact of an expanding secularization, or marginalized by the deepening privatization of religion into psychological interiority, where it could easily be reduced to psychological therapy. As human workers, the rest of nature, and human spiritual energy became subordinate to the autonomous development of mechanistic technologies, these very technologies became social gods.

The consequent divinization of mechanistic technologies expressed itself in the pseudoreligion of consumerism. In the consumerist vision, sex was uprooted from its familial source of spousal bonding and from its related link to the regeneration of the species. It was promoted as a trivialized consumer commodity, granting instant gratification. Instant sexual gratification in turn became a propaganda symbol for capitalist consumption, as evidenced by modern advertising. Not surprisingly, symbols of violent power accompanied symbols of consumerist sexuality, with both increasingly celebrated in the mass media.

With this "privatization" of so much of society—of family and religion to weaken their power, and of the economy to expand its power—the mediating institutions of society began to erode. The result was a growth of individualism, but one in which individuals felt naked and powerless before centralizing mass bureaucracies—the overt power of the giant political state and the covert power of the giant economic corporation. Political and economic organizations were also uprooted from the organic communal system of family and religion and based instead on a secular and instrumental theory of voluntary individual contracts, mediated by the social technology of the expanding legal profession. These developments also carried positive gifts, but in the crisis of late modernity we are discovering their negative face.

The Decisive Event of Television

Modernity's cultural control of values took a decisive step in the electronic era with television.

In capitalism, the macro-society of the "external" or "objective" world of work (now beyond the family) is guided by the supreme value of warlike competition. Hobbes rightly described this as "the war of all against all." Before the event of television, however, this macro-society of competitive war was softened by the opposite values in the micro-society of the family and privatized religion. Here the reigning value was loving cooperation, at least in theory.

The contrast of these two values—warlike competition in work and cooperative love in family—took expression at the cultural level in sexual symbolism. The economy could thus be seen according to the phallic image of male sexuality as external, aggressive, and hard. By contrast, the family could be seen according to the womb-like image of female sexuality as internal, receptive, and soft. Men were largely in charge of the world of work; women, the world of home. In theory, the brutalizing of the male in the harsh workplace was to be healed and checked in the evening when he returned to the gentle home of wife and children. Despite the patriarchy and violence which often existed in the home, the values of family life did flow over into the economy to check its harshness.

But with the micro-electronic revolution and the deepening cultural influence of corporate-controlled television, the reverse became true. *Rather than the family's exercising a softening influence on the economy, the economy through television began to shape, according to its destructive values, the cultural life of the home.* Through television, the warlike competition of the economy, with its cultural celebration of violent power, trivialized sexuality, and idolatrous consumerism positioned itself as the basic mediator of values in the heart of the familial process.

Today, in cultural terms, television is the truly dominant cultural socializer. In the words of Neil Postman, a professor of communication arts and sciences at New York University,

Television has become. . . the command center of the culture . . . .
Right now television has the culture by its throat.[4]

The traditional socializers of family, religion, and school have weakened before television's power. Because of an increasingly "value-free" orientation, the public educational system has often become valueless, abdicating its cultural responsibility. Religion, in turn, has often become highly privatized and, at least in the mainline Christian bodies, largely ignores the religious potential of television. As a result, families often gather together only to receive the televised propaganda of the economic corporations.

Finally, the late modern shifting sexual division, drawing ever more women into the paid labor market outside the home, imposes one more burden upon the already overburdened family system. The solution is not to confine women once again to the home, nor simply to liberate women from the home, and especially not to impose on them the double burden of work outside the home and most of the work inside the home.

All of this, and especially the changing role of women, precipitates a new debate within liberalism over the meaning of sexuality, the function of sex roles, and the status of family.

II. THE NEW DEBATE WITHIN LIBERALISM

In this new context, the "liberal center" erodes and splits into right and left wings. Although, in the United States, the left wing is generally called "the liberals" and the right wing "the conservatives," I prefer to describe them respectively as "left-wing liberals" and "right-wing liberals" to help keep in view the fact that this is a split within the liberal view of culture. Both these wings call for a revision of the liberal ideology, but only to preserve liberalism as still viable in the new context.

Liberalism's Left Wing

The left-wing liberals seek mechanistically to rationalize the economy by public (state) regulation of the market and social welfare service of individuals. But, at the deepest cultural level, this state-led reform of the economy has the instrumental goal of providing a structural platform for a highly individualistic and privatized interpretation of cultural freedom. This view of cultural freedom reveals itself especially in left-wing liberalism's privatization of sexuality. The left wing sees sexuality as a matter of individual preference or choice, with family life as only one preference among many, but in every case with no public consequences.

For this side of liberalism, sexuality has become an autonomous means of self-fulfillment, uprooted from the social fabric and from the species' generative process.

This wing correctly criticizes the heritage of patriarchy in received family structure, but then it seeks only to rescue its individual victims (women and children) and ignores family as such. On this left wing, there is no normative theory of family, not even in a wide sense, and family is implicitly treated with suspicion.

The liberal stream of feminism (which is not the only stream) has embraced this left-wing perspective in order to compete with men on the ground of autonomous freedom. The competition is played out in the "male" world of the political economy, while the "female" world of the family is undermined and goes into crisis.

Liberalism's Right Wing

The right-wing liberals perceived quite early this cultural threat from the left. They realized that the permissive cultural orientation of the left would undermine family and society, in turn precipitating an all-encompassing state. They also realized that moral permissiveness and state expansion would interfere with the control of labor and the freedom of the market. The right wing therefore pursued the opposite strategic course: using the state publicly to support the micro-realm of family (especially sexuality) and religion to defend the macro-realm of the economy as private. But this meant defending the patriarchal family and a nationalistic form of religion. *In this wing, the restoration of traditional values provides the discipline and purpose needed to make the free market function, and also to prepare for the noble sacrifice of the family's sons in war to defend this vision of macro-freedom.*

Right-wing liberalism also tries to continue the patriarchal mythology in which men are linked to the external world of work and women to the internal world of home. This has disastrous consequences for family and society, especially in the new social context. First, it fails to deal with the real oppression of women precisely when consciousness of this oppression disrupts the traditional "balance" of marriage and family life. In the new social situation, if a partnership model of intimate communications and sharing of family responsibilities does not replace the classical sexual division of labor, many marriages will not survive the new pressures. Second, this return to the patriarchal model allows the expanding ethos of warlike competition from the macro-society of work to continue unchecked in its expanding macro-role and its invasion of the micro-society of family. Such unchecked expansion of the alienated masculine symbol at the foundation of cultural life increases the threat to life's ecological-social-spiritual whole.

The Failure of Both Wings

The liberal left wing revises the liberal ideology by making the economy public as a platform for deepening privatization of family (and sexuality) and religion. By contrast, the liberal right wing wants to make family and religion public to provide patriarchal security and discipline for a privatized economy.

The left wing compromises the macro-level of economic freedom in the hope of expanding the micro-level of psychological freedom, while the right wing compromises the micro-level of psychological freedom in the hope of defending the macro-level of economic freedom. The left wing sacrifices Adam Smith to expand Sigmund Freud, while the right wing sacrifices Freud to defend Smith.

The left wing of liberalism, including its liberal feminist stream, aggravates the late modern erosion of life's ecological, social, and religious whole by tending to dissolve the familial and religious framework for the micro-level of the self—seeking especially to make the sexual self autonomous.

Quite logically (in this view), a leading issue for the left is abortion, the "right" to kill the child in the womb who infringes on the rights of the autonomous self. Thus liberated by abortion, both women and men are free to compete in the macro-level of the economy—unfettered by reproductive responsibility. As liberal feminists join so many men before them in this uprooted vision of sexuality, the destructive energies of modernity accelerate.

By contrast, the right seeks to preserve traditional religion and the traditional family as the psychic defense of the economy. But its vision of religion and family is patriarchal and linked to an ethos of violence. The right thus reasserts the traditional male warrior symbol as the divinely inspired ruler over the family and defender of the nation. While the left wing of liberalism tries to expand state-sponsored social security and to reduce state-sponsored military security, liberalism's right wing seeks just the opposite—to reduce the state's social security and to expand its military security.

The left wing's threat to the family comes primarily from the micro-level, while the right wing's threat comes primarily from the macro-level. The left-wing threat comes from the micro-level by condoning the killing of children in the womb, trivializing sexuality into an autonomous source of individual gratification, and dissolving the family before the expansion of an individualistic-massified society. The right-wing threat comes from the macro-level by increasing the danger of rapid nuclear holocaust or slow ecological contamination, but also by a reassertion of sexism, racism, and classism, all imposing economic burdens on poor and middle-income families. This is further compounded by the right's defense of a patriarchal model of family, which does not provide an adequate model of mutual communications and support necessary to resist the pressures of late modern life.

We might say therefore that *the left-wing attack on family proceeds from the psychological side (where culture is subjectively rooted), while the right-wing attack on family proceeds from the economic side (where culture is objectively institutionalized).* But the left wing's psychological disintegration of family from within has the paradoxical effect of economically victimizing family members, especially women and children, who then must face the public world in economic isolation. Similarly, the right wing's continued privatization of the free market has the paradoxical effect of psychologically victimizing family because, through the free-market approach to television, corporate values become the basis for socialization.

Similarly, both left and right wings of liberalism further the modern degradation of work, but again beginning from opposite poles.

The permissive culture of the left also expresses itself as adversarial—challenging authoritarianism in work. But adversarialism as a principle is incapable of building a creative community of work. *Under the left-wing vision, accordingly, the workplace degenerates into a fragmented cluster of self-seeking defensiveness.* Even unions seem often to fall victim to this cultural adversarialism.

By contrast, the authoritarian culture of the right is manipulative, even repressive. Patriarchy, the right-wing model of family, becomes the right-wing model of work as well, with workers treated as children. Because childlike workers do not know what is best for them, patriarchal management must make workplace policy and punish workers if they fail to conform. But manipulation and repression cannot build a creative community of work. *Under the right-wing vision, the workplace is forced to become a hierarchical machine.* And this machine is increasingly oriented toward the production of *violence*— violence to the earth, violence to society, and consequently violence to the Creator. The power of the military-industrial-university complex is a threatening fact of global life, East and West, North and South.

Both wings of modern liberalism, despite their polar opposition, feed the late modern ecological, social, and religious destruction of life's creative communion.

TABLE 7.1
Contrasting Strategies of Liberal Right and Liberal Left

Liberal Left	Liberal Right
private family	public family
public economy	private economy
psychologial freedom	economic freedom
Sigmund Freud	Adam Smith
micro-level	macro-level
liberation of women	promotion of patriarchy
individual as foundation	family as foundation
expand social security	reduce social security
reduce military security	expand military security
threat to family	threat to family
from micro-level	from macro-level
of psychological self	of economic institutions
paradoxically leaves family	paradoxically leaves family
as economic victim	as psychological victim
adversarialism in work	authoritarianism in work

III. THE CLASSICAL ROOTS OF THE MODERN CRISIS

Secularization as a Misdiagnosis

Often within the conservative wing of Catholicism, the crisis of the modern world is diagnosed as due to the loss of certain classical spiritual values, particularly from Western Medieval culture. The problem is described as "secularization." The prescription generally offered for this diagnosis is a healthy "restoration" of classical values, especially hierarchical authority and imposed discipline, as well as spiritual transcendence.

But in exploring the spiritual dimension of the crisis of modern culture, I found myself unexpectedly coming to the conclusion that a restoration of classical spiritual values would only compound the modern crisis. I increasingly discerned the deepest cultural root of the modern crisis to be classicism itself. The essence of the modern crisis is that production is abandoning reproduction, in turn yielding the destruction of the life system. More fully stated, the modern systems of mechanistic production (the macro-level) and psychological atomization (the micro-level) are eroding and attacking the reproduction of life. But this process did not begin with modernity. Modernity only deepened the process by giving it the technological weapons to carry it out on a vast scale. Rather, the process began within classical civilization and was carried to the present, especially in certain streams of Western spirituality.

Dualism as the Deep Root

Classical Christianity ordered Western culture into a double dualism. First, it was religiously ordered (for Christians) into the hierarchy of a "lower" way for the laity who lived in a "secular" world, and a "higher" way for the "religious" who allegedly rejected the world. Second, it was politically ordered into a hierarchy of "superiors" who ruled and of (implicitly) "inferiors" who were ruled over. If monasticism and subsequent forms of "religious" life legitimated the first dualism, clericalism legitimated the second. I should make clear that this critique of religious and clerical dualism does not negate the important roles for the Catholic communion of evangelical celibacy, intentional Christian communities, or the leadership authority of the episcopate and presbyterate. The debate is over not their validity but their cultural style.

Both of these dualisms were mutually supported in a transcendent framework based on the classical Greek understanding of the chain of being, descending away from pure being (God) into less and less pure realms. Just as "higher" transcended "lower" on the philosophical chain, so "religious" transcended "seculars" (laity and "secular" clergy), the "secular" clergy transcended the laity, and "superiors" transcended "inferiors," on the religious scale.

The dualism was further deepened by extending the monastic "religious" model to the "secular" clergy. Monastic or "religious" men and women, the spiritual elites of Catholicism, lived in monosexual institutions based on a monopoly of celibacy. In the Middle Ages, as the power of monasticism reached into the episcopate and even the papacy, the "secular" clergy were also pressed into the life style of the monastic monosexual celibate monopoly. The net result was that religious elites in Catholicism came to form an ecclesial sub-culture segregated from the laity.

I do not criticize this embodiment of Western Christianity in its classical context. That model of church was a strategic response to the contextual challenge of the surrounding culture. Perhaps for that context it proved a creative way of being faithful to the Gospel, especially in the struggle with lay investiture. It also made enormous contributions to Western civilization, and indeed to the entire human experience. But whatever its creativity in the Medieval context, in the late modern context such spiritual flight from the "lower" and "secular" cycles of nature fails to celebrate the spiritual principle of regeneration so profoundly needed as an antidote to the late modern assault on life. To understand why that is so, we need to see that *the modern understanding of science is really a secularized and democratized development of the classical understanding of transcendent "sciencia."*

Science, Sexuality, and Secularity

In the Medieval period, only a few religious elites could reject the world, that is, try to rise above the webs and cycles of the natural and social ecology and so be free from rootedness in family and the work of "the world." The key to this symbolical rejection of the world by religious elites was the requirement of celibacy. Celibacy was the means to be free from the secular world.

The word "secular" provides the key to the cultural meaning of this rejection. In its Latin origins, "secular" comes from the word for *secus,* whose variant is *sexus,* which of course means "sex." For the classical mind, the secular world was the world caught up in the need for sexual reproduction, that is, in the necessity to reproduce because of the presence of death. In Greek mythology, *eros* (the sexual urge) and *thanatos* (the death urge) were closely linked. Sexuality was a requirement of secular finitude.

By rejecting the reproductive cycle of sexuality, classical celibate religious elites claimed to transcend both *eros* and *thanatos,* both birth and death, and thus to be free from the webs and cycles of the sexual-secular world. Having abandoned finitude, they symbolically passed, by means of contemplation, into the infinite and absolute realm of the eternal universal, namely the Divine understood as transcendent over the world (not as immanent within its creative energies). The fruit of this identification with the transcendent dimension of the Divine through contemplation was called "sciencia."

Paradoxically, freed from the burdens of family and worldly work, these religious elites of the West had the leisure to experiment with empirical manipulation of the very earth they had theoretically rejected. *The monasteries were thus the womb that brought forth modern science. But once the baby started to grow up, the monastic womb could no longer contain it.* As a result, the pursuit of knowledge in the West undertook a long journey from the ideal of transcendent "sciencia" to the modern norm of secularized science.

The two key negations of monasticism, freedom from biological family (responsibility for reproduction) and freedom from the responsibilities of the world, became, in a secularized and inverted way, the ideals of modern culture. Through mechanistic freedom and progress, modernity came to hope that all people could be free from the webs and cycles of nature. Just as "religious life," by its spiritual hegemony based on an exclusively transcendent understanding of the Divine, had implicitly diminished the profoundly religious meaning of sexuality and of work, so modern secular life in its paradoxical inversion trivialized sexuality and degraded labor. The autonomous individual, freed from social bonds and economic limits, became the modern ideal. Work and family were not modern sources of meaning, just as they had not been for classical "religious."

For classicism the religious meaning of sex and work had only been "lower," but modernity carried the classical uprooting of religious experience through to its ultimate consequences. It removed all religious meaning from sex and work. Classical and modern culture are indeed different, and classicism certainly could not have foreseen or intended what modernity would create. But one still flowed into the other, like parent into child, even if the child proved rebellious. *The problem of modernity is therefore not that modern science developed technologically while failing to develop spiritually; that is a restatement of the old dualism. The problem is rather that the dualistic spirituality of classicism, by failing to celebrate the spiritual depths of the secular world, especially its sexuality and work, passed on no adequate religious resources for the newly born modern scientific vision to understand its own religious depth.*

For this reason, rather than appealing to the classical age as an antidote to modernity, we need to be even more traditional than the classical traditionalists. As Thomas Berry has argued, we need to recover in postmodern form the pre-dualistic primal tradition of the tribal-shamanic roots of human culture, which preceded classicism and which in fact provided the powerful cultural foundation for much of classicism's creativity.[5]

Here, tapping the most ancient memories of human culture, we can learn from our deepest roots that *sexuality and work are holy precisely because they embody the webs and cycles of nature.* These webs and cycles are holy because creation is holy. Creation is holy because it reveals the holiness of the Creator.

The primal peoples, whose experience is most approximated in the tribal peoples among us, always had this immanent sense of a holy creation. But classicism was grounded on the transcendent flight from creation, and on a certain blinding to nature's immanent revelation of the Divine Mystery. *Transcendence remains a valid dimension of interpreting the Divine, but alone it is unbalanced and ultimately proves threatening.* Modernity grew out of this imbalance and expanded technologically its destructive consequences. The healing of modernity's spiritual and technological imbalance is intimately linked to a recovery of the immanent holiness of creation.

Often the charge is made against this recovery of the immanent holiness of creation that it fails to take sin seriously. Christians certainly must see creation as disrupted by sin. But Catholic Christians, at least, believe that sin did not fundamentally corrupt nature, that it only wounded it, and that a residual goodness is still present in nature. The saving act of Jesus is, in turn, a healing re-creation which does not reject nature but takes it as its basis. This theological view is generally described as sacramental. The recovery of the immanent revelation of the Divine in and through creation is an act of sacramental healing for our imbalanced and destructive late modern culture.

IV. TOWARD A PATH OF CULTURAL HEALING

The primal creation-centered vision of spirituality needs to become the natural foundation for the attempt of Christian spiritual energies to guide the postmodern scientific paradigm and postmodern technologies. Only such a retrieval will enable postmodern spirituality to guide science and technology toward a life-giving healing of the sinful destructiveness of modernity's hostility to life.

The fertile encounter between our primal past and our postmodern future is the cultural framework for Christianity's engagement in the recreative healing of the creative ecological, social, and spiritual communion of life. By contrast, both pure modernization and the synthesis of modernization with a classical restoration are paths of further degradation and disintegration. But what does this mean for family and work?

A Postmodern Vision of Work and Family

Work is the process by which we humans become conscious cocreators with each other, with our ecological matrix, and ultimately with the Creator from whom all creativity arises. We humans need consciously to reflect on our work, continually to reshape it through technologies, and always to name its cultural meaning. Because the heart of culture is spirituality, culture ultimately reveals the deepest spiritual values of a society's work. For this reason, economic experience becomes a matter of profound spiritual meaning.

Family is the creative communion of the kinship system across time and space—reaching back across past generations of ancestors, into future generations of the as-yet-unborn, and into present generations of relatives whose lateral extension reaches outward in concentric circles to friends, community, and ultimately to the entire human family. Family is the fundamental cell of all society, the biological root out of which society grows. Society in turn is the family blown large.

If family is the fundamental cell of society, then family is the fundamental cell of the work process. For most people in times past, family and work were the same reality. Again, only since the industrial revolution have work and family been dramatically fragmented. We might describe the social principle of the rootedness of society and its work in family as *the priority of family.* This principle is linked to a second principle bearing on work, *the priority of labor,* which sees labor as the subjective source of economic creativity, not simply as an objective force to be hired and extrinsically managed.[6] The priority of family and the priority of labor are two sides of the same coin. Let us look at family and work together from this perspective.

Family means something much more than marriage or the parent-child relationship. While these are the heart of family, standing alone they are a naked heart. It is a strategic mistake of modernity to view the family simply as the nuclear family, or the household. The vast majority of the human race has not seen family in this narrow way, neither in times past nor even at present. If family is defined from the household or nuclear unit, then family easily becomes one particular "lifestyle choice" among many others. But the various "lifestyle choices" often enumerated—such as two-parent families, one-parent families, singles, celibates, homosexuals—are not alternatives to family but parts of wider biological kinship systems extending across time and space. For example, while singles are not married, they are never alone: they are always part of a kinship web of parents, grandparents, ancestors, and probably siblings, cousins, aunts and uncles, nephews and nieces. Even if people do not know their family, they still have one, and must come to terms with its meaning.

When society so severely reduces the meaning of family, it in turn impoverishes itself. It is perhaps the deepest social tragedy of modernity that it has so diminished family, first to the nuclear unit, then to the household, and now threatens this diminished family with disintegration. Our inability to imagine a profound social role for family is simply a result of our impoverished sense of family.

For our purposes, there are three basic statements about the relationship of family (in the rich sense) and society.

1. *The family is the fundamental cell of all society.* It is not one more institution among many other social institutions. Nor is it simply an economic, political, or cultural institution. Rather, the family is the social root of all institutions. Family is the micro-society, out of which the macro-society grows. As such, family contains in seminal form all social life—economic, political, and cultural (including religious).
2. *The family is strategically central to ecological, social, and religious transformation.* Because family and society are related as micro and macro of the same reality, the struggle over the form of family is simultaneously the struggle over the form of society, and vice versa. Changes in family and society can, of course, be creative, destructive, or ambiguous.
3. *To deny—in theory or practice, explicitly or implicitly—that family is central to social structure and to social transformation is to undermine both family and society.* Institutions and strategies not centered in family erode society at its cellular foundation. This erosion of society is in turn an undermining of life in the creativity of its full ecological-social-spiritual communion.

Such thoughts may seen naive and nostalgic, but they may become quite realistic in the postmodern electronic era.

Let us first recall that the basic economic, political, and cultural functions of the family were uprooted from it only because of the growing sophistication and complexity of modernity's social and material technologies. When industrial machinery became too big to fit into the house and too expensive for the family to afford, it migrated to the factory and converted the family into an exclusively consumer unit. When the functions of health, education, welfare, law, and religion were vastly developed by the modern university system, they developed into the relatively autonomous professions and institutions we know today as separate from the family. Similarly, as modernity fragmented and mobilized individuals, politics lost its rooted fabric in the kinship system and moved instead into the combination of mass political parties and mass political bureaucracies, whose political campaigns are increasingly spectacles of consumerism. Over time, politics became uprooted from the stable and familial communities, with the empty space filled by interest-group competition.

Today, because of the micro-electronic revolution, we will probably see a return of many of these functions back to the family, not in opposition to the larger professions and institutions developed out of classicism and modernity, but in partnership with them. We are already familiar with the phenomenon of desk-top publishing, so rapidly utilized now by the explosion of successful home-based businesses (mostly started by women). Its imminent successor is desk-top manufacturing, returning the workshop to the home, yet with greater sophistication than that possessed by industrial manufacturing. Very soon, families will also have sophisticated health advice available to them, with in-home computerized diagnostic and monitoring procedures for critically and chronically ill members. The same will be true of legal services, general information, and education. As a result, families will recover a sense of their creative power as more than consumers. In a Christian parallel, as we already see beginning, there will be an explosion of basic communities, really a new version of early Christianity's family or household churches. Such house churches will also have available to them through electronic communications the best of Christian educational materials.

Objections are sometimes offered that such technologies are too expensive for poor families, and so should not be stressed. But note how the poor invest in televisions sets, which they quickly see as essential to life. Many micro-electronic technologies are far less expensive than the family automobile, and could provide the family with important means of avoiding external expenses and of internally generating income.

For poorer countries, such technologies could become village investments, or investments by extended families. Very soon, for example, a Kenyan coffee farming family could go to a village computer, powered by a solar collector and in communication with a global satellite, to find the current world market price of coffee, throw out a bid, contract a buyer, arrange international transport for the crop, and have the money deposited electronically in the family account. Bypassing the Kenyan Coffee Board and the global commodities cartels, the farming family could have a much larger margin of profit.

Strategic Principles

While it is still too early in the birth of the new culture to know just how the reempowerment of family and the recentering of work in family will take place, perhaps some tentative strategic principles can be offered to guide society's thoughts and actions.

A first step would be the *cultural celebration of life as creative communion,* striving toward richer consciousness of itself as rooted in the webs and cycles of nature and society and in turn arising from, and immanently revealing, the love of the Creator.

A second step would be *public recognition that family is the first social expression of this creative communion,* the cell and root from which all else in society flows.

A third step would be to see *work as the expansion of the familial process to the macro-level.* Family and work, rather than being guided by the opposite ideals of love and competition, would instead integrate both, with love in the defining position.

A fourth step would be to pursue *experiments in rerooting work in the family,* through new models of home-centered work and family-centered community development, all made possible on a vast scale by the micro-electronic revolution. Labor unions that wish to be creative would do well to learn how they can help humanize these new familial possibilities.

A fifth step would be to develop explicit *family criteria for all public policy,* for example, family-impact analyses for all decision-making, and public policy favoring the coordination of workplaces and schools with home life.

All of this would require the articulation of a social vision that breaks beyond the narrow imagination of both the left wing and right wing of late modern liberalism. This articulation in turn would require creating a fresh space in politics. But none of this will happen unless the postmodern social vision can draw deeply on fresh spiritual energy that celebrates the immanent spiritual meaning of family and work in the holy process of the universe.

Should this happen soon in Christian communions, there will arise a *vast reservoir of spiritual energy* capable of joining with other spiritual traditions to heal the frightening destructiveness arising simultaneously at the macro- and micro-levels of late modern culture. If that happens, we shall rediscover for a postmodern context the healing and recreative power of the same Spirit who brooded over the waters of Genesis.

NOTES

1. On the postmodern thought of Pope John II, see my essay, "The Cultural Vision of Pope John II: Toward a Conservative/Liberal Postmodern Dialogue," in David Ray Griffin, William A. Beardslee, and Joe Holland, *Varieties of Postmodern Theology* (Albany: State University of New York Press, 1989).

2. See Paul Shervish, "Family Life and the Economy: Graver Responsibilities and Scarcer Resources," *Families, the Economy, and the Church: The U.S. Bishops' Pastoral Letter on the Economy and its Relation to Family Life* (Washington, D.C.: National Center for Family Studies, 1985).

3. See Harry Braverman, *Labor and Monopoly Capital: The Degradation of Work in the Twentieth Century* (New York: Monthly Review Press, 1974).

4. Alvin P. Sanoff, "A Conversation with Neil Postman," *U.S. News and World Report,* Dec. 23, 1985: 58-59.

5. See various essays by Thomas Berry in his multi-volume collection *The Riverdale Papers,* in photocopied form and available from The Riverdale Center for Religious Research, 5801 Palisades Avenue, Bronx, New York 10471.

6. See Gregory Baum, *The Priority of Labor: A Commentary on Laborem Exercens Encyclical Letter of John Paul II* (New York: Paulist, 1982).

8

FROM INDIVIDUALISM TO PERSONS IN COMMUNITY: A POSTMODERN ECONOMIC THEORY

John B. Cobb, Jr.

My interest in economics arose from practical concerns. In 1969 I was aroused to the effects of economic growth on the environment. Nothing that I have learned since then has reduced my dismay.

Until that time, I had assumed that economic growth was needed to deal with the acute suffering engendered by poverty. When I came to oppose growth, therefore, I was distressed to find myself in the position of the comfortable North American rejecting growth for the sake of the environment. I felt the need to examine the situation more closely. That examination led to the discovery that most of the growth that damages the environment does not benefit the poor. Indeed, economic growth requires the exploitation of the poor, and in many instances growth leaves them worse off even by economic measures. When considered in terms of real human satisfaction, the rich do not benefit either.

Finally, problems of world hunger led me to focus on agriculture. There, too, I found that growth was not the answer. For the present, global supplies of food are sufficient. The problem now is inability to pay. But precisely those agricultural policies designed to generate growth increase the number of the poor who are unable to feed themselves. They also reduce the arable land which will be available in the future when food requirements will be greater. My disillusionment with the economy of growth was complete.

But my personal disillusionment, and that of tens of thousands of others, has had no effect on the course of events or on public policies. Both political parties have remained growth oriented. And, of course, business continues to try to grow. Economic efficiency aimed at growth is taken to justify wave after wave of depopulation of rural America, as capital and energy are substituted for labor, and the family farm disappears. Whence comes this commitment to growth? Is it simply the natural expression of greed?

I. The Modern Commitment to Growth

Examination shows that the modern commitment to growth cannot be explained by greed alone. Equally greedy people in other times and places have not been committed to growth of the economy in general; they have been satisfied to improve their relative standing in a static economy. Growth appears not as an expression of greed but as an ideal, a commitment. We have come to believe that growth will enable us all to improve our situation together. With growth, the gain of one need not mean the impoverishment of the other.

This idea is intuitively plausible. Yet no one can deny that the industrialization through which growth occurred was accompanied by enormous suffering in England and subsequently elsewhere, and that it is accompanied by such suffering also today. The gain of all is not apparent. Indeed, much sacrifice is needed to accomplish growth.

The intuitive plausibility of the idea that a larger pie would enable all to have more would not have survived the empirical evidence of the increased suffering of the poor had it not been for economic theory. The theory in question arose in the eighteenth century at the height of the Enlightenment and is, accordingly, rightly called "modern" economic theory. Because belief in the truth of this modern theory leads to commitment to growth quite apart from empirical evidence, the theory requires examination.

Adam Smith observed in the Scottish market that sellers were free to get as much as they could for their goods, and that buyers were free to seek the lowest prices and the best quality. The participants in the market understood what they were buying and selling quite well. No one bought or sold unless he or she gained by doing so; everyone gained through exchange. Also producers, observing the market, gauged their output accordingly and thereby met the needs and desires of the consumers. In this way they profited, and the consumers got what they wanted at a favorable price. When each seeks personal gain without regard to the consequences for others, all benefit. Smith spoke of an "invisible hand" which transforms the self-seeking of individuals into the good of the whole.

Because all gain in the free market, the larger the portion of the economy that can be brought into the market, the better. Primarily, for Smith, this principle meant an end to governmental controls. These controls necessarily inhibited the mutual gains which the market is ideally equipped to provide. From Smith's time to the present, enthusiasm for the market has been the hallmark of non-Marxist economics. Today the actors in the market include industrial organizations of vast size and enormous economic and political power, and the role of government has greatly expanded. Business uses advertising to create demand for products that few consumers are able to understand and appraise realistically on their own. But these historical changes have had little effect on the basic model with which most economists work. Divergences from that model are viewed as obstacles to be removed or, at best, as unfortunate necessities. Needless to say, the model has, in some respects, been brilliantly successful.

It is important to remember that a major part of what is exchanged in the market is labor. In the free market, the individual can seek the most lucrative employment. Of course, the employer seeks the cheapest labor. These opposite aims should lead to the most efficient outcome beneficial to both.

In fact, however, the strength of the parties in the early days of the industrial revolution was quite unequal. There were more people needing employment to survive than there were jobs to be filled. Wages settled at the subsistence level. That is, employers paid just enough to enable their employees, together with a limited number of dependents, to survive in a state of extreme poverty.

At first, economists expected that this would be a temporary condition. As industry prospered from low wages, it would expand, requiring more workers and bidding up wages. But others saw that this increase in wages would not last. As wages rose, more of the workers' children would survive. The increased labor pool would bring wages back down. Industrial workers would always be paid at subsistence levels.

This was depressing news and gave to economics its name of "the dismal science." There was only one escape. Production per worker, or productivity, would have to increase faster than population. Then there would be enough for all, and wages could rise above the subsistence level. Productivity could rise as the worker was given better tools and equipment. This required capital. Growth could be restored in a way beneficial to all as capital supplemented labor in the productive process. Growth based on improved productivity, rather than on the number of workers employed, has accordingly been the central commitment of economists from that time to the present. The success of this strategy has been enormous. In the fully industrialized world, few workers now live at the subsistence level.

We can now appreciate the idealism associated with the commitment to growth. And we can understand why the criticism of growth is so resented. As economists see it, their role is to guide nations in the process of continuing growth, reducing as far as possible the stresses and strains of recession, unemployment, and inflation. The criticism of growth is felt to be an attack on the vocation of the economic community rather than as a request for the development of supplementary theories.

However understandable, the commitment to growth as the solution to the major economic problems is still distressing. It was a brilliant solution to the problems of nineteenth-century England. Today it is a major source of problems. We must join the handful of economists who are calling for reconsideration.

Thus far I have been using "growth" in the way economists use it. It is an increase of goods and services passing through the market. The economic community as a whole regards the Gross National Product (GNP) as a sufficiently accurate measure of growth to be usable for most purposes. Indeed, most economists by "growth" *mean* increase of GNP unless they clearly specify a preferred measure, such as Net National Product (NNP) or Gross Domestic Product (GDP). For our purposes, these distinctions are unimportant. The debate about economic growth is the debate about the desirability of directing our efforts to the indefinite increase of the GNP. (No one is opposing growth in wisdom, grace, knowledge, and love!) The question in the First World is whether the need for growth applies where the threat of rapid population increase has gone and plenty of goods are already produced for all to live far above subsistence levels.

Let us consider the situation more closely. According to economists, the function of the national economy is to contribute to the total well-being of its individual citizens. The contribution made by the economy is goods and services passing through the marketplace. Its contribution is proportional to the consumption of goods and services by these citizens. As consumption increases, accordingly, well-being increases. Measurements of production correlate with quantities of consumption.

These assumptions of modern economics can be questioned at several levels. Some of the questioning is taken seriously in the economic community. Does individual consumption correlate highly with production per capita? On the one hand, much of the production goes into military hardware, expansion of industrial plants, and police protection of a sort made necessary by the production itself. This expansion does not add to the individual consumption in which we are interested. On the other hand, many economic services are performed in the household, so that much of what is consumed escapes measurement by the GNP. GNP increases if the wife works and domestic help is employed. But it is not clear that well-being increases proportionately.

Two Yale economists, William Nordhaus and James Tobin, took account of these criticisms in an important article in 1972 entitled, "Is Growth Obsolete?"[1] The question meant, as I have indicated: Is increasing the GNP no longer desirable? To answer this question, they developed an index for more accurately measuring consumption. This index they called the Measure of Economic Welfare (MEW). The question was whether changes in GNP correlate well with changes in MEW. Their assumption was that, if they do, then the commitment of the economic community to increase of GNP is justified. They concluded that the correlation is sufficient for GNP to suffice as an indication of economic welfare.

Their evidence, however, was far from decisive. Their figures show that from 1929 to 1947 per capita GNP grew around 30 percent while per capita MEW grew around 33 percent. During that period the correlation was high, and their conclusion is supported. From 1947 to 1965, however, the comparable figures are 47 percent and 6 percent. During that period the correlation was very low.

To those not committed to the sufficiency of the GNP, the question of what has happened since 1965 is important. Has the high correlation of the earlier period been renewed, or is the low correlation of the post-World War II years continued? If the latter is the case, then the argument of Nordhaus and Tobin, that the overall correlation suffices to justify continued use of GNP to guide policy, grows weaker and weaker.

Unfortunately, no one has brought the figures of Nordhaus and Tobin up to date, and the efforts by a group of us in Claremont to do so turned out to be fruitless. Some of the statistics needed are not available, and some of the assumptions made in formulating MEW have become increasingly difficult to justify or even to interpret in the changing situation. Accordingly, our group devised its own measure of welfare, an

Index of Sustainable Economic Welfare (ISEW), following MEW in many ways but also introducing different considerations.

Our calculations lead to conclusions more favorable than those reached by Nordhaus and Tobin for the period they studied. For example, from 1950 to 1965, while per capita GNP rose at an annual rate of 2.08 percent, per capita ISEW rose at a rate of 2.14 percent! Clearly our different assumptions are not unfavorable in principle to the conclusion drawn by Nordhaus and Tobin. In the 1970s, however, while per capita GNP rose at the rate of 2.04 percent (approximately the same rate as in the earlier period), per capita ISEW remained almost constant, actually falling at an annual rate of minus 0.14 percent per year. From 1980 to 1986, while per capita GNP rose at the rate of 1.84 percent per year, per capita ISEW fell at the rate of minus 1.26 percent annually. These results show that there is no necessary correlation between economic growth as measured by GNP and changes in real economic welfare.

II. THE ENVIRONMENT AND THE FUTURE

My realization of how deeply commitment to growth, defined as increase of GNP, has come to characterize market economics, and of how dangerous this commitment is, has led me to examine the assumptions underlying the theory. The assumption that is most striking, at least to one concerned about what is happening to the environment, is the assumption that the effect on the environment is not a factor to be considered in economic theory. Nordhaus and Tobin, for example, take no account of pollution or the depletion of natural resources in the calculation of economic welfare. If they did consider depletion and pollution as negative factors, it is probable that the 6 percent gain in welfare shown by their figures from 1947 to 1965 would disappear. The 47 percent growth in per capita income during that period would then be accompanied by no gain at all in economic welfare! To me, the exhaustion of resources and the pollution of air, water, and land have obvious importance for human welfare. Why are these physical realities ignored by economists?

Originally, modern economic theory did include consideration of land. Capital, labor, and land were seen by Adam Smith as more or less equal factors in the production of goods. Malthus went further in emphasizing the importance of land. He thought that increasing population would force up the price of food. Accordingly, he theorized, while capitalists and workers were kept by competition from increasing profits and wages, landlords would profit greatly. In other words, land would be the primary source of wealth. Had this view continued, it is probable that the condition of the land as well as its quantity would have been of interest to economists. Resource exhaustion and pollution would have played a role in economic theory.

But this changed with the shift of attention from the quantity of production to productivity per worker. The application of capital to land increased the yield. Hence capital, rather than land, became the variable that determined production in agriculture as in industry. In Kenneth Boulding's words, economics focused on the "exchange, production, consumption, and accumulation" of commodities.[2] Only capital and labor counted.

Of course, economists know that land is needed to supply raw material for production and as a sink into which wastes are discarded. But economics developed at a time when, relative to need, resources and sinks were both very large. For purposes of economic theory, they were treated as infinite, and no value was assigned to them. Since then, as shortages appeared, capital and human ingenuity have been used to develop technologies to overcome these shortages. For example, as agricultural land was used up, deserts have been irrigated; as accessible high-grade ores disappeared, new technology has made it possible to mine previously inaccessible ores and to process low-grade ones; as the quantity of wastes has increased, new ways of processing these for reuse have been found. Nordhaus and Tobin reflect the general view of economists when they say that "reproducible capital is a near-perfect substitute for land and other exhaustible resources."[3]

With such assumptions, economists have omitted natural resources and sinks from their calculations. They are not led by their science to examine empirically what happens when farmland erodes and waters are polluted. In the recent debate about limits to growth, almost all economists have retained their faith in technology as making possible virtually unlimited growth, regardless of the physical limits noted by ecologists. The results are understandable but distressing.

The lack of importance land has in contemporary economic theory entails complete disregard for the interests of living things other than human beings. The rapid extinction of plant and animal species that accompanies economic expansion does not appear as a relevant consideration within economics. Domesticated animals are included as commodities, no different from clothing or machinery, and wild animals lack even this consideration.

The threat of dominant patterns of the economists' thought to the environment stems not only from their neglect of the value of the natural world, but also from their practice of discounting the future. This discounting follows from the fact that the price of goods in the market is taken to be the only measure of their value. The price is the result of what the participants here and now desire. This desire does not exclude the future altogether, for people want to secure or improve their own futures and that of their households. But the "rational" person, according to economic theory, does not place the same value on future enjoyments as on present ones.

The rational discounting of the future can be connected with depreciation and interest rates. Suppose I purchase a piece of land. I can farm it so that at the end of twenty years it will be as productive as it is now. Or I can farm it in another way such that I will earn more annual income, but the soil will become so eroded and exhausted that I will have to sell it after twenty years for a lower price. If I am "rational" (in the sense of the modern economist), I will decide between these two methods of farming solely in terms of one question: Will the amount of money that I will earn from investing the extra income earned by the exploitive method of farming be greater than the reduction in the value of the farm? If so, the rational procedure is to use up the soil.

III. INDIVIDUALISM AND COMMUNITY

As I paid attention to the working of the economy, I discovered that its harmful effects are not only on the natural environment; they are also on human community. I was puzzled by this. Because economists are dedicated to showing how human needs can best be met, why is the outworking of their theory so destructive of communities?

The answer has not been hard to find. The economy works against human community because it is based on a radically individualistic view of human beings. Because what is valued is not community, but only per capita consumption of goods and services, community is destroyed whenever it stands in the way of increasing the total quantity of goods and services.

The strongly individualistic bias of modern economics expresses the eighteenth-century Enlightenment milieu in which it arose. Enlightenment thinkers took community for granted and accented the rights and liberties of individuals. Much was gained by this emphasis that is worthy of our gratitude, and we need to remain vigilant lest we lose what is precious in this heritage. But, like many reforms, it was *too* successful. Our need today is to renew community among free individuals. In this context, we cannot be content with an economy that works against community.

Furthermore, we now see that the political, economic, and cultural individualism of the Enlightenment was rooted in a physical and metaphysical individualism which has also proved inadequate and misleading. Modern science thought of the world as composed of indivisible units—atoms—which related to each other only externally. Their relative spatial locations could change, but this change had no internal effect on them. An atom remained self-identical and unchanged forever!

Of course, no one supposed that individual human beings remained wholly unchanged forever. Political theorists and economists chose, nevertheless, to think of them atomistically. They did not consider how they were mutually affected and even constituted by life in community. Individuals were instead viewed as essentially separable from one another, unaffected by the breakup of community. The only concession made by economists to the communal character of human life was to speak in terms of individual households, rather than individual persons, as the atomic units whose welfare was sought.

Economists often make clear their continuing preference for viewing people as a collection of atomic units by using Robinson Crusoe as their model for explaining how the market works. He has his Man Friday as his household and his island as his property. If he has the opportunity to trade, he will do so only if what he receives is of more value to him than what he gives. The exchange, accordingly, will necessarily benefit him or his household.

Using Robinson Crusoe as the model works well to make the market attractive, because the atomic unit, the household, is self-sufficient without trade. Crusoe is not only free to trade for his best advantage, he is also free not to trade at all. In the real world, however, few people have this freedom. Most people have no means of production at their disposal. They must sell their labor in order to live. Their choice is only to whom they will sell it. Their dependence on others is, therefore, much more drastic than the individualistic model implies.

Economists sometimes claim that their science is descriptive only, that its use is to be governed by the values of those who use it. But this claim is profoundly misleading. Description passes very easily into prescription and, in any case, exists for the purpose of guiding policies. The categories of the description profoundly affect the implications for policy formation.

Where the existing community resists the changes required to bring about economic growth (perhaps through increasing the productivity of agricultural workers or through industrialization), those informed by the study of economics will point out the need for rationalization, called "modernization." This modernization requires that systems of mutual support give way to systems of competition, so that the total supply of goods and services will increase. When new communities form around the new economic systems, improvements in productivity will require that they, in their turn, give way. Today, whole towns disappear as factories close, because the produce of those factories is more cheaply manufactured elsewhere. Economists frown on any protection of such factories, and thereby of such communities, from competition, because it is this competition that increases the total product.[4] Community counts for nothing in these calculations because households are conceived atomistically.

IV. POSTMODERN ECONOMICS AND COMMUNITY WELFARE

That I am dissatisfied with modern economic theory is obvious. There is certainly much in it that is true and valuable. We cannot do without it in the sense of simply returning to premodern theory. We need a theory that can incorporate much of what has been learned into a wider context. What we need, in other words, is a *postmodern economic theory.* My own thinking on this issue is heavily influenced by the philosophy of Alfred North Whitehead.

Today postmodern physics is well advanced and the outlines of a postmodern medicine and a postmodern agriculture are quite visible. But postmodern economic theory does not yet exist. Kurt Dopfer has edited a collection of papers entitled *Economics in the Future: Towards a New Paradigm.*[5] His fine introduction summarizes the paradigm of modern economic theory and offers four propositions with respect to the new paradigm: the need for a holistic approach; the need for a long-run view; the need to view economics as an empirical science; the need to view economics as political economy. I commend this essay to you as pointing in the right direction. I am pleased to say that he quotes Whitehead and specifically refers, in connection with holism, to Jan Smuts, who was important to Whitehead. If there are any similarities between his new paradigm and the postmodern theory of which I shall speak, they may not be entirely coincidental.

The most sustained contribution to a postmodern economic theory has been made by Herman Daly, the leading writer on "steady-state economics" in contrast to "growth economics." He is keenly sensitive to the environment and to the need to adjust economic thinking so as to make life on this planet sustainable. He has made specific economic proposals that have influenced what I have to say in this paper. I am glad to say that he also is familiar with Whitehead and recognizes affinities. A full postmodern economic theory should include great chunks of his work.[6]

The modern theory begins with admiration for the ability of the market to distribute goods optimally, to the advantage of each actor in it. It assumes that this advantage is the good for which the economic order exists. The increase of market activity is therefore assumed to increase welfare, and only very reluctantly will most economists engage in more careful analysis of what human welfare really is.

The postmodern theory should begin with this latter question. When it does so, it immediately rejects the Robinson Crusoe model. Human welfare is not the sum of the welfare of individuals, each inherently independent of the others. Human beings are communal beings. We belong to one another and do not exist apart from one another. In more technical terms, we are internally related to one another. We can improve human welfare, accordingly, only as we build and improve communities.

Personal freedom is as important as economists have supposed, but it is not modeled well by Crusoe bargaining with another island owner. Freedom is the ability to attain our ends, not simply the choice of items in trade, although this choice may be contributory to freedom in the larger sense. How free we are depends on the nature of the community in which we participate. Whitehead's discussion of freedom contrasts markedly with that of modern economists:

> In modern states there is a complex problem. There are many types of character. Freedom means that within each type the requisite coordination should be possible without the destruction of the general ends of the whole community. Indeed, one general end is that these variously coordinated groups should contribute to the complex pattern of community life, each in virtue of its own peculiarity. In this way individuality gains the effectiveness which issues from coordination, and freedom obtains power necessary for its perfection.[7]

Thus far, I have spoken of the community at which we aim as purely human. Our mutual human relations are clearly of primary importance. But we are internally related with other creatures as well, and they with us. The community with which we are concerned includes the land, with all its animate and inanimate elements. The good of the whole community is that to which the economic order should contribute.

Whereas the focus on individuals and their decisions in the market "discounts" the future, a focus on the well-being of the community does not. A community that is destroying the possibility of its own continuance into the future is not well off. If the good of the community is what is sought, then the end is necessarily a sustainable community. A sustainable community need not be static. Indeed, without variety, change, and interest, a community cannot be sustained. But the modes of change must be those that do not undercut the freedom of the future.

Whereas the modern theory proposes that each individual act from pure self-interest and leave the coordination to the market, or Adam Smith's "invisible hand," the postmodern theory sees that communities are interdependent. Each community must seek its own good in a way that does not impose undue problems on others—indeed, in a way that gives others greater freedom to deal with their problems. The welfare of each community is enhanced by the welfare of the others, because communities too are internally related. A postmodern community will be concerned not to deplete the global resources unduly, or to pollute the air and sea, or to change the global weather patterns. The local community will not sustain itself at the expense of the whole. Nevertheless, the more local the self-determination the better, because individual participation is thereby enhanced. This principle should apply equally in politics and in economics.

Dopfer noted that the new economics, unlike modern economics, must not be caught in the trap of seeking to be a value-free science. What is needed is a *more reflective value-laden inquiry about the economy as a part of the total society.* This type of inquiry characterized economic thought from Adam Smith through the nineteenth century and is called "political economy." But of course an announcement of goals and ideals does not suffice. I am beginning there, but political economy must include practicable economic programs. The clarification of goals and ideals is only romantic daydreaming if no economy can be devised to support these ends.

Neither the centrally planned economy nor the market economy as now constituted provides the needed programs. Although both central planning and the free market have roles to play, what is needed is not simply a mixture of the two. To determine what must be centrally planned, what left to the market, and what ordered in other ways, is a major task. I am certainly not going to fulfill it in this essay. But I will indicate a few economic directions and goals that might help to make this kind of sustainable global community of communities a possibility: (1) conservation of stock; (2) regional self-sufficiency; (3) economic priorities within regions; and (4) population stability.

V. Conservation of Stock

First, economists will need to shift their primary attention from consumption to capital stock. Kenneth Boulding proposes this shift, and defines capital stock as all the artifacts useful or desirable to human beings as well as the human beings themselves. A community is well off when the quality of such things is high and the quantity sufficient. This capital stock is more important than consumption. Indeed, consumption diminishes the stock, so that in many respects a reduction of consumption is desirable. For example, if homes are built to last two hundred years, they are "consumed" much less rapidly than if they are built to last only thirty years. A shift of emphasis from consumption to stock will encourage the making of more durable goods and will slow down the exhaustion of resources and the production of waste.

In addition to capital stock, economists need to take account of natural stock. Abundant topsoil, forest cover, and pure water are important parts of the whole community. Their reduction impoverishes the community, their increase enriches it.

In measures of production and consumption, distinctions are needed between resources that (i) are unlimited, those that (ii) are replenished by themselves when not overused, and those that (iii) are strictly limited. No restrictions need be placed on resources in the first category. Those in the second should be used only within the limits of sustainability. Herman Daly has proposed for resources in the third category a quota system. If the decision were made that one percent of the proven reserves of a mineral could be mined each year, then rights to mine that much would be auctioned. The cost of those rights would add to the market price of the mineral, encouraging frugal use. If additional resources are proven, more could be mined. If not, there would be a slight reduction from year to year, but exhaustion could be indefinitely postponed. Recycling would be encouraged, and the transition to other resources would be gradual.

VI. REGIONAL SELF-SUFFICIENCY

Second, political economics should seek regional self-sufficiency. This self-sufficiency may, at first glance, seem contrary to postmodern thought, in which interdependence is emphasized. Persons in community are profoundly dependent on one another. It might be concluded that the increase in interdependence fostered throughout the world by modern economics is a mark of its excellence.

In fact, however, the type of interdependence developed through the international trading system works against community. A Third World nation entering into this system loses much of its freedom to make decisions about its internal life. That loss of freedom means a great reduction in the possibility of its citizens participating in the determination of the conditions under which they live. To be dependent for one's livelihood on decisions that one cannot influence is not the form of interdependence that makes for community. For whole communities to be dependent for their survival on decisions they cannot influence is clearly contrary to the postmodern concern for persons in community. The market mechanism, the invisible hand of Adam Smith, will work to increase the total global production of goods and services. It will not work for healthy community.

That many smaller nations find themselves powerless in the face of great economic forces is evident. Thus far their efforts to attain greater influence over the terms of trade have failed. But even if they were to succeed, even if the New Economic Order were realized, the whole system would continue to work against community.

Basic to the modern system of international trade is specialization in production. If each region concentrates economically on what it can produce most efficiently, the total global product will increase. To realize this modern goal, many regions concentrate their agriculture on export crops. As a result, many peoples who were once able to feed themselves now depend on importing food. The poor often cannot afford to buy this imported food. Although GNP rises, diets deteriorate.[8]

To aim at the well-being of communities will mean rejecting this ideal and direction. Instead of tying its economy into the global system, each community should undertake to become relatively self-sufficient, especially in basic needs. Given such self-sufficiency, they can, like Robinson Crusoe, trade only when they really want to. Relative self-sufficiency makes possible relative self-determination. (The most successful stories of economic development since World War II have involved programs for food self-sufficiency based on land reform. Japan, Taiwan, and South Korea all followed this procedure.)

At what levels that degree of self-sufficiency is possible or desirable is a very complex question. For some purposes, the relatively self-sufficient community may be the subcontinent of India! Nevertheless, the term "community," and the emphasis on "persons in community," do accent those smaller groupings in which persons can have a larger sense of participation and a larger share in making the decisions that govern their lives. For many people in India, the most important community is the peasant village. To enhance the self-sufficiency of the village, to improve its quality of life, including its material well-being, through empowering the people of the village to shape more of their own destiny, would be a goal of an economy focused on the community instead of on individual households. (The affinities of this theory with that of Gandhi are obvious.)

In short, the modern economic arguments for complete freedom of trade, whether among villages or among nations, are not convincing from a postmodern point of view. Trade between communities would occur when relatively self-sufficient agents saw mutual benefits to be gained that would not be harmful to the global community. No doubt, as modern economists warn us, this approach would lead to higher prices and slower global increase of gross product. But low prices and global growth should no longer be our priorities. We should be more concerned that people eat well and that family and community flourish. The reduction in trade would reduce the use of energy in transport as well as the pollution of air and water. That reduction would slow economic "growth" in a very positive way.

Community self-sufficiency will often be in tension with economies of scale. With respect to some products, such as steel or automobiles, communities will have to be quite large to be self-sufficient in reasonably economic ways. However, when growth is abandoned as a goal, many economies of scale will no longer be important. The postmodern economy will be more concerned with the efficient use of energy and natural resources than with labor productivity. Small-scale production near sources of renewable energy can often prove efficient in these terms.

VII. REGIONAL PRIORITIES

The third principle for political economists involves establishing priorities within the relatively self-sufficient regions. The first call on the economic product should be meeting the basic needs of all. The second should be to provide interesting and enjoyable work for all who desire it. The availability of abundant goods and services should be the third priority.

Relatively self-sufficient communities will be free to enact policies to meet basic needs of all their members. Food is most important. In much of the world, the first step in dealing with food needs is to return many people to the land. Redistribution of land in this country and many others is an urgent need. This redistribution can further reduce energy consumption. In most cases, landed farmers can meet their basic needs. To meet the needs of the urban poor, the first claim on tax funds would be to provide food stamps or, better, a guaranteed annual wage sufficient to meet the most basic of human requirements.

The second priority within the region is to make work more interesting. In addition to land distribution to farmers, family business should be favored, and larger businesses should have worker participation in management and ownership if not outright worker ownership. All of these policies will tend to strengthen community in the process of production. Where the use of energy to increase productivity has freed people from drudgery, this use should have priority claim on energy resources. But where the use of energy has routinized jobs and created unemployment, it should be heavily taxed or forbidden. It is true that such regulations in favor of interesting work might make some products noncompetitive with those from other communities that did not so regulate, but if so, that problem can be handled by tariffs. Competition within the community will be among firms with similar rules imposed upon them. In any case, the quality and quantity of work improve so much with the increased interest and involvement of the worker that there might not be any problem.

Some boring work or drudgery will still be necessary. Because everyone will have basic needs cared for, and because more desperate persons from the community (such as undocumented workers) can no longer be exploited for this work, the pay for it will have to rise dramatically and the working day be shortened. People might then choose to work four back-breaking or monotonous hours for the same wages as for eight hours of more attractive work. At some point there would be enough takers. Of course, some prices would increase as a result. But because the goods would be protected from external competition as necessary, this increase would not be critical.

With respect to the third goal within the region—an abundance of goods and services beyond necessities—quantitative measures of market activity will have their place. But other considerations will be of more importance, even here. First, the goods must be produced with as little environmental disturbance as possible. Second, their distribution is as important as their quantity. If all of the abundance beyond necessities goes to the top quintile of the population it will provide less enjoyment than if it is more widely shared. Although any attempt to achieve full equality should be eschewed because of its incompatibility with freedom, efforts to spread both wealth and income more evenly will be appropriate. Indeed, when there is real experience of community, the hardship of the poor subtracts more from the well-being of the rich than additional luxuries add to this well-being.

VIII. POPULATION STABILITY

The attainment of healthy community life in most of the world is incompatible with rapid growth of population. Such growth requires growth of the economy as well, and we have seen how the procedures demanded for this growth work against community. Furthermore, the carrying capacity of many regions has already been reached or exceeded. Population stability is an essential feature of any hopeful future. Its urgency is accentuated by a focus on community.

In a world made up of relatively self-sufficient communities, population problems of one community cannot be solved by exporting its surplus to others. Before a community reaches the carrying capacity of its own region, it must take thought. We may hope that few communities will be required to take action as drastic as that of China. But as painlessly as possible most of them must bring population growth under control. The assurance of having basic needs met in old age will help reduce pressures to expand. Granting to women rights over their bodies and opportunities for interesting work, either in or outside the home, will help. Literacy education, dissemination of birth control information, and the availability of abortion, when necessary, will also help. Economists, too, can make interesting and useful proposals. Economic disincentives can be built into tax structures, but these tend to penalize the children. As an alternative, Herman Daly among others has proposed that the right to have one child be given to each man and woman. These rights could either be exercised or sold. Those who strongly desire more children, and are prepared to pay the price, could buy rights from those who are less interested. The total number of births would be controlled. On the whole, children would be brought up by those who want them very much.

To be certain that communities accept responsibility for attaining a sustainable pattern, restrictions on the movement of people will be necessary. The very rapid turnover of population in so much of the United States works against community. Much of this movement today is out of economic necessity. This necessity would be greatly reduced if postmodern economic principles were applied. Insofar as the present level of movement is based on current economic practices, economic changes would suffice to stabilize communities.

On the other hand, we can assume that some communities would achieve their goals more successfully than others, whether because of better location and resources or because of better leadership and community support. Persons from less successful communities would naturally like to take advantage of this success. But a large influx of people would quickly reduce the attainment. I see no alternative but to continue restrictions on immigration among countries and even to add them among states or other regions at which relative self-sufficiency is possible and desirable.

IX. MODERN AND POSTMODERN ECONOMICS: A SUMMARY

In this section I review the significance of the labels "modern" and "postmodern" as I have used them.

They have their clearest exemplifications in physics. Modern physics viewed the world as composed of self-contained units, or atoms. These atoms change only in their spatial relations to one another. How they are grouped together has no effect upon their internal constitution. Postmodern physics, by contrast, portrays the world as composed of entities that are profoundly constituted by their relations to each other. One cannot separate an event from the field in which it occurs. Whitehead shows that the model of organism-in-environment works better than the modern model of parts-of-a-machine for natural physical units at many levels.

Modern political theories followed the lead of modern physics. For political thought, the self-contained units were individual human beings. In its influential Lockean version, these human individuals form political units, not out of necessity for survival, but so as to protect their ownership of the property they have acquired. Government exists largely to protect private property rights of essentially self-contained and self-sufficient individuals.

The postmodern view says that individual persons are important, but that we are what we are *only in and through our relations* with others— both other people and creatures of other types. Community is thereby inherently valuable. Postmodern political theory recognizes that the primary way to serve individuals is by improving communities.

From the contrast between atomic individuals and persons in community follows the difference between the modern and postmodern economic theories. Modern economic theory measures economic welfare by total production divided by the number of people. To increase this ratio it advocates policies that weaken and even destroy both human community and the wider ecological community. This destruction does not appear as a loss in its theory or in its statistics. Postmodern economic theory seeks, by contrast, the welfare of communities of persons, of persons in community. Accordingly, per capita consumption becomes less important than the satisfaction of the basic needs of all, opportunities for interesting work for all who want it, participation in decision-making, and the community's control over its own life.

I do not intend to suggest that a postmodern political economy will move us painlessly toward utopia. I can foresee no society without serious problems. We have wounded and overpopulated the planet; we cannot undo what we have done; and options that were once live are now dead. But among the options that remain to us, we can still make important choices. We can continue the path of modern economics, with its destruction of human community and natural environment in hopes of increased consumption by all individuals at some future date. Or we can try the path of postmodern economics, preserving and regenerating community at all levels. My view is that a decent human survival requires the latter choice.

X. GOD, INTERCONNECTEDNESS, AND THE POLITICAL ECONOMY

I began by pointing to the practical concerns that aroused my interest in understanding the commitment of so many economists to the increase of production. I have written throughout as though the issues were practical and factual. I believe they are. Yet the level at which questions are raised and answers are sought reflects another dimension—the dimension of vision and commitment. Most practical and factual inquiries about the economy have failed to raise these questions, because they have been guided by different visions and commitments. It is when one views the natural world and human economic activity in their inclusive interconnectedness that the questions I have raised are asked and answered. When one cares what happens not only to human beings but also to all living things, some of these issues are pressed further still.

Belief in God has often worked against these concerns. Sometimes God has been understood to ordain all that happens, especially all nonhuman events, so that humans are to cultivate resignation to them. Sometimes God has been understood to guarantee a consummation of the process, so that concern about human threats to the survival of life is pointless. Sometimes God has been understood as having to do only with personal salvation, so that attention to social and ecological issues is a distraction. Sometimes God is understood as so fully immutable as to be unaffected by the fate of creatures, so that, the more attention is directed to God, the less the sufferings and activities of creatures seem important.

With such ideas of God in view, many have denied God for the sake of a full-orbed commitment to the health of the interconnected world. That choice is understandable and admirable in its way. But atheism, however laudable its motives, has its dangers. If there be no standpoint more inclusive than those of human beings, these human standpoints will tend to be treated as final or absolute, justifying anthropocentrism, ethnocentrism, or even egocentrism. Or, this lack of an inclusive standpoint can so lead to the relativization of all truth and reality that every idea and action is considered equally good and equally bad with every other. In this case, there is no longer any reason to challenge the regnant view of economists, or those of Marxists or Maoists, for that matter.

Alternatively, some favored part of the whole—humanity, the biosphere, or Gaia—may be accorded divine attributes, with the inevitable limitations that eventually arise when something less than the whole is treated as of ultimate importance.

There is a third option, a postmodern one: the affirmation of God as interconnected with the whole interconnected creation. In this vision, God is the life of the world and the world is the body of God. What is done to the least of creatures is done to God; to love God is to love all creatures; to serve God is to participate with God in the enlivening and enrichment of the interconnected world. It is in fact this vision that has given rise in me to the practical concerns and perceptions expressed in this essay.

NOTES

1. William Norhaus and James Tobin, "Is Growth Obsolete?", in *Economic Growth* (New York: National Bureau of Economic Research, 1972).

2. Kenneth Boulding, *Beyond Economics: Essays on Society, Religion and Ethics* (Ann Arbor: University of Michigan, 1968), 192.

3. Nordhaus and Tobin, "Is Growth Obsolete?", 14.

4. Robert Heilbronner is an important exception. See *An Inquiry into the Human Prospect: Updated and Reconsidered for the 1980s* (New York: W. W. Norton, 1980).

5. Kurt Dopfer, *Economics in the Future: Towards a New Paradigm* (Boulder: Westview Press, 1976).

6. Herman Daly, *Steady-State Economics* (San Francisco: W. H. Freeman and Co., 1977). Although I revised it slightly before publication, adding in particular the final section, the present essay was substantially completed before I began collaboration with Daly on the book that has recently appeared as *For the Common Good* (Boston: Beacon Press, 1989).

7. A. N. Whitehead, *Adventures of Ideas* (New York: Macmillan, 1933), 67.

8. See Dean Freudenberger, "Agriculture in a Postmodern World," in David Ray Griffin, ed., *Spirituality and Society: Postmodern Visions* (Albany: State University of New York Press, 1988).

9

ESCAPE FROM MODERNISM: IN SCIENCE, RELIGION, POLITICS, AND ART

Frederick Turner

Consider the process by which a modern integrated circuit is made. A wafer of silicon is doped with impurities, exposed to light that is shone through a template to form a pattern of shadows, treated with new impurities that differentiate between the irradiated and unexposed areas, etched by a bath of corrosives, blanketed with a new surface of silicon, exposed to another pattern of light, and so on, until a marvelously complex three-dimensional system of switches, gates, resistors, and connections has been laid down. This system may be destined to form part of a computer which will in turn help design new integrated circuits. The technical term for this process is "photographic." Essentially an integrated circuit is a very complex silicon photograph. Photographic techniques are now being used to make all kinds of very tiny machines—pumps, solar energy collectors, and measuring devices.

143

We normally think of a photographic process as one that makes pictures of things rather than things themselves. A photograph is significant as a piece of information, but as an object itself it is just a bit of sticky paper. But our silicon photograph does not just *represent* something—the pattern of light with which it was irradiated; it *does* what it is a photograph of. In a sense it is a miraculous picture, like that of Our Lady of Guadalupe: it not only represents, but does; it is not just information, but reality; it is not just a piece of knowledge, but a piece of being; it is not just epistemology, but ontology.

Consider, moreover, the digital, or "Soundstream," method of reproducing music. The music is scanned every forty-four thousandth of a second or so; the sound wave activity in that forty-four thousandth is given a numerical value, and this value is recorded in terms of a binary sequence of laser-burned holes and unburned spaces on the record. To play the music you just scan the holes with another laser and synthesize a sound every forty-four thousandth of a second which corresponds to the number you get.

The point is that the digital recording is really just a very sophisticated "score" of the music. It in no way reproduces the actual shape of the music, the way the grooves on the vinyl of a normal record do; any more than the five parallel lines, the clef, and the little black ellipses with their tails reproduce the actual shape of the music—or indeed, than the letters on a page reproduce the sounds of speech. In a sense, the digital recording harks back to an old method of reproducing music: the player piano.

But the interesting thing is that digital recordings are much more accurate than any analog recording, which attempts to match the actual shape of the music, could be. They are literally as accurate as you want: you could scan every hundred thousandth of a second—though it would be useless, as the highest pitch we can hear is lower than a twenty-thousandth of a second in frequency. Moreover, a digital recording is theoretically almost invulnerable to wear, whereas an analog recording must suffer and shriek to give up its musical information.

The paradox is that an analog recording, which is the actual reverberation of the original performance of the music—as if we were to put our ear against the wall of the Sistine Chapel Choir—is less accurate than the entirely new performance generated by machinery from the meticulous numerical score of a digital recording. It is as if, knowing the right language, we could write the names of foods so accurately that if you ate the paper it would be more tasty and nourishing than the foods themselves.

So: photographs can now, magically, do what they are pictures of; and a score of a piece of music can be more accurate than the sound of the music itself. We live once again in a world of runes and icons, efficacious and full of virtue; a world in which the distinction between how we know and what we know, statement and referent, meaning and object, has begun to break down. Indeed, quantum physics tells us that these cloud-capped towers, these gorgeous palaces, these solemn temples, the great globe itself, are made out of statistical domains of information—numerical likelihoods called electrons, photons, and so on; and the Big Bang theory says we are all made out of light.

Remember the scene in *Close Encounters of the Third Kind* where the kids' mechanical toys all wake up and, in their dim electronic awareness, run about on the floor and clap their hands and flash their lights? And recall that the music of the Aliens is actually—as you realize at the very end—a simple variation of the Disney tune "When you Wish Upon a Star"? We have met E.T., and he is our toys, our animated cartoons, our computer programs. The Magic Kingdom—Anaheim or Orlando—is the American Eleusis where spirits are invoked to transubstantiate inanimate matter.

Our children are growing up on computer programs and fantasy role-playing games—"Voyager," "Greyhawk," "Dungeons and Dragons." The space program was too slow to bring them to those other worlds, and therefore they constructed them right here on Earth. Play has become increasingly concrete and even practical and profitable. It is almost as if an evolutionary necessity in culture dictated that from our most infantile and inconsequential and unnecessary behaviors—"a waste of time" —comes the solid future of the species. Just as it began to seem as if political, economic, and technological forces were combining to organize the human race into a rational, centralized, and anonymous unity, and the world was, as they say, becoming a small place, counterforces of great power and unexpected provenance have taken us all in an entirely new set of directions. The new electronic technology is by its nature playful, decentralizing, individualizing, and pluralist. The strong hand of the corporation and the still stronger hand of the state, which were once able to coerce the population into their service by cutting off its sources of energy and information, are becoming more and more impotent to get a grasp on the individual. Quite soon a family equipped with its own solar power generator and its own computer will have a kind of practical sovereignty once possessed only by nations.

Once the city, which was the central machine of production and the access to the power of information and communication, could be used by the authorities to maintain their power; proximity to the city was the reward for compliance, and banishment to the state of nature was the most effective punishment. But now there is no way of denying the city to anyone who has the curiosity and energy to appropriate it. The telephone and the C.B. radio have replaced the city street, the home computer with a modem replaces the office block, the dish antenna and videotape recorder have replaced the movie theater, and the digital stereo music system has replaced the symphony hall and opera house. Information is the means of production, and there is now no way of plugging the leaking joints where the public can feed on the rich flow of free information.

We are reentering at last the ancient animist universe, populated by genies and geniuses of place, in which every object possessed a spirit or daemon that one might control and use. But the nymphs and dryads are now microprocessors, inhabiting our machines, tools, toys, cars, stoves, clocks, chess sets, and typewriters. Soon every human artifact will have its own helpful and dedicated little intelligence, its own nisus or animating will; and we shall surely not stop there. Already electronic prostheses are a regular part of medicine, and they have begun to be used in livestock management and agriculture. We are teaching Nature how to speak with us, at the same time as we are learning the languages of the natural species.

The world is becoming a *bigger* place, more densely packed with information. A few years ago the amount of information contained in the world's libraries, computer memories, and so on, doubled every ten years; now the doubling-time itself has gone down to eight years and is continuing to shrink. This process has a cosmological significance, because the universe itself is made of information: Matter and energy are only more or less simple forms of information, and are by no means as fundamental as they were once thought to be. And whereas matter and energy can indeed decay according to the laws of entropy, paying for their durability of form by their eventual death into more primitive states of organization, information itself is not only immortal but also self-propagating. On the level of matter and energy, the world is running down; on the level of information the world is growing and becoming more and more elaborately organized. And *our* activities, tiny as they appear in space and time, are a significant part of that growth.

Pascal said that the silence of these infinite spaces terrified him. But we now know that those spaces, large as they are, are not infinite; and that space itself is generated by an evolutionary process which is more primary than space itself. Once the universe was no bigger than a baseball, and before that it was smaller than an atom. What counted then was not how big or how old it was, but its capacity to generate new information: to derive in turn, from its single law of relation, first gravitation, then the strong and weak nuclear forces, and at last electromagnetism. Measured in terms of space and time, humankind is indeed, as scientists traditionally remind us, a tiny speck in the vastness of the cosmos. Measured in a more fundamental way, by density and complexity of information, we are already the largest objects in the universe. Indeed we are the cortex or cambium of the universe, its skin, its bud, its growing surface, and our new laws—of morality, aesthetics, government, and games—take their appointed place next to their predecessors, the laws of biology, chemistry, physics, and mathematics. Our laws, though latecomers, are no less real for that; it is a matter now of embodying them in their constituency, as a new statute gradually takes its place in the legal system through judicial interpretation and precedent. As Thoreau put it, punning between the leaves of the trees, the leaves of books, and the "new leaf" we shall all turn over:

> No wonder that the earth expresses itself outwardly in leaves, it so labors with the idea inwardly. The atoms have already learned this law, and are pregnant by it. . . . The very globe continually transcends and translates itself, and becomes winged in its orbit. Even ice begins with delicate crystal leaves, as if it had flowed into moulds which the fronds of water plants have impressed on the watery mirror. The whole tree itself is but one leaf, and rivers are still vaster leaves whose pulp is intervening earth, and towns and cities are the ova of insects in their axils.[1]

The evolutionary biologist Alexander Graham Cairns-Smith has suggested a very exciting hypothesis.[2] To put it in an oversimplified way, there were, before the DNA-based life that we know today, more primitive forms of self-replicating and metabolizing chemistry, of which the organic molecules, proteins, and amino acids of contemporary life were once only part of the phenotype, the somatic machinery. Domains of electromagnetic polarization in certain clays, he suggests, could print replicas of themselves in growing columns which would in gross structure and behavior differ according to the pattern of the polarization. These structures and behaviors could differentially affect the survival of the whole organism, and thus the three forces of evolution—mutation, reproduction, and selection—could come into play. Cairns-Smith is able thus to explain the otherwise highly improbable origins of DNA.

Not least among the fascinating intellectual implications of this idea is the notion that what is now the genotype—the blueprint—of a living organism was once only part of its phenotype—the expression of this blueprint in physical terms. Indeed, we do not need to go to Cairns-Smith's work for an illustration of this idea. There are many cases in viruses and bacteria where a piece of machinery used by the genetic material to promote its survival has actually become incorporated into the genetic material itself, as in the case of the plasmids; and the messengers of the DNA sometimes perform some of the functions of DNA itself, as when viral RNA takes part of the responsibility for carrying the genetic inheritance.

A fascinating analogy suggests itself: Perhaps our traditional cultural ways of storing and passing on information—through speech, the development of socially-maintained individual personalities, writing, and electronic data processing—are now taking over the central genetic tasks of our species; just as the organic molecules that were once its tools superseded the genetic functions of the clay ur-life, if Cairns-Smith's theory is correct.

The distinction between being and consciousness, which to Descartes and Berkeley seemed so absolute as to require divine intervention to enable them to communicate, has now become only a matter of degree. Being has dissolved before our eyes as we examined it more and more closely, until, in quantum physics, matter proves less durable than the light in which we see it; and it evaporates into energy, pure event, if we try to take it apart any further. Matter, then, was only an arrangement, a mutually-supporting collection of probabilities, in the first place; and its only existence was as and in its relations, internal and external. The universe is made up of the differential sensitivities of its components to each other. Our clever toys, our microchips, are only a concrete demonstration that the physical world is inherently sensitive and potentially aware. And if we are to take the theory of evolution seriously, which says that a conscious human being is an advanced ape, a sophisticated vertebrate, a highly-developed bit of matter, a complex arrangement of energy, then the corollary must also be true: the apes are primitive men, the phenomenon of life is undeveloped human awareness, matter and energy are unorganized or diffused forms of human consciousness. The universe is only and always its own registering, measuring, calibrating, and recording of itself; and we are the most active example of that process.

One consequence of this view is that the old notion of humankind's alienation from Nature was only a cultural illusion, which is now utterly exploded. That Nature from which we were supposed to be alienated never existed: the great quantum experiments—the parallel-slits light experiment, the polarizing filter light experiment—show that Nature has not made up its own mind about what it *really* is, and is quite happy to have us help it do so. That whole tradition of philosophy which saw us as cut off from our "true" way of being has in fact collapsed, and simply has not realized it yet. *We* are Nature, and we are as at home here in the world as anything has ever been at home: for the whole world is made up of such as we. Its physical components are, just as much as we are, tourists, outsiders, amateurs, getting by on a smile and a shoeshine, and deriving what being they have from the recognition of their fellows. All nature is second nature.

The new quantum theories of cosmology suggest that the probabilistic and chance-governed behavior of the elementary particles is a sort of "living fossil" of the state of the whole universe in its first moments of existence during the Big Bang. In other words, the order and determinateness of the physical world as we know it through conventional physics and chemistry did not at first exist, and evolved out of a chaotic prior state. Given a random chaos, not only in the physical world but also in the rules (or lack of them) which govern it, lawful regimes tend to persist and propagate themselves into the future, by definition, while chaotic regimes are inherently unstable and evanescent. The laws of physics and chemistry—and of biology and human society—evolved because they promoted survival.

At the very beginning of the universe, there existed an infinite number of possible states, each with a probability of one in infinity. Even nothingness was only one possibility, sharing the same infinitesimal likelihood of being true. "Existence" itself, as a sharply defined state completely incompatible with nonexistence, had yet to establish itself clearly. All the possibilities "existed," with an infinitely small efficacy. The quantum-statistical nature of the electron, for instance, is a remnant of that indeterminacy, as is the statistical-mechanical character of the pressure of gases, indeed any physical process when we analyze it to a point at which our unit of measurement is smaller than the acuity of the system's minimum behavior as a system. The sharpness of reality is the result of a harmonious synchronizing of many fuzzy elements.

Human technology is, in some senses, the continuation of the process of evolution by which the indefiniteness of the world gave rise to greater and greater certainty. Technology is the realizing of the possible, and our machines are only the last in a series which goes back through the chemical servomechanisms of our bodies and the bodies of animals, the persisting and self-maintaining organization of crystal structures and stable molecules, and the durable coherence of the elementary particles, to that first moment when possibility resolved itself into a burst of identical photons.

We are at a curious juncture in the history of science and technology. The empiricism of the Renaissance gradually, over the next three hundred years, flattened out the ancient hierarchic coherence of the universe and broke up the great chain of being. Just at the moment when the world

seemed to have been reduced to a valueless collection of objective facts—
the world view of Modernism—a new order began to come into being. A
gigantic hierarchy is appearing more and more clearly, as the jigsaw
puzzle pieces of science are put together: geometry the microstructure
of physics, physics the microstructure of chemistry, chemistry the microstructure of biology, biology the microstructure of the human sciences.

That new Great Chain of Being is, unlike the old one, dynamic and
fluid: it is the great branching tree of evolution. As long as evolution was
conceptually confined to the realm of biology, it did not seriously threaten
the Modernist conception of the world as "value-flat"; it simply made
Life into a mystical anomaly, or a pullulating disease, a "fever of matter,"
as Thomas Mann put it, in the "frozen chastity" of the inorganic. But
now we can construct viruses out of "dead" chemicals, proving they
were not as dead as we thought, and the link has been made. All of the
world is alive, as it were, and its life becomes more and more intense as
it evolves, more and more self-referential, more and more self-measuring
and self-certifying, more and more sensitive to the rest of the universe,
and thus determinative of its nature.

The destruction of the old coherence can be traced and epito-
mized in the etymological collapse and fragmentation of the word "art."
In *The Tempest* it is Prospero's "art" that makes temporary sense of the
airy nothing the world is made of, rendering it into cloud-capped towers
and gorgeous palaces, solemn temples, even the great Globe Theatre
itself. For Shakespeare "art" meant science, philosophical knowledge,
technical power, craft, theatrical sleight of hand, liberal education, magic,
and "art" in our modern meaning, all at once. The moment of *The
Tempest* was the last moment of full cultural health and integrity until
our own time now. "Art," the word, was gradually torn to shreds, until in
our century art and science, science and technology, philosophy and
science, art and philosophy, magic and science, craft and art, education
and art, have all been set against each other, like demons bred out of the
corpse of the great mother.

But now that coherence is swiftly returning. Film and science fiction testify to the convergence of science and art. The indeterminacy
principle, which destroys the distinction between observation and action,
makes all science into technology and all technology into science. Academic philosophy has died and passed its inheritance on to the theoreti-
cians of science and to art criticism; the anthropologists have revealed
other cultures' magic as science and our own science as magic. In all the
arts, the death of Modernism has given birth to a new rapprochement
between craft and art; education is at last being recognized as a valid
experience in itself; and art is, once more, properly required to be

moral. All of these assertions are prophetic more than scholarly: but watch the event.

Not that the empiricist detour or diaspora was unnecessary. Shakespeare's magic did not work outside the theatre, and we needed three centuries of self-imposed alienation, of tearing things to pieces to see how they worked, to be able to come back to a coherent and valuable world, this time with the powers and knowledge we always felt were our birthright—powers and knowledge we had mimed with our magic. But now that we have come back we must cast away the habits of our exile—the self-contempt, the illusion of alienation, the hatred of the past, the sterile existentialism, the fear of the future, the willful imposition of meaninglessness on a universe bursting with meaning.

Another way of saying the same thing is that we are undergoing a religious revolution. In about 1600, a new religion appeared on the scene, which we might call materialism. Its practice is what we usually call "economic activity," and its higher religious emotions include the sense of the beauty of Nature, awe at its workings, and the sense of triumph in technological achievement. Its theology was atomistic: like God, the atom of matter was indivisible, eternal, invulnerable, responsible for all events in the world. Unlike God, though, it was not aware, conscious, or personal. As with other great religions—and it was a great and in many ways noble religion, and much of our own best and most significant behavior consists in its observance—it gave rise to magnificent heresies, systems of morality, and even good science: dialectical materialism, existentialism, the theory of evolution.

If it be protested that materialism is not a religion, a cross-cultural view would rapidly convince the objector. People living in the medieval world did not call their everyday rituals religious, or even rituals. They were just the way one lived one's life. Animists or totemists, before contact with Europeans, would say the same thing about their own practices and value systems. What enabled materialism to triumph all over the world was precisely the fact that it did not claim to be a religion at all, but labeled other systems as religious; and, just like monotheism, polytheism, animism, totemism, and ancestor-worship, there are elements of it in all human value-systems.

But materialism is now going through the same crisis that Christianity did four hundred years ago. Christianity resolved its crisis by coexisting with the new religion, to the usual enrichment of both, while accepting certain modifications and limitations in its relevance, the chief of which was the recognition of itself as *a* religion, rather than "the way things are." Perhaps a similar adjustment will take place to the new religious conceptions that are now beginning to burst on the world.

The chief challenge to materialism, as I have already pointed out, was the disappearance of the atom as atomic or irreducible, and the consequent dissolution of matter into event, relation, and information. One of the advantages of materialism was that the further one reduced the complex and ambiguous behavior of the apparent world in the direction of simple atomic events, the more concrete and unambiguous it seemed to get. Religion seeks certainty, and for a long time materialism delivered it. But one more reduction, one last simplification, spoiled everything. Suddenly the world, as it was revealed by quantum physics, had become utterly ambiguous again; and far from offering an escape from the relativism of human perception, the pursuit of material explanations had now totally implicated the observer in the behavior of reality.

Much that is good can be salvaged from the old religion: the world of matter, though it is now revealed as a provisional one, without the appealing absoluteness it once possessed, is still a beautiful and exquisitely ordered one; and it is surely legitimate to give it a share of worship. But if we do so, we must give a greater share to ourselves, both as the supreme product and expression of matter given its chance to do what comes naturally, and as the supreme observer and determiner of the material world. That aspect of religion which desires to worship something outside of, and superior to, ourselves, will not be satisfied any longer with materialism.

And materialism always carried a dangerous and perhaps evil flaw: its fundamental and ultimate realities, the atoms of matter, were impersonal, insentient, and unintelligent—that was precisely what made them intelligible. But the elevation of matter also implied a valorization of those characteristics—impersonality, insentience, unintelligence. We began to regard the personal, the sensible, the conscious, as a second-class reality, which must face up to the impersonal "real world" and submit to the "reality principle," or to the blind forces of economic change, the dialectics of class struggle, or the survival of the fittest. And perhaps our great political and technological monsters—communism, fascism, the hydrogen bomb—are the final expression of that inbuilt suspicion of the personal: they promised to eradicate persons from the face of the earth. Even the impiety that one may sense in this essay comes from its violation of the materialist theology.

But we *are* entering a new age, one which will see a reconvergence of the old meaning of "art" upon a more efficacious basis, and a reestablishment of the great chain of being with a new, dynamic, evolutionary aspect. It will be an age of return of the classical philosophy, ethics, aesthetics, and economics, but with solid scientific foundations, and enriched immeasurably by the cooperation of all the human cultural traditions.

In fact, this is the most startling aspect of the postmodern synthesis as it comes into shape: its classicism. In the heyday of high modernism the world of the future seemed more and more impersonal, cool, centralized, inorganic, tidy, sharp-edged: a world-state with equal prosperity for all, tall rectilinear buildings, cool atonal or serial music, abstract art, imagistic free verse which caught and froze a moment of sensory experience in an exact verbal image, the "new novel" purified of the fetishism and hierarchy of plot and character, a leveling of all sexual, religious and ethnic differences, and a psychological style without repression, without alienation, without ego, absolutely free from the shibboleths of honor, beauty, sexual morality, patriotism, faith, idealism, religion and duty.

But, oddly enough, this future now appears more and more dated, even dreary. The marvelous cross-cultural studies of the human ethnologists, linguists, and comparative religionists have shown that yes, indeed, humankind *does* have a nature; there are cultural universals. But this nature is neither a limitation nor a totally protean adaptiveness. Rather, it is a system of neurobiological and developmental rules which make possible an immensely productive and infinitely versatile, but characteristically mammalian and human, *generativeness*. The rules must be followed, or the freedom, the limitlessness, the generativeness, will not come about. And those rules include not only the grammar of language, but also the classical laws of harmony, melody, color, proportion, poetic meter, narrative, rhythm, and balance. The human nervous system is designed by its evolutionary adaptation to cultural selective pressures to be sensitive to certain culturally-universal qualities found in the arts all over the world. The Modernists believed those classical qualities to be arbitrary and reactionary limitations and tried to sweep them away, thus deeply damaging the art forms they were trying to liberate and also depriving them of their audience. But now we are beginning to discover the nature of our humanity as well as the humanity of nature. To put it aphoristically: we have a nature: that nature is cultural: that culture is classical.

Of course, we must redefine "classical" to include the tonality of Chinese, Indonesian, and African music, and the visual representational conventions of the Tlingit, the Maori, and the Navaho, and the verse forms of the New Guinea Eipo, the Eskimos, and the Yanomami. But there *are* rules to be derived from this pan-human study; and to break them is not a daring innovation but a pointless exercise—akin to shining a light in our eyes at a wavelength invisible to the human retina, or to speaking a sentence whose grammar works on no humanly-comprehensible principle. We must change our romantic attitude to the rules, too, and recognize them not as a tyrannical imposition but as our own biologically and culturally agreed-upon code of communication, our constitution, the foundation of our freedom. The great mistake of the Modernists was to identify randomness with freedom. Freedom lies on the far side of order; it is an order that is now so complex that it has become self-referential and thus self-governing, autonomous. The random is the most complete of tyrannies.

The future now looks quite different from the way it once did. Not only is a world-state, thank heavens, quite out of the question; we may even be in the last days of the nation-state, which can no longer fulfill its original function of protecting the population from the external and internal disruption of productive activities. A much more decentralized world seems most likely, more personal, warm, custom-made, organic, untidy, decorated. Our music will be full of enchanting melody again, though it would sound strangely foreign to the ears of Brahms or Beethoven; more dark-skinned, more rhythmic, with an Oriental quaver, more incantatory, with more improvisation in performance. Our visual arts will be mainly representational, with abstraction usually reserved for decorative function, but there will be a rich play of modes of representation; it will once more seek after beauty, nobility, truth, and the sense of wonder. Our architecture will recapitulate the pan-human village clutter, with all functions, domestic, religious, retail, industrial, educational, horticultural, political, jumbled in together, and it will be splendidly and comfortably decorated. Our poetry will be, as all human poetry was until seventy years ago, richly metrical and rhetorical, full of stories, ideas, moral energy, public statement, scientific speculation, theology, drama, history. Indeed, many of these changes have already begun, though an entrenched rearguard of Modernist reactionaries still holds much of the political and economic power, and middlebrow taste will need decades of deprogramming from its masochistic preferences.

The new world will also be a more oral and aural one, as the written work takes its proper place as only one of a number of modes of verbal information storage and transmission. The arts of speech, of rhetoric, will rise again. The word as performance, as part of the living colloquial present of a culture's experience of itself, will take on greater importance, and the folk arts and popular arts will be reconnected with high art.

There will also be a refeminization of the arts. The Modernist reduction tended to write off sexual differences as trivial cultural impositions, and thus, paradoxically, to reform all of its ideals and norms upon an exclusively masculine model. What followed was a tragic destruction and dismissal of the arts of the traditional feminine culture, and an attempt—pathetic as it now seems—to provide equality for women by demanding that they imitate the achievements of the traditional male culture. Now, however, the scientific study of sexuality and gender, and of human social and biological evolution, is showing distinct statistical differences between men and women. A full, rich, and human culture is impossible upon an exclusively male model, even if women are trained to fit that model; and we are now seeing a rediscovery and revalorization of the female side of culture.

I suspect that some readers winced a few pages ago when I cited a list of values: honor, beauty, sexual morality, patriotism, faith, idealism, religion, and duty. That wincing reflex is an indication of a set of biocultural factors related to value-creation and reward systems which is both fascinating and almost unexplored.

In order to understand these factors we must first make an essential connection. A value system, despite Kant, is a reward system. Not that there is anything base about reward. The nobler a value, the nobler—and the more intangible to an ignoble mind—is the reward which goes with it. The nature of a value will be determined by the nature of the reward. The human body, we now know, has a very complex hierarchy of reward systems, the lowest associated with what is evolutionarily most archaic and automatic, and the highest with what is most recent and voluntary.

Materialist ethics came together with materialist biology in the nineteenth century and agreed that there were only two types of rewards: those obviously associated with physical survival, and those obviously associated with reproduction. Two brilliant systems of value—Marx's, which essentially reduced all value to the economics of physical survival; and Freud's, which reduced all value to sexual libido—were the result. Existentialism struggles ambivalently between accepting these rewards as preferable to the more complex socio-cultural value systems and rejecting them, and all rewards, as bribes to make us give up our freedom, which it identifies with randomness.

Under the pressure of these theories of reward, which postulated very coarse rewards even for very refined behavior, the value systems of world culture themselves changed and coarsened. When an audience winces at the sound of "duty, honor, and beauty," and so on, it is doing exactly what a Victorian audience would do upon hearing words like "passion," "desire," "sexuality," or even "money," "fees," "honoraria." The Victorians, in a last-ditch defense of the older, more complex value system against the efficient and economical new reductions, would naturally be pained by references to the enemy's rewards. We, the inheritors of D.H. Lawrence and Albert Camus, feel the same old blush come to our faces when we are reminded of all the old rewards—the joy of duty, the satisfaction of honorable conduct—that we have given up. Not that we are not often honorable and dutiful, but we are so in a spirit of taking nasty medicine with a good grace, and we are deeply suspicious of those who enjoy doing their duty.

But a new biology is forcing on us a new value system. The pleasures of eating and sex, which our evolutionary inheritance has provided to encourage us to perform activities which are metabolically rather expensive and time-consuming, are not the only rewards. The study of the chemistry of brain reward has begun to uncover a remarkable variety of rewards, suppressors of rewards, suppressors of the suppressors, linked rewards which in the absence of each other are punishments, and so on. The pleasures of achievement, of insight into the truth, of heroic exertion or sacrifice, of good conscience, of beauty, are *real* pleasures in themselves, not repressed and sublimated derivatives of sexual libido or the fetishism of a food-controlling class. Certainly the higher pleasures *enlist* the coarser and more obvious ones to reinforce them; and indeed society uses the coarser and more obvious ones—food, for children, and sex, for adolescents—as ways of training, calibrating, and stimulating the higher reward systems, "priming the pump," so to speak. But the "endorphin high" is as real a reward as are orgasm, or the pleasures of eating.

Nor are food and sex any longer the simple survival drives they seemed to the materialists. The study of human evolution shows that very early on the division of food played a central role in the religious rituals that defined the human community. What food *represents* soon became more important to us than the two thousand calories, the proteins, and the vitamins we required for mere survival. A Hindu would die rather than eat of the sacred cow. Food, as the anthropologists Mary Douglas and Claude Lévi-Strauss point out, has become more than bread alone. So too sex. The comparative study of sexual behavior shows that, far from possessing a feeble and watered-down version of brute sexuality, we are the most sexual of all animals—we are in heat all the time, we copulate face-to-face, and our females have as powerful a libido as our males. Our sexuality is much more powerful than that of our closest relatives, the chimpanzees and gorillas; it is far more powerful than is needed for reproduction. Many anthropologists suspect that our sexuality evolved in tandem with our brains, and that it took on an important social and cultural function: to encourage the creation of family and social groupings that could nurture the young through the extended human infancy, and promote cooperation through personal affection. Nevertheless, without the discovery of the higher reward systems, theories of sublimation that kept motivation on a materialist basis would still be plausible. It was the brain-chemicals that broke the old ideology.

But there is a terrible tragedy here. The endorphins were discovered because certain researchers into the physiology of narcotics and drug addiction asked the obvious yet brilliant question: Why should the brain have receptors designed precisely to respond with extreme sensitivity to the sap of an Oriental poppy? What evolutionary necessity could make such sensitivity adaptive? The answer, of course, was that those receptors were designed to respond to something else entirely, and that the poppy-resins simply happened to possess a molecular resemblance to that something else: an opiate produced by the brain itself to reward itself for doing its very hard work. The tragedy is this: the materialist theory of value had the result of cutting off many of the pleasures produced by the brain-chemicals. Just as our sexual and digestive deprivations were finally being satisfied by the new morality and the economics of abundance, we were being starved of the pleasures of the mind, spirit, and soul. Twentieth-century culture is full of an angst, an unsatisfied and inexplicable yearning, which we can now identify as a thirst for things like glory, sanctity, conscience, and heroism, which were forbidden to us by the doctrines of existentialism. Worse, we began to replace those pleasures with their artificial counterfeits; and as the doctrines of materialism triumphed first among intellectuals, then among the population at large, so did the use of opium, cocaine, mescalin, and cannabis. (Of course those individuals at the bottom of society, who felt themselves outcasts from its value system, have always used such drugs when they could get them.)

We are only now beginning to realize the horrible effects of tampering with the brain's own reward system by means of drugs. It touches us, with the hard thrill of permanent damage, in the very center of our will, our freedom, our selfhood. It eats the soul, because the soul is a process of transformation between what is and what ought to be, a hunger that is elevated when it is satisfied, and the drug destroys the tension and the hunger and thus the process of transformation. Who can forget those rats that would ignore females in heat and even starve to death, pressing the pedal that would deliver their shot of mental happiness? Or the teenage mugger, sniffing and shaking with his addiction, interested in nothing but the high?

But—turning again to the future—as the theory of reward changes to encompass those higner brain rewards, so we will once again educate the young to create their own highs, and the demand for the artificial substitute will decline. After all, the real thing is, chemists say, fifty times more powerful than the false, though harder to obtain.

What are the brain-rewards for? This is one of the most fascinating questions in the current study of evolution. Some of them—the pleasures of honor and duty—clearly have a function in the promotion of social cohesion and community. Others—the pleasures of insight and puzzle-solving—reward us for our naturally human scientific and technical capacities. Others—love and tenderness—encourage us to nurture what we have reproduced rather than abandon it. Others still—the pleasures of beauty and creative synthesis—are rewards for the world-creating activity which is our single greatest specialization as animals. But they all require a cultural medium that feeds and encourages them, if they are to develop into their full expression.

The origins of the peculiarly human use of endorphins as a reward for ethical, intellectual and aesthetic activity can be plausibly located in early hominid ritual behavior. Many of the higher vertebrates engage in complex rituals, usually at some point in their life-cycles where two contradictory behaviors are evoked by the same situation—for instance aggression and sexuality, territoriality and sexuality, territoriality and flight, flight and sexuality. The ritual always involves inappropriate, out-of-context, nonutlitarian, "as-if" behavior, which creates an alternative nonfactual or nonpresent model of the situation: for instance, in the triumph ceremony of the geese, where the courting male makes a symbolic attack on a nonexistent hostile rival or enemy.

The early human mating/hunting/housewarming ritual evidently involved more strongly than with any other species the creation of alternative worlds. We see those worlds later on the walls of the caves of Altamira, Lascaux, Zimbabwe, the Chumash Indians. And the ritual began to be passed down traditionally as well as genetically, and therefore it could change quite swiftly from generation to generation. Since success in the ritual led to success in mating and reproduction, it thus exerted a powerful selective pressure—an intra-specific selective pressure, like that which produced the brilliant scales of the stickleback, the feathers of the peacock, the antlers of the elk. The ritual very rapidly domesticated the human species, causing its cortex to mushroom out to three times normal size, and producing the loss of body hair, upright posture to carry the fetish objects of the ritual, a long period of infancy to program the brain, greater life-span to instruct the young, the face-to-face sexual posture to encourage the development of personality, extension of the period of being in heat to the status of permanence, so as to increase the social intensity, and most of all the development of the endogenous brain-reward system to encourage the expensive activity of alternate world construction.

It is this development which explains the addictiveness of the activity of computer programming. For the creation of a program is the most direct way yet devised for a human being to create alternative world-models, to try out the future in advance, to play, to enter the subjunctive or extraterritorial space of "as-if." This is why it is so great a boon to public education, which has largely destroyed all its old techniques for stimulating and calibrating the inner reward system.

Any good teacher will recognize the phenomenon of the potentially gifted student, whose self-reward capacities have been stunted from birth by parents and teachers who would not challenge them and who feared to inculcate in the student an undemocratic pride and pleasure in achievement. As you force the unaccustomed juices of pleasure—in learning, in truth, in beauty, in work—to flow, your students are almost incredulous. Surely you do not expect them to *enjoy* it? It's obscene. You're teaching vile and monstrous joys. And in fact you are giving them their inheritance— an inheritance paid for by millions of our remote ancestors in their caves, humanizing themselves by ritual, the development of kinship structures, the agonizing and delicious effort to articulate the wordless.

Paradoxically, then, materialism as the supreme religion began to sicken when we were able to make thinking machines, and died when we began to see ourselves as machines for the production of spirit, soul, value. Materialist politics is dying too, as we came to see our traditional cultures as machines to support and promote that productive process of soul-making. All over the world, the revolutionary forces are now what the reductionist revolutionaries of the nineteenth century would call "reactionary": they champion complex cultural and traditional value-systems—ethnic, religious, and political—against reductionist materialism, whether liberal, fascist, capitalist, socialist, or communist. What makes the Vietnamese, the Shiites, the Poles, the Iranians, the Afghans, the Israelis, the Palestinians, and the Irish such dangerous adversaries is not materialistic socialist ideology but religion, traditional education, kinship structure, patriotism, the sense of beauty, honor, heroism, duty, and all the rest: the endorphins blazing in the head like a lantern, more fiercely than any sexual passion, or thirst, or hunger for bread.

To a materialist or an existentialist all those values and beliefs are only games, a distracting play by which we hide death and the reality of our material condition from ourselves. But the strange thing about the human race is that it is more deeply motivated by a game than by a reality, and fears losing more than it fears death. From the point of view with which we began—the collapse of knowledge and being, information and reality, representing and doing—the paradox is no paradox. Reality was always a game, and our games continue the evolution of reality. We evolved as idealists, teleologists, essentialists, because we survived better that way. Essentialism is the only practical form of existentialism. Teleology is the best policy. Less idealistic animals have less control over the future.

This essay began by showing how technological change might alter some of our fundamental philosophical distinctions—between knowledge and being, animate and inanimate, epistemology and ontology. It continued by showing how the sciences themselves confirmed these changes. And then it demonstrated how, when we understand our own bodies and brains as a chemical technology directed toward higher goals, our useful and serviceable materialist ideology must be laid aside for a more personal and humanly responsible view of the world. Let me conclude by showing how in one field of human activity, poetry, the changes I have described might have specific effects.

Some effects I have already described: once our biogenetic predilection for metered verse, narrative, drama, and communal meanings is understood, poetry will gravitate back towards its ancient center, represented by the *Ramayana,* the *Heike,* the *Iliad;* it will take back into itself the capacities of the novel, which only developed because poetry had given up plot.

Other changes are foreseeable. In his most famous poem, "A Blessing," James Wright describes an Indian pony:

> She is black and white,
> Her mane falls wild on her forehead,
> And the light breeze moves me to caress her
> long ear
> That is delicate as the skin over a girl's wrist.
> Suddenly I realize
> That if I stepped out of my body I would break
> Into blossom.[3]

This poem is imagistic, and it expresses, finally, a terrible alienation from the world of nature, a gap which the anthropomorphic imagery (the skin over a girl's wrist) attempts, with self-conscious futility, to bridge. After all, to join the horses Wright must step out of his human body. Keats said the same thing in "Ode to a Nightingale." Now Homer is not imagistic because his characters are at home in the world, and his natural objects—olive trees, mountains, caves—take their place in human purposes. Imagism attempts to anticipate human interpretations of objects and show them in themselves, naked to the naked senses. The attempt is, of course, always unsuccessful, because, as we know now, nature does not know any better than we do what it should look like. But the failure feels to imagists like the consequences of a fall, a casting-out from our proper nature as nature's insiders.

Of course, we were always nature's insiders, and our solidarity with nature is based on the fact that nature, like us, is fallen and still falling, outwards from the chaos of the Big Bang, into order and complex beauty and freedom. Once we realize this, the image will be released from its old ideological bondage and can take its place in the human story, the human argument; pure imagist poetry will have lost its ideological basis and will become a minor, if delightful, form of decorative verbal art.

The nature of metaphor and symbol will also change. Before the materialist revolution, we robustly persisted in the belief that objects possessed the powers that the poetic imagination conferred on them. We believed in magic, magical properties, efficacy by correspondence: the rose was sick with love, the sword hated its enemies, jewels could enchant or heal, the moon was intelligent and a little mad. Our world made more human sense to us than it did to the materialists, but it was almost completely intractable and inhabited by uncontrollable powers.

For the materialists, metaphor and symbol are terribly sad reminders of that human sense of the world that was lost, of our alienation from nature. The rose does not really love, nor the sword hate, nor the jewel heal, nor the moon enchant; they only arbitrarily symbolize these things. Metaphor is technical failure. All significance is a pathetic fallacy, canals of Mars that we put there by the weakness and hopefulness of our eyes. There is no magic any more.

Within the materialistic framework, we had to choose, as Freud saw, between technical power and psychic health.

That time is now over. We shall be making intelligent and crazy moons, and passionate roses, and fierce swords with microprocessors in their hilts, and medically efficacious jewels. No doubt we will build canals on Mars, and make it into exactly the place of Edgar Rice Burroughs' poetic visions, if we so choose. Metaphor and symbol will become a program for technical transformation, and invented technology will be the new metaphors and symbols of the world. In one sense, our poetry will become less obviously metaphorical and symbolic—only because the metaphors and symbols will not be plastered on to the outside of reality, but will be a concrete and accepted part of its plot, as the technical hardware is in a science fiction novel. Facts will be significant, and symbols will be facts. It is not that we shall rise above nature—one of the goals of Modernism—rather, we shall *be* nature, naturans, naturing. We will once more see life, as Edgar says in *King Lear*, as a miracle—as magic, but at the same time an "art lawful as eating," like the enchantment that, in *The Winter's Tale*, brings the statue of the dead queen to life.

NOTES

1. Henry David Thoreau, *Walden* (Columbus, Ohio: Charles E. Merrill, 1969), 327.

2. Alexander Graham Cairns-Smith, *The Life Puzzle: On Crystals and Organisms and the Possibility of a Crystal as an Ancestor* (Toronto: University of Toronto Press, 1971).

3. *The Norton Anthology of Modern Poetry,* ed. Richard Ellmann and Robert O'Clair (New York: W. W. Norton, 1973), 1180.

10

STORIES IN THE POSTMODERN WORLD: ORIENTING AND DISORIENTING

William A. Beardslee

There's very little drama left and very few
good scripts. Stories no longer have a
beginning, middle, and end.
                                    Bette Davis[1]

Not only in film, of which Bette Davis was speaking, but in all the imaginative expressions of our culture, stories are being refashioned, often in
drastic ways. Often, as she says, the conventional expectation of beginning,
middle, and end is dealt with as a mere convention, and many storytellers
intend the reader to understand that the storytelling art is wholly arbitrary,
and that plot as such does not tell us anything about the way things are.

Yet stories are told in every culture, and they are being told and will be told in the postmodern world. And stories are told for many purposes. Let us ask ourselves about one particular thing that stories do for us, and think about the way that is changing in the postmodern world. I am thinking about the way in which stories help us find ourselves, find out who we are. The way it used to be was that my life was a story, and I found myself by fitting that story into the great story of the world in which I lived. My little story retold, on its tiny scale, the great story into which I believed it fitted. In between my story and the great story came all sorts of other stories, but especially the story of my role model, some key person who had already discovered the way she or he made sense out of life by being part of the great story, thereby serving as an example or inspiration for me as I grew, experimented, and learned about life.

Although we have known since the time of the classic discussion of plot in Aristotle's *Poetics* that stories are indeed artificial creations, and that the plot is to a large degree shaped by the teller, the project of locating myself by fixing my story to a larger story did nonetheless presuppose that both my story and the larger story had the form of something like the conventional plot of the made-up story.

Something such as this kind of discovery of identity through story takes place in virtually all cultures, I dare say, and we may ask, how will it be different in the postmodern world? We start with the easy part. Formerly, the big story into which we fitted was the story of my particular faith, or perhaps my particular country. Of course, I was not living in just *one* big story; the story of my faith and that of my country, or the story of my social class and the story of my romantic life, might be in some conflict. A great deal of the adventure and interest of the classic stories arises from this kind of tension. The central figures in the great nineteenth-century novels are often not firmly anchored in their social location, and their unfixed position provides room for the development of the story and for the moral development of the character—Fanny Price in Jane Austen's *Mansfield Park* and Esther Summerson in Charles Dickens' *Bleak House* are two examples. But despite the fact that the protagonists, both those in novels and we ourselves as we struggled through life, were in situations of conflict among different stories, the assumption was that there was an overall story. It was one that in the end would turn out to be a unified story, coming to a conclusion that tied up all the loose ends. By becoming part of this overall story, my own story, unfinished and broken as it might be, could hope to find its own eventual unity.

So what is new? What has changed? It still sounds very familiar, at least to those of us who grew up in that world. What has changed is that, although there were competing great stories into which you and I and the characters in novels had to fit ourselves, there was nevertheless one overall story that gave the orientation and provided the resolution in the end. The stories of Judaism and Christianity have been the classic "great stories" in our culture, and if they were replaced by the story of the nation or of the "culture," at least the general pattern was much the same. Our liberal tradition, whether explicitly religious or not, believed that the overall story was the human story—although that story was interpreted all too imperialistically and patriarchally as a generalization of the story in which we liberals felt at home.

Now, however, there does not seem to be any single story into which I can fit my life in the old-fashioned way. The postmodern world is a world of the interweaving of many stories, and a world in which we recognize the positive value of stories in which we do not take part. The very stridency with which so many people are still trying to deny this is a sign that the old way is not working very well. Whether in politics or religion, we quickly sense a great fear of moving away from the traditional way in which we organized our lives, theoretically at least, around a single story, and dealt as well as we could with the conflicts between the various stories in which we were actually engaged. To me, the American flag is still a very positive symbol—we used to fly it every day at our summer cottage, until the cottage burned down. But when we built the new cottage, we left out the flagpole. Our doing so was a sign that we saw that we were in a new situation.

To give another example, in a recent essay, David Griffin makes clear that, in the postmodern world, we cannot hold the older Christian belief that Jesus Christ appeared at the "middle of time." He says, ". . . there can be no idolatrous notion of a 'middle' of history."[2]Yet how deeply that image of the Christ appearing in the middle of time is embedded in traditional ways of telling the Christian story![3] Those of us who are of that tradition will have our imaginative work cut out for us, if we are to live in our tradition and also in the postmodern world.

But in the world as it is, one single story is no longer sufficient to give us direction. Whatever the orienting story is with which we identify, it has to be woven into others, and how we do that and still find a way of expressing a genuine loyalty to our faith, or to our country, is what we need to discover. To learn to live in our organizing stories as part of a rich and complex fabric of interwoven, interdependent stories is one of the tasks of storytelling today.

If this were all, the question of stories in the postmodern world would be straightforward enough—difficult, but clear. The clue to the postmodern world would be that its vision of an interlocking web of interdependent stories can give us a fresh start in weaving together the conflicting stories in which we find ourselves.

But this is not all. In fact, the real reason I am included in this volume is not that I am a great storyteller, or even a great theorist of narrative. My role is to discuss, in relation to this issue of stories or narrative, the two great meanings of *postmodern* which are competing in our world. The postmodern world of this series of essays is an open, hopeful world, a world of new possibilities because a wide range of new insights in physics, biology, psychology, religion, and even in economics is leading us away from the deterministic models in which we were almost locked in the so-called modern world with its Newtonian science.

When we look at the world of the creation of art and literature, and the study of these subjects, however, we find a very different post-modernism. This world is one where, to quote Jacques Derrida, we live in "the joyous affirmation of the play of the world and of the innocence of becoming, the affirmation of a world of signs without fault, without truth, without origin."[4] In the theological field, this kind of postmodernism has been summarized by Mark C. Taylor in the title of his book, *Erring*.[5] The title suggests that the course of human life is "erring" both in the sense of "wandering" and in the sense of "transgressing."

A key point in this shift of vision is that the older story could com-bine tradition and creativity. Something new meant a turning point in the story. One thing that has become questionable in the artistic post-modernism is precisely the creativity that is so prominent in the other kind of postmodernism. A recent *New Yorker* article described the work of a young New York artist, the point of whose work is that there is no point in being original; her work is explicit copying. Sherrie Levine became known by a show entitled "After Walker Evans," which consisted of a professionally copied series of Walker Evans' famous Farm Security Administration photographs, which she signed and exhibited as her art. This was followed by "After J. M. W. Turner," twenty reproductions of paintings by Turner cut from an art book, and signed by Levine.[6] Granted that there is a strong and conscious irony in this, one of the great marks of the postmodern world in art and literature is the deep suspicion of the creative person, the expressive individual of the old Romantic tradition. If we were to turn from narrative to poetry, we would behold the same landscape. A recent work on postmodern poetry comments on how bleak and unpromising a scene the postmodern world is for the poet.[7]

What does this tell us about stories? Sherrie Levine's art tells us that there is nothing new in our story, even though it seems so new and origi-nal to us. Charles Altieri's comments on postmodern poetry tell us that the poets can find little to write about except words, language. Mark

Taylor's *Erring* tells us by its title that the story line is now "erring," that is, both wandering (without direction) and transgressing—the remnant of direction is the direction of breaking the rules or breaking the accustomed pattern. That motif ties in with the emphasis on shock or subversion in so much postmodern art.

In this kind of postmodern world, the loss of a story that locates or orients us leaves a place for another kind, the disorienting story, the story that assaults our expectations and pulls us out of the world to which we have become accustomed.

Let me illustrate this point from the field of biblical studies, where the study of stories or narrative has been one of the main lines of interest for some years. The October 11, 1986 *Los Angeles Times* reported that Robert Funk's seminar on the historical Jesus had voted that Jesus did not expect the imminent end of the world. Perhaps a more cautious interpretation of the group's action would be that the expectation of an imminent apocalyptic end of the world was not a constitutive part of Jesus' message. The ground for this judgment expressed in the *Times* article was that it is in the parables that we find what is distinctive about Jesus, and one scholar is quoted in that article as saying that the parables "are trying to identify the activity of God where the people are. They are not interested in talking about angels and God in heaven and what a particular age will bring."[8]

This scholar notes that the shift away from an apocalyptic interpretation of Jesus has been going on for some fifteen years. That is about the time since the important work of the founder of the historical Jesus seminar, Robert Funk, and of John Dominic Crossan began to call fresh attention to the parables.[9] Not all the members of the seminar would follow Funk and Crossan, but we should note that their work is extremely important for our question, for both of them interpret the parables of Jesus as disruptive, disorienting stories rather than as traditional religious stories which are orienting ones. Although the "Jesus Seminar" is explicitly focused on the *historical* question of what Jesus did and did not say, at a deeper level these excellent scholars are saying that disorienting stories, not orienting ones, are those that point to that which is most important. For they assume that Jesus told important stories—hence, disorienting ones. It is true that the this-worldly versus other-worldly question is also important. But I believe that it is more fundamentally the case that the postmodern culture in which academic professors find themselves does not see the traditional orienting story as still functional, while the disorienting story indeed may enable us momentarily to glimpse something beyond the daily round.

Perhaps it is worth noting that the late nineteenth century saw the rediscovery of the apocalyptic orienting Christian story, while at a little later time the orienting Marxist story achieved a widespread acceptance.[10] It is not too much to say that for many, both in Europe and in other parts of the world, the Marxian story became the secular replacement for the Jewish or Christian story, which had been the deep-level orienting vision even for those in Western culture who were not practicing adherents of either of these faiths. As we turn to our own time, we see that, parallel to the scepticism about the orienting story we have noted among religious thinkers, there is a similar scepticism about the Marxian story. Listen to these remarks by a thoughtful and sympathetic student of Marxism: "[Marxism's] character as a total ideology or a worldview, which once seemed to guarantee that it was grounded in reality and which made it politically vibrant for so many, stands revealed to us as a delusion in some respects and a nightmare in others."[11] Marxism's "total ideology or worldview" was presented through its "story." To this author, Walter Adamson, Marxist thought has been purged of its narrative elements, and what remains is a methodological torso. Still exceedingly valuable as a tool of social analysis, it has lost its narrative character.

What holds together these different comments about the post-modern world (this term is not used by all those cited) is precisely their sense of the lack of connectedness in the passage of events. To cite Derrida again: "The future can only be anticipated in the form of an absolute danger. It is that which breaks absolutely with constituted normality and can only be proclaimed, *presented,* as a sort of monstrosity."[12] A different figure, which sums up very well the postmodern view of narrative for so many, comes from Marcel Proust. He was writing about a very restricted area of what we mean by society, the society of the "salon," when he said, ". . . a kaleidoscope which is every now and then given a turn, society arranges successively in different orders elements which one would have supposed to be immovable, and composes a fresh pattern."[13] But the image of historical change as a turn of the kaleidoscope sums up very well a whole wing of the postmodern sensibility about historical change.

One of the factors contributing to the breakup of faith in an over-all story is terribly clear: in our century, the liberal faith in a gradually improving human story, the Christian faith in a world transformed into or at least toward the Realm of God, and the Jewish faith in God's care for God's people, have all been shaken and in many cases destroyed, simply by what human beings have done to one another. If the Holocaust has been balanced for Jews by the creation of the State of Israel, the rigid state of life in Eastern Europe, along with the chaotic course of contemporary history, has brought about the loss of faith in the Marxian story which I noted above, and this loss is no doubt one of the principal stimuli to the emergence of the negative kind of postmodernism. For many European intellectuals, Marx had provided the principal clues to the modern world for looking beneath the surface movements of history to its deeper forces, and the disillusionment with Marx has led to that sharp separation of the present from the future which is shown in the quotation from Derrida above.

A second factor, very different in kind, is the increasing elusiveness of the "subject" or the self. If Marx gave the modern world its principal social-historical clues, Freud opened the discussion of the subject or self. Here, too, the modern view was marked by "suspicion": What happens on the surface conceals a deeper dynamic, which Freud undertook to disclose. While many postmodern thinkers are strongly revisionary of Freud, especially because of his male-oriented perspective, he is a key figure in postmodernism, and the suspicion of the self-conscious subject is a centerpiece of postmodernism. This theme is not unrelated to the former one. A part of the reason for the suspicion of the self or subject is the experienced powerlessness of the self to bring about historical change, for instance in France in the 1960s.

But the center of this new view of the self is the postmodern study of language. We used to suppose that language was at the disposal of the self. Increasingly, the point is made that the self is shaped, is indeed constituted, by the interwoven network of language. The shift from existentialist theories of interpretation, in which the choosing self was central, to structuralist analysis was the key change. Structuralism tried to show how meaning was produced as the expression of tensions between opposing pairs of terms: life/death and male/female, for instance. The "deep" meaning of a text is controlled by these oppositions, rather than the meaning's being "controlled" by the author. Early structuralism was strongly rationalistic, and much of it attempted to recover a single meaning. Later it appeared that important meaning is pluri-significant; a text expresses a bundle of possibilities. Either it is said that there are a multiplicity of structures of deep tension at work, or that the deep structure produces an indefinite range of meaning in its expression. In either case, the subject is no longer in control of meaning, but is rather a vehicle for its expression.

Thus the subjectivity of the author and that of the reader are not regarded as autonomous, but as cultural products: ". . . the subjectivity itself, and the meanings with which it plays are not disembodied ideas, coming to us from some Idea of Absolute Being 'out there'; they are historically produced and socially created."[14]

Such a postmodern stance is often torn between two inferences: one, that recognition of the social relativity of the subject frees critics (read, us) to reexamine the shape of our subjectivity, and to use those forms of subjectivity disclosed by texts as critical leverage in this task; and the other, that the subject is so strongly controlled by its social production, and in addition is so dissected by the situation in which it is produced by such diverse factors, that we understand ourselves almost entirely as products, and not as actors.[15] It is evident that the relativity of the self makes the question of ethical standards for critical reevaluation both of selfhood and of society an urgent problem. It is also the case that this whole effort to look below the surface ideational or logical meaning in order to find a deeper dynamic is a quest to uncover power factors that shape ideology. A pervasive theme of postmodern reflection about the self is the way in which traditional selfhood is shaped by male/female stereotypes, a theme which unites the two elements just noted. Hence Kaja Silverman, in discussing the work of the feminist film critic Jacqueline Rose, indicates how the basic technique of the camera's "gaze" is derived from the male gaze at the female, and notes that the "imaginary excess which haunts the system" offers not only (by its excess) a return of a repressed femininity, but also the possibility for destabilizing the symbolic order, for throwing into jeopardy its Oedipal identifications.[16] I might note as well that from this point of view, the very basic relationships and self-images that are suggested by the Oedipal language are understood themselves to be linguistic, that is, cultural, creations. Hence they can be changed. We see again the note of disrupting the continuity of narrative as the typically postmodern stance—a disruption that can be liberating.

If we ask what the connection is between the first antinarrative theme noted above (the experienced loss of meaning in the traditional orienting narratives) and the second (the discovery that the self does not stand apart from narrative, but is constituted, even at the unconscious level, by the narrative conventions of the society in which it comes to be), the connection that I see is the following: the postmodern self is capable of small-scale purposive actions, but there is little confidence that these can cumulatively bring about meaningful changes. The link provided by the "myths" of the premodern and modern worlds has been eroded away. The small-scale acts of purposiveness are not thought to fit into a larger story. Or, to come at it from the other side, the flow of life seems not to be a narrative, but a stasis, a flow indeed, but one that is repetitive and, indeed, repressive. That is why meaningful action is subversive. If there is meaning in stories, it will be in the subversive stories, not in the connected mythological patterns which build continuing communities. So it is not surprising that whether we look to theologians of the parables of Jesus, to Marxist or feminist liberation thinkers, or to so-called purely literary analysis, the recurrent emphasis is on the shattering of patterns, on breaking open the rigid and enclosing forms of language and society which restrict and limit us.

The frequent assertion that there is no "truth" in the postmodern world is a result of this move. Truth is associated with the existing social structure. Whether as "Christian," "Marxist," or "capitalist," it is understood to be an ideological bulwark of a system that benefits a few, not a description of how things are.

What are we to say about this literary postmodernism, from the point of view of the open postmodernism we are trying to elaborate in this series?

First, we recognize the many strengths of this analysis. It would be irresponsible to try to develop an open postmodernism that ignored the chaotic and broken experience of this century. The temptation to utopianism is aptly rebuked by the whole tenor of literary postmodernism.

Second, the familiar pattern of "hermeneutics of suspicion," so closely associated with the names of Marx and Freud, will continue to be a mark of open postmodernism. We will always need to look beneath the surface meanings, to discern forces shaping us and our world of which we are not immediately conscious. From what has been said above, it is clear that neither of these great thinkers offers a total worldview that is viable today. But their ways of getting beneath the surface are still important tools also for postmodern thinkers who do see an openness and freedom in events which was not clearly articulated by either Marx or Freud. The point is that openness and freedom always operate within the sorts of framework of constraint which Marx and Freud elaborated.

Third, the way in which postmodern literature and art have thrown the traditional orienting stories into question needs to be taken seriously. In particular, the element of "closure," the element of rounding off the meaning by bringing the story to a conclusion, needs to be reimagined by any of us who stand within one of the traditional stories. The closure of the end of a narrative effectively excludes meanings that have not participated in the story. The traditional, if often caricatured, picture of heaven and hell in the Christian story makes the point—but it is equally visible in, say, a Western film or a traditional romantic novel. We will still need and want to tell stories in their traditional form, but we have to learn to relativize their endings. That is the truth for us that lies in the loss of traditional story form to which Bette Davis alludes in the epigraph of this article.

But we must challenge the assumption that the alternative to rigid, constricting, existing form is simply disruption. Actually those who advocate the disorienting move have, behind their negative action, an often hidden longing for a wider justice—a remnant, in fact, of the Jewish and Christian traditions and the secular offshoots from them. The fate of narrative is tied to the social process; it is indeed an imaginative question, but not one for the imagination of the isolated subject, and the orienting story to which we attach ourselves will have to relate to the brokenness and suffering of our world.

There are two ways in which what I have called the literary postmodernism needs to be augmented or transformed by the wider, open postmodernism of this series. First, the erosion of the self is only half the story. The self or subject is indeed many-layered. It is "composed" by social forces and especially by language. It is never wholly unified, and it is always partly driven by forces that are never wholly conscious. In the language of our topic, the subject always participates in a bundle of stories, although usually consciously relating to only one or a few. The self nonetheless does have a center, even though one that is never wholly actualized. The events of the life of a subject are momentary unifications of experience, and these unifications are purposive. There is hence a clear basis for the small-scale purposiveness that keeps appearing, often without any apparent basis, in the works of literary postmodernism.

Furthermore, although the world is without a center in the sense that none of the historical routes of tradition has privileged access to any center, and indeed these routes of tradition continually claim more "centrality" than they actually share, nonetheless the world—the universe in which we live—is not simply the random accumulation it often appears to be in postmodern writing. There is a central perspective on the universe, a perspective that ensures a ground for moral judgments. Although our access to this central perspective is limited by precisely our own perspectives, we can have knowledge of it.[17]

If our own stories are created by the interaction of data from the past with continual purposive events of unification of experience, then narrative is far more than the arbitrary play it often seems to be in literary postmodernism. Stories are indeed an interweaving of many strands, and not the single story which they often seem to be. A principal task of postmodern imagination is to help us see ourselves in this more complex way. To do so, we still need to relate ourselves to overarching stories. These stories cannot simply be invented. We are, as the French are fond of saying, "bricoleurs," tinkerers, cobbling together a structure out of rather miscellaneous elements given to us by our pasts. But the elements from the past are not mere unrelated fragments, despite their miscellaneous character. They offer us tracts of meaning, directional, transformative possibilities as we relate our own stories to them.

At first, the meaning we put together might seem unrelated to those past meanings, the fragments of which we build together into new patterns. This is the way in which the matter is often presented in postmodern writing. But if we remind ourselves, or if we discover, that the great overarching stories of the past are not simply the rigid, imprisoning structures they are often taken to be, we can relate to them, indeed stand in them as our own stories. To do so, we must look in these stories for their own hints or elements of self-transformation. Then we will find them to be astonishing resources rather than imprisoning structures. Then "story" will again be able to relate us to patterns of "rightness" that are grounded in reality, although not in the static "reality" against which so much both of modernism and postmodernism have revolted.

In religious terms, a strong theme in much postmodernism is that that which is most important and beyond immediate experience can be encountered in narrative only as narrative is broken. As George Aichele puts it: "In order to exceed the limits, theology must uncover the non-itself which lies unnamed at its center, its hidden eccentricity and non-identity. It must become concrete."[18] This route opens the way to an awareness of the undifferentiated creativity which is manifested in all events. It is a theme richly developed in Eastern religions. We honor this kind of postmodern exploration. But we set beside it another fully valid route, the route that continues to find meaning in continuing, developing story, precisely because story is built on value-judgments. This route will not so immediately disclose the undifferentiated creativity, but it will put us in touch with the "rightness" which, in spite of all scepticism, we long to know, and which is disclosed in the interwoven web of stories within which we live.

To put it in terms of types of story, we can continue to recognize the often very unwelcome role of the disorienting or subversive story, which is such a recurrent feature of postmodernism, without failing to see that the orienting story in which we find ourselves is also still central today. We will have to reimagine the fundamental story as an open one, without the closure of a final ending, but that reimagining will still make place for the many small endings of the substories within which we live and which we are.[19]

NOTES

1. Quoted in *U.S. News and World Report,* Dec. 8, 1986:76.

2. David Ray Griffin, "Postmodern Theology and A/theology: A Response to Mark C. Taylor," in David Ray Griffin, William A. Beardslee, and Joe Hol-

land, *Varieties of Postmodern Theology* (Albany: State University of New York Press, 1989), 51.

3. This point was made with especial clarity in Oscar Cullmann's *Christ and Time: The Primitive Christian Conception of Time and History,* Floyd V. Filson, trans. (Philadelphia: Westminster, 1950), in which the dramatic, single-story plot of Christianity was defended theologically. Hans Conzelmann's *Die Mitte der Zeit* (translated as *The Theology of St. Luke* by Geoffrey Buswell [New York: Harper, 1960]) recognized the prominence of this theme in Luke and Acts, but was not sympathetic to it theologically. Conzelmann's theological view was an existentialist one, which overcame the single-story character of the Christian vision by sacrificing the dramatic, story quality of Christian existence.

4. Jacques Derrida, *L'ecriture et la différence* (Paris: Editions du Seuil, 1967), 427, cited in Gayatri Chakravarti Spivak, "Translator's Preface," in Jacques Derrida, *Of Grammatology,* G.C. Spivak, trans. (Baltimore, Md.: Johns Hopkins University Press, 1976), xiii.

5. Mark C. Taylor, *Erring: A Postmodern A/theology* (Chicago: University of Chicago Press, 1984).

6. Janet Malcolm, "A Girl of the Zeitgeist," *The New Yorker,* Oct. 27, 1986: 60-61. (The person in the title is not Sherrie Levine but Ingrid Sischy.)

7. Charles Altieri, *Self and Sensibility in Contemporary American Poetry* (Cambridge: Cambridge University Press, 1984), 203, observes: "By reducing the scope of our questions we find a realm of playful, half-serious reflections important precisely because there is virtually no content until the poet produces the *mots justes.* However, within this framework there is very little way for the *mots* to be *justes.*" Altieri's sober assessment of the position of contemporary American poetry is the more striking because of its contrast with the "early postmodern" poets whom he examined in *Enlarging the Temple: New Directions in American Poetry during the 1960s* (Lewisburg, Penn.: Bucknell University Press, 1979). Altieri's treatment of the poets of the 1960s dealt with a group of writers, many of whom were affirming a broader postmodern vision, sometimes explicitly derived from Alfred North Whitehead. Of them he said: "While the other contemporary arts, in the throes of what John Barth has called "Exhaustion," continue to reinterpret the subjective aspects of a dying social order, the best postmodern poets are at work articulating the shape of a new temple that may provide the locus for a new image of man" (239).

8. Vernon K. Robbins, *Los Angeles Times,* Oct. 11, 1986, Sec. II: 6.

9. Robert W. Funk, *Language, Hermeneutic, and Word of God* (New York: Harper & Row, 1966); John Dominic Crossan, *The Dark Interval* (Allen, Tex.: Argus, 1975). Crossan's view is also stated in earlier publications.

10. In the Christian tradition, at least, the apocalyptic story is an orienting story, although it functions in situations of stress and expresses a great deal of disorientation.

11. Walter L. Adamson, *Marx and the Disillusionment of Marxism* (Berkeley: University of California Press, 1985), 228.

12. Jacques Derrida, *Of Grammatology,* 5.

13. Marcel Proust, *Within a Budding Grove,* G.K. Scott Moncrieff, trans. (New York: Vintage Books, 1970), 66-67. I owe this citation to Kaja Silverman, *The Subject of Semiotics* (New York: Oxford University Press, 1983), 13.

14. Timothy Reiss, "Critical Environments: Cultural Wilderness or Cultural History?" *Canadian Journal of Comparative Literature* 9 (1983), 198, cited by Robert Detweiler, "What is a Sacred Text?" *Semeia* 31 (1985), 228.

15. The first stance is well-represented by Kaja Silverman, *The Subject of Semiotics.* The second is exemplified by Jean-François Lyotard, *The Postmodern Condition: A Report on Knowledge* (Minneapolis: University of Minnesota Press, 1984). I have discussed Lyotard's views at some length in "Christ in the Postmodern Age: Reflections Inspired by Jean-François Lyotard," in *Varieties of Postmodern Theology* (see note 2 above), 63-80.

16. Kaja Silverman, *The Subject of Semiotics,* 235. She is referring to Jaqueline Rose, "Paranoia and the Film System," *Screen* 17/4 (1976-77), 85-104.

17. For a fine statement on this theme, see David Ray Griffin's paper mentioned in note 2.

18. George Aichele, *The Limits of Story* (Philadelphia: Fortress Press, and Chico: Scholars Press, 1985), 138-39. He is advocating a theology of Dadaism.

19. For a fuller discussion of the potential and problematic of the disorienting story, see William A. Beardslee, "Parable, Proverb, and Koan," *Semeia* 12 (1978), 151-73.

Allan McCollum, "Plaster Surrogates," 1984, (enamel on hydrostone).
(Photo courtesy of Rhona Hoffman Gallery, Chicago.)

11

THE REENCHANTMENT OF ART: REFLECTIONS ON THE TWO POSTMODERNISMS

Suzi Gablik

In the visual arts, the era of the early
'70s believed itself to be a great flowering
of postcapitalist culture. It believed
that the commodity and its mind-set
would be replaced by performance and
by site-specific works. The artist would
perform in real time, enacting an example
of nonalienated work. The artist would
play out the role of the free subject,
creating a model that would be emulated
elsewhere in society. But the '70s
represented not the last flowering of a
new consciousness, but rather the last
incandescent expression of the old
idealism of autonomy. After this, no time
would be real, no labor would be living,
no cultural expression could be outside
the commodity system.

Peter Halley

I think that almost everybody is potentially
a shaman. What is needed is to wake up
that potential and begin to explore
experientially one's spiritual relationship
to the universe, to other forms of life on
the planet, and to each other. . . . Respect
is a key word in this regard because the
experiences that come from shamanism
tend to foster a great respect for the
universe, based on a feeling of oneness
with all forms of life. By getting into
harmony, one has much more power
available to help others because harmony
with the universe is where true power
comes from.

Michael Harner

Our particular point in culture, more so than any other in the history of
humanity, appears to be at a critical threshold where the option of continuing as we have before is being perceived as no longer viable. The
message is out on all sides that we are having to choose between survival
and ecocide, and there has been an increasing demand at the creative
edge of our society to shape a new social order. It is a task in which we
may, of course, choose not to take part. But my own personal concern,
for some time now, has been the question of what role art might play in
response to this need for "accelerating the transformation," as Riane
Eisler has put it, "from a dominator to a partnership model in all aspects
of our lives."

As the art world undertakes the fateful closure of modernism and
its failed utopian ambitions, two postmodernisms seem to be emerging
within the world of artistic practice. Only one of them so far is visible
and dominant within the mainstream, and that is *deconstructive* postmodernism, which is playing out the Weberian process of disenchantment
with medicinal forms of nihilism not meant to ward off an otherwise
irredeemable reality but to come to terms with it. Deconstructive artists
reject what they perceive as the modernist myths of stylistic innovation,
change, originality, and uniqueness, which are now viewed as the worn-

out trappings of a chic but totally impotent radicalism. Often they work by stealth, assuming the posture of counterfeiter or charlatan, a sort of trickster figure, who is not going to get us out of the mess we are in but will engage in the only legitimate cultural practice possible for our time— which is, in the words of Jean Baudrillard (a seminal theoretician of the deconstructive scenario), "the chance, labyrinthine, manipulatory play of signs without meaning."

The other postmodernism, happening simultaneously if rather less visibly (because so far there has been, at least in the art world, no comprehensive or workable framework for it), is what I choose to call *reconstructive* postmodernism. It is challenging the very ground of our materialistic worldview and, as such, is part of a larger project of "reenchantment" occurring in many arenas of our culture. Put simply, reconstructive postmodernism implicates art in this awakening sense of responsibility for the fate of the earth and of the high levels of psychic and physical toxicity in our environment. It differs from deconstruction in that it does not merely react to the present state of affairs; it actively seeks pragmatic solutions and to restore health and aliveness through an empowered new vision.

Although the two postmodernisms are quite discrete and separate events, what they share in common is an understanding that the belief system that belonged to the modern worldview has become dysfunctional. Among the key questions at stake on both sides are how to respond to the demands for cultural renewal and change, and whether art (once the primary architect of modernist ideals) can actually be effective any more, given the proven resistance of twentieth-century capitalism to radical transformation. Reconstructive artists believe that art has the potential for radically reshaping the beliefs of society, whereas deconstruction involves a withdrawal of belief and a hollowing out of authenticity, based on a retrospective reading of modernism that is fully aware of its limitations and failed ambitions. Deconstructionists believe that positive action is doomed either to impotence or co-optation by an economic system that has become virtually uncontrollable. In this circumstance, art can no longer present itself as the hope of a better civilization; it can only iterate the certainty that such a hope is no longer possible. To believe in the transcendent power of art at this point would be self-deluding: the very term has to be overheated for picking one's way through the vast junkyard of consumer culture. Art may reveal the problematic nature of this situation by mirroring it, or transforming it into a hollow parody of itself, but it is helpless to change anything.

Reconstructionists, on the other hand, are trying to make the transition from Eurocentric, patriarchal thinking and the "dominator" model of culture to a more participatory aesthetics of interconnectedness, aimed toward social responsibility, psychospiritual empowerment, deep ecological attunement, good human relations, and a new sense of the sacred— all that the old industrial paradigm has tended to exclude. More resonance and communion seem to be the key, and a willingness to search for options beyond the pursuit of a career and upward mobility, for options beyond individualism and secularism.

Where the two postmodernisms differ, obviously, is in their solutions, and in the fact that each believes its scenario, its view of the future, is the correct one and that the other is hopelessly deluded. But I would like to suggest that the differences between these two perspectives are more than merely philosophical, because it is precisely between the role of mirroring (where the artist is a detached observer) and the role of shaping (in which we are not merely witnesses or spectators, but orchestrators of culture and consciousness) that the shift from old-paradigm into new-paradigm thinking is likely to occur. Indeed, the new paradigm has been said to represent a kind of reenchantment because it opens up the future to new possibilities and in it you see new options, not closure.

By presenting these incompatible claims in what I hope is a nonantagonistic relation, I intend to show that one philosophy no longer accurately represents our culture, which is best revealed right now in the dynamic of its opposing tendencies, knowing that the most fruitful developments often take place where two different lines of thought meet. With this in mind, I shall now offer some examples of artists working from each of these perspectives, which are drawn from my forthcoming book, *The Reenchantment of Art.*

I. DECONSTRUCTIVE POSTMODERN ART

Deconstructive aesthetics, as I have already suggested, starts from the premise that strategies of protest are no longer effective, having been neutralized or "bought off." In a recently published article entitled "Hover Culture: The View from Alexandria," the artist/critic Ronald Jones asks what the wisdom would be of formulating another confrontational culture when the fate of such a counterculture is already so assured. It is difficult to imagine, he claims, that a counterculture that actually possessed the deftness to rearrange the terms of the dominant culture, or to inspire fundamental reform, would be allowed. The culture industry likes to create the illusion that the culture is transforming itself, but actually to act as if it will, according to Jones, is counterproductive, a kind of false-hearted, self-delusory promise. The nondeluded individual of today is the one who has given up naive hopes, comforting beliefs, and pointless idealizing—which is like smearing with luminous paint after the light has gone out. Jones writes:

> If the last degree of authenticity has been drained away from the development of our culture, so that it now subsists at the level of a programmatic charade, isn't the decision to refuse change the moment it appears at least sincere? As freakish as it must sound, spurning change . . . reasserts the artist as the arbiter of a radicalized culture.

Instead of creating anything new, the artist slows things down and "hovers" in place, as a way of not feeding the cultural demand for change—moving into slow motion where nothing seems to change.

Rather than trying to carry forward the betrayed ideology of the old avant garde, the deconstructive artist may resort to fraudulence, becoming, for instance, a counterfeiter who simulates the work of other artists, as when Sherrie Levine rephotographed the work of Walker Evans and Edward Weston and exhibited it as her own, or when Mike Bidlo painted "Magrittes" and "Jackson Pollocks." A recent project by Bidlo involved copying to scale some eighty-four paintings of Picasso's Women (he always works from color reproductions, never from originals). These actions directly violate our notions about creativity, particularly according to the modernist canon, as being based in innovation, authenticity, originality. To simulate is to play what Baudrillard has called the "disappearing game" of postmodernism, where the true has become a moment of the false. "The effects of disappearance . . .are the best we can afford today," he states. "Nothing is true, so a few gestures become hip. . . . You don't believe in it, but you do it anyway and you even get to like it in the end."

Nowhere are the "beautiful effects of disappearance" better illustrated than in the paintings of Allan McCollum, which simultaneously dramatize and thwart our desire to look at pictures. On close scrutiny, McCollum's paintings reveal themselves as simulacra—as pseudoartifacts in which picture, mat and frame are all one seamless object, molded in plaster—but there is nothing to see. In place of any communicating image, there is a dark, thick substance, like pitch: a pure screen of black, whose emptiness would seem to express the posthumous death of culture and art. These simulations of conventional art objects are usually hung in groups, often by the hundreds, to resemble a crowded salon show. "I'm doing just the minimum that is expected of an artist and no more," McCollum has stated. "I'm trying to orchestrate a charade."

Because in an age of simulacra nothing separates true from false, how can we assess the reaction of the power structure to a perfect simulation? By feigning a violation, suggests Baudrillard, and putting it to the test. "Go and simulate a theft in a large department store," he has written. "Or organize a fake hold-up. . . . How do you convince the security guards that it is a simulated theft?" You will not succeed, because the web of artificial signs will be inextricably mixed up with real elements (a police officer will really shoot on sight, or a customer will faint from fear). Likewise, how do you convince an art dealer that McCollum's pictures are not "real" works of art, but are simulations? You will not succeed, because collectors will buy them, dealers will show them, and critics will write about them; even simulations cannot escape the system's ability to integrate everything. And so it is that art survives its own disappearance; somewhere the real scene has been lost, but everything continues just the same.

How does one attack cultural inauthenticity if one's means and materials are indistinguishable from those of the cultural reality one is attacking? In the absurd but alluring "product art" of Haim Steinbach, works of art represent themselves as objects of consumption, becoming more commodified than commodities. Steinbach buys many of his art objects ready-made at Conran's, or the supermarket. He seductively arranges and displays tea kettles, digital clocks, lava lamps, water pitchers, trash receptacles, boxes of cereal, radios, cooking pots, towels, and boxes of detergent on specially constructed Formica shelves, for the viewer-customer. In a work entitled *supremely black,* three boxes of Bold detergent are displayed with two gleaming black, deco-style water pitchers, and in *pink accent*[2] we have two rubber Halloween masks, a pair of stainless steel trash cans and four tea kettles. This reduplication has its own particular fascination, that of the pure look: Steinbach does not criticize the mechanisms of consumption so much as he objectifies the commodity as spectacle. What would it take for an entire society to recover from the addictive system in which we live? There is little encouragement to change our orientation because compulsive consumption keeps our culture going and is supported by it. The artist's consciousness has been fatally enriched with this knowledge.

"It is one thing to speak about this situation, it's quite another matter to recognize how we participate emotionally in this ecstasy, how we should monitor it," Steinbach stated recently in a symposium on "Avant-Garde Art in the '80s" at the Los Angeles County Museum. "We live in a culture of pornography; we are engulfed by it, contained in it. We are not standing by the river bank watching this excess of shit flow by, rather we are flowing with it, in it." If Steinbach's work dissolves the difference (which no longer exists) between our desire for commodities and our desire for art, and if this state of things is pornographic, we must look at it and ask ourselves how we partake of it: in the logic of the commodity, when even culture itself is disseminated as a product, everything acts to commodify consciousness. Steinbach continues:

> On an emotional level, artists are recognizing the extreme state of ambivalence they find themselves in, feeling revulsion and fascination at the same time. They also recognize that this is not going to change. . . . But sooner than look elsewhere, sooner than conclude that we are in an artificially excessive culture of meaninglessness and that we'd better jump ship as fast as we can, we choose to have fun and play this particular computer game. Sooner than look from above at how others live, we choose to live in our own culture.

Is there, then, no way out of the alliance of capitalism and culture? Is deconstruction the only plausible answer—cultivating the paradox and leaping, as it were, over one's shadow? "I think an understanding of the limits is less paralyzing than going off on some silly campaign based on false assumptions," the painter Peter Halley comments. "To me, that would be really paralyzing." Implosive strategies demand going to extremes —or doing nothing—until the system devours its own empty forms, absorbs its own meaning, creates a void and disappears. Halley defines this as "rearguard action"—which he takes to be the only response possible—a rearguard action

> of guerilla ideas that can disappear back into the jungle of thought and reemerge in other disguises—of fantastic, eccentric ideas that seem innocuous and are so admitted unnoticed by the media-mechanism, of doubtful ideas that are not invested in their own truth and are thus not damaged when they are manipulated, or nihilistic ideas that are dismissed for being too depressing.

And so we have this policy of going nowhere, of not occupying a position, becoming nothing, having no positive horizons, no optimistic goals, no constructive alternatives. "Right away people ask, 'What can you do with that?' " writes Baudrillard. But that, it would seem, is just the point: there is nothing to be had from it. The only thing you can do is to let it run, all the way to the end. The *tabula rasa* certainly clears the ground. But, as Sylvère Lotringer says to Baudrillard, "there is a high price to pay in terms of emptiness and disenchantment. There you have all the seduction, and the sadness, of nihilism."

II. RECONSTRUCTIVE POSTMODERN ART

If it is accurate to trace many of our present dilemmas to what has been called "the disenchantment of the world," then the solution, according to reconstructive postmodernism, must somehow involve the reenchantment of the world, a process that will depend on our ability to break the circle of routines and beliefs built up by modern culture and to begin the transition into a different stream of experience: one that transcends the consumer environment and moves away from the idea that only one model of the universe —the modern one—explains all of reality. Mysticism, it was claimed by Max Weber, was out of tune with modern societies, so if ever mysticism reared its head, something was going awry. The truth is we are only beginning to perceive how our development has been blocked by mechanistic models; how the images with which we have programmed ourselves actually run our lives, unconsciously determining our outlook and reinforcing the negative conditions they represent. The world as an emanation of spirit, of visionary powers and mythical archetypes, is not congruent with the world of mechanization, which requires matter-of-factness as the prevailing attitude of mind. "Myth orchestrates the culture and consciousness of entire civilizations," Jean Houston has written. "It provides a template for the forms of culture, so much so that it becomes possible to change both culture and consciousness by changing a myth." We are just beginning to perceive how the ideological world-picture in terms of which the individual experiences his or her life plays a crucial role in setting the expectations and ideals of what it is possible to achieve.

Many people continue to believe that entering the visionary mode will draw them away from the world of modern consciousness and fix them in archaic states that are unsuitable to contemporary life. But if the mythology is as bad as it is in our technological world, then creating the proper connection with our collective dreambody becomes nothing less than a major cultural task of our time. Far from being romantic or regressive, the return to mythic consciousness seems laden with pragmatic implications for a culture that has been so intolerant of mystical experiences which transcend consensus reality. Really to let go of this systematic denial and repression requires a willingness to empty oneself of old programming. It means correcting what quantum physicist David Bohm has called an "entrained mistake" of the whole culture—our overidentification with the rational process. Such a mistake is harder to correct than a merely personal one, because it has been programmed by an entire historical epoch. Another whole dimension of intuitive, nonrational knowledge is added to our sense of the world by the dreaming mind, which demonstrates that mechanistic consciousness is not the absolute it presents itself as. It would seem, then, that those artists who perceive the need for postmodern consciousness to be remythologized—who are attempting, in their work, to gain access to these deeper levels in order to reactivate a sense of the mythic and the sacred like a great force field, and to bring the dream images of a mythology to manifestation—have already begun the task of transcending our alienated and mechanistic models. In hooking us back up to our collective dreambody, they begin to transform what James Hillman so aptly calls "the retarded state of external reality"—the dead and ugly, soulless and mechanical, world we currently inhabit. Peter Halley writes:

> It is the essence of modern consciousness to be irrevocably structured by the technological aspects of industrial production. The individual of today transfers the engineering ethos of modern technology and bureaucracy to his personal consciousness and emotional life. This ethos, characterized by mechanicalness, reproducibility and measurability, produces in consciousness the traits of abstraction, functional rationality and instrumentality.

Mythic thinking is a force against the literal mind, which insists that things are only as they appear. It is also an opening into the numinous, transpersonal dimensions of the psyche (which can be either ecstatic or terrifying), where there is no separation between inner and outer, between "real" and "imagined," where there are no boundaries, so that all things flow into each other. In shamanic consciousness, the world is not experienced as separate from ourselves—a perception which I find embodied in Richard Rosenblum's sculpture *Manscape:* the boundary between self and world has been allowed to dissolve, and the figure of a man becomes a walking landscape. If a paradigm refers to the pattern of beliefs, perceptions and ways of seeing that are characteristic of a culture, then Rosenblum's sculpture breaks through the dualism of the Newtonian-Cartesian worldview, which has dominated Western consciousness for over two hundred years. The essence of our culture of estrangement is that we are bewitched by the vision of separateness: we do not see ourselves as part of the world. There is a split between mind and matter. Modern scientific consciousness insists on a rigid distinction between observer and observed—the mechanistic idea that we can know the world only by distancing ourselves from it, by knowing it from the outside, rather than through psychic participation and through the emotional identification of subject and object. Rosenblum, who lives and works in Newton, Massachusetts, transforms the roots of dead trees into visionary sculpture (which he then casts). Uprootedness, so much a part of modern alienation, with its peculiar forms of distancing and detachment, seems resolved in this aesthetic metaphor of *belonging:* rerooting ourselves in the cosmos, realizing the bodily unity of ourselves and the world.

"With hands grounded in earth and hay," writes Rachel Dutton, an artist from California who creates sculptures resonant with genetic memory of the ancestral animal chain that is woven into the cells and tissues of our body, "I was able to enter the immense fertility of the dream world directly through my art. I crossed over into a land far older than my dreams, where I felt echoes of other ancestors, clusters of innumerable animals, birds, insects, fish, secreting, weaving, digging. . . ." From this dream-memory emerged such unusual sculptures as the *First Mothers,* who, when they entered creation, learned to make paper nests, and whose sharp eyes would have seen the ancient great lizards, forests of ferns, daylong twilight under constant clouds. Another sculpture emerging from Dutton's dream-memory is *Feet of Song,* whose skin is black, whose arms are without elbows or wrists, who talks with his feet, and the world vibrates, shifts from one foot to another, shakes, and dances its dance. For Dutton, the repeated gestures of bundling and tying hay around an armature, of kneading and shaping mud and, later, coating it all with papier-mâché, takes on a ritual quality, while the gestures of her figures are frequently influenced by her experience as a dancer.

> When I work [says Dutton], I feel a kinship with ancient working rhythms, with totem builders of early primitive societies, with ancestral memories from deep time, simple common memories below the threshold of myth— the rolling motion of a hip joint as weight is shifted from one leg to another, the coolness of shadow on skin, the heat of the day radiating from hard, packed earth at twilight.

Mircea Eliade once said that it is not enough, as it was half a century ago, to discover and admire the art of the primitives; we have to discover the sources of these arts in ourselves, so that we can become aware of what it is, in a modern existence, that is still "mythical" and survives in us as part of the human condition. To participate directly in shamanic consciousness in our culture can be associated with deep metaphysical fear, because we are not accustomed to experiencing worlds other than the everyday world. We do not cultivate trance states in which not only deep experiential identification with animals and plants may occur, but in which there may be a spontaneous experiencing of archetypal presences which do not belong to ordinary reality. This dying to

Richard Rosenblum, "Manscape," 1984-85. (Photo courtesy of Addison Gallery of American Art, Andover, Massachusetts.)

Fern Shaffer, "Winter Solstice," Lake Michigan, 1985. (Photo courtesy of Othello Anderson, Chicago.)

the world of the senses, this dying to the literal perspective, can be dangerous territory, as attested to by Jos. A. Smith, a New York artist who has trained himself to make precise drawings of experiences he has in trance states. *Priest of Dark Flight,* standing at the entrance to the underworld during one of Smith's shamanic journeys, is a numinous figure from another world—ambivalent, perilous, unpredictable, with clairvoyant eyes. The modern rational mind is likely to dismiss such an apparition as a hallucination, or the effects of a drug. But to shamanic consciousness, it is totally, and terrifyingly, real—to the point where, in virtually all cultures other than our own, the remarkable healing and transformative potential of these nonordinary states has always been known and systematically explored. When the ego-personality is allowed to dissolve, it creates an opening onto the numinous, or the *nagual,* onto a whole spectrum of consciousness not normally admitted to the reality of modern civilization—but this shifting of mindsets, or contacting alternate "supernatural" realities, is a skilled practice, not to be undertaken lightly:

> The first time I saw *Guardian of the Deepest Gate* walking towards me [Smith writes], the twisted roots forming the mouth of the shield were stretched open and it was screaming. It was an endless stream of sound that was pain and anger and fear all intertwined. A voice that seemed to come from no particular direction said, "This is the guardian of the deepest gate." I knew without being told that at some point I have to pass it and I would be in a totally different world. It obviously entails another death beyond the one I experience upon entering a deep trance, and I was too afraid to go farther at that time.

Are these things real? Do they actually happen? A young medicine man, in training, telling of his initiation in an Australian tribe, remarks to the anthropologist Lucien Lévi-Bruhl:

> After that I used to see things that my mother could not see. When out with her I would say 'Mother, what is that out there yonder?' She used to say, 'Child, there is nothing.' These were the *jir* (ghosts), which I began to see. The fact that they cannot be seen by ordinary persons only means that they are not gifted with sufficient power, and not that it is not there.

We have been conditioned to believe that that which cannot be grasped by ordinary rational thought is hallucination or illusion. The spectrum of consciousness in our culture has been drastically reduced to the narrow sense of identity associated with ego-consciousness. As the boundaries of consciousness expand, however (and this is what shamanism can teach us), we become aware of things that remain unreachable for our ordinary eyes. If Michael Harner is correct, almost everybody is potentially a shaman, if he or she wakes up that potential and begins to explore it experientially.

At the edge of a frozen lake, a woman dances herself into a visionary state. She wears an extraordinary garment of raffia and string that transforms her into the supernatural being she is impersonating. Her presence in the landscape is like a numinous symbol of wings and flight, signifying the possibility of transition to another mode of being, the freedom to abolish a petrified or blocked system of conditionings. The woman is Fern Shaffer, an artist from Chicago, enacting a personal empowerment ritual, called "Crystal Clearing Ceremony," on the shore of Lake Michigan at winter solstice. The temperature is well below zero, and, although it is dawn in Chicago, the scene feels ancient, from another time. We obviously cannot interpret this work through current art-world discourse or deconstructive aesthetics, but its mythic, "Dreamtime" aspect makes a direct hit on the psyche. One escapes from historical and personal time and is submerged in a time that is fabulous and transhistorical. One enters another rhythm than that in which we are condemned to live and work: a reactivation of primordial, mythic time, which makes possible an approach to other states of consciousness.

For Shaffer, the process of creating a shamanic outfit to wear can be likened to creating a cocoon or an alchemical vessel, a contained place within which transformation can happen. Magic clothes are often the means whereby shamans pass from one world to the other to achieve the necessary communication with spirits—perhaps a cap of eagle and owl feathers, or a cloak adorned with ribbons and stuffed snakes. This "sacred wardrobe" acts as a lure for spirits; it serves as the means to gain access to alternate states of consciousness. We have no prescribed way to do the spirit quest in our culture, no ceremony for meeting the gods in the magic circle. Those who want to learn once again to enter the "Dreamtime," to communicate with spirits, have to find ways of effecting a release of archetypal memory, by rekindling ancient fires from the energy of the unconscious. One must begin, however, by separating oneself from the world of ordinary, everyday activities, in order to find that inner core of myth that has been made by our culture to seem archaic.

On another occasion, Shaffer went to Cahokia Mounds, Illinois, to an ancient ceremonial site similar to Stonehenge, in order to enact her "Spiral Dance," a ritual she performed in collaboration with the photographer Othello Anderson during the spring equinox of 1987. "I wrapped string rope around the outer post," she writes, "and then began unwinding the string in a clockwise fashion, doing this spiral dance. As the universe unwinds, so did I. I was told as I was there that I was awakening the spirits from this place." Farther on, there is a kind of temple to the sky, but with no walls or roof and bereft of statuary. The temple is the place of magical encounter. This one is very old. It is, they say, a tomb; whose, no one can remember. The stairs lead to the top of a very large ceremonial mound. I wonder if in times now forgotten the initiates came in procession up this staircase to the rites. Shaffer says about her work:

> If I am able to rediscover my own first experience of the basic spiritual existence with nature, it might help others rediscover and honor the same things in themselves. It does not matter that I possess no expert training or special knowledge, only the ability to open up and channel the intuition of my own self. I would let my experience of the primitive pattern of creation speak for me, since I have taken part in the most ancient workings of the human spirit. I am merely bridging the patterns of things from the past to now. What the world lacks today is not so much knowledge of these things of the spirit as an experience of them. Experiencing the spirit is all. To believe is ok, but a personal experience is better, a direct feeling with something. You can call it a shamanic state if you like.

The point in all this is not the simplistic one of a romantic return to nature or an idealizing of archaic cultures, but the deeper issue of recognizing that we do not live in a dead, mechanistic world. Much of the sense of emptiness in our culture comes from the fact that we are deprived of meaningful ritual and contact with the great archetypes that nourish soul life. We have lost any sense that doing rituals is important for the earth; we have chosen to ignore the healing and transformative potential of nonordinary states of consciousness. Yet trance methods and direct ecstatic experience are ways of dissolving the boundaries of our own system, of stepping outside the present cultural context, with its surfeit of depersonalized, violent and mechanized images, in order to let go of the hold this picture of the world has on us. The physician Larry Dossey has put it very well in his essay, "The Inner Life of the Healer":

> What we desperately need from shamanism is far more important than the shaman's trappings: it is the *soul* of the healer we need to recover, for that is what we have lost. . . . "Soul" is a new mode of awareness . . . a way of seeing that rescues all of life from the

sterile vacuity that has become synonymous with modernity. . . .
This, then, is the great legacy of shamanism for the modern healer:
a way to make life alive; a way to discover that the world is
enchanted and not dead.

The remythologizing of consciousness through art and ritual is just
one way that our culture, having eliminated all magic from its picture of
reality, can regain a sense of enchantment. But I would like to stress that
this reenchantment does not have to take us back to some sentimental-
ization of the archaic. Effective shamanic work can be carried out just
as well in a modern, urban setting, in places where the atmosphere of
disenchantment is normally most acute. For a year and a half, from
mid-1979 through 1980, the artist Mierle Laderman Ukeles, who since
1978 has been unsalaried artist-in-residence at the New York City Department of Sanitation, walked around with sanitation workers and foremen
from fifty-nine municipal districts, talking with them. Then she did an
art work, called *Touch Sanitation,* that went on for eleven months, during which she went around the five boroughs of New York and personally shook hands with everyone in the department. "It was an eight-hour-
day performance work," she told me.

> I'd come in at roll call, then walk their routes with them. I made
> tapes and a video. I did a ritual in which I faced each person and
> shook their hand; and I said, "Thank you for keeping New York
> City alive." I hope that my handshakes will eventually burn an image
> into the public's mind that every time they throw something out,
> human hands have to take it away.

Modern factories and offices and other workplaces are not exactly
spaces of enchantment, but through the example of the enlightened touch,
a compassionate gesture of the hand which embodies a nonthreatening
openness to others, a space of enchantment is opened up, if only for a
moment. The archetypal reach of this gesture—like a Buddhist *mudra,* a
gesture of generosity—goes beyond the horizons of our social world; it
responds to needs so deep they are not even recognized until the gesture
has touched them with its kindness. In a related performance, *Following
in Your Footsteps,* Ukeles followed the workers around and pantomimed
their movements, pretending to be like them, as a way of showing her
appreciation for what they do, and acting as a stand-in for all the people
who do not do this work. New York produces twenty-six thousand tons
of garbage a day, so if they did not do their job, the city would die.
"We're looked down upon, and I try not to let it bother me," commented

one member of the department, "but it's nice that someone is standing with us." Stated another: "Sanitation men are not like a bunch of gorillas. Some of us have college degrees. Mierle has made us feel good about ourselves. If that's what art is, it's fine by me." Ukeles has been appointed Honorary Deputy Commissioner of Sanitation and been made an honorary teamster by the union.

In a Marine Transfer Station, an enclosed pier on the Hudson River where sanitation trucks dump their loads into barges for transport to the Staten Island landfill, Ukeles mounted a series of "maintenance installations"—minimalist stacks and piles of shovels, rakes, chains, ropes, and cyclone fencing, and a ten-foot-tall wire basket filled with thousands of discarded work gloves collected for over a year by the workmen as an indication of the massive work they do for us. In another aspect of her work, Ukeles sees herself as heir to the Constructivist tradition of choreographing machine dances. Workers helped her with the *Ballet Mécanique* she created for six street sweepers, which went along Madison Avenue as part of New York City's Art parade in 1983. When the ballet was over, the six drivers turned the huge machines to face the audience and took a bow, raising and lowering the sweepers' brooms and backing up slightly with their beepers on. Ukeles has also created a special "contextual sculpture" for the Sanitation Department, called *The Social Mirror*—a city garbage truck, completely decorated with mirrors, so people can see who makes the garbage.

Ukeles' effective shamanic work is more pragmatic than ideal. Her extraordinary ability to knit herself empathically into the community of sanitation workers manifests an art in which empathy and healing are the parameters, the test of whether the work is being carried out paradigmatically. The image of the shaman strikes at the roots of modern estrangement: merging her consciousness with the workers, she converses with them, learns from them. There is no critical distance, no theoretical violence, no antagonistic imperative; but as something more than art, her work becomes an exercise in model-building, in the construction of an alternative to the professional role model. When one develops the worldview of a shaman, one becomes a healer in all one's activities. One becomes a positive, transforming influence, releasing spiritual potential, shaping new frameworks and regaining the power to enchant.

III. WHITHER POSTMODERNISM?

Having looked at these opposing tendencies and incompatible claims, the question remains: what determines the direction in which art evolves? Personally, I choose to believe that the old-paradigm drives for power and profit, which currently form the cultural "ground rules" of art-making, will increasingly subside as the shift from objects to relationships—a central aspect of the emerging new paradigm—begins to affect the old studio model of artistic practice. Obviously, art that is totally the product of the way of life of this civilization is not likely to reorient it in any significant way; the innovating force is more likely to come from those individuals who are willing to break with the market context in which we have been trained to act, and who are prepared to engage in the collective task of reenchantment—who have come to understand that the problem we are facing is how to deal with a belief-structure that has significantly blocked both psychological and spiritual development. There will always be individuals for whom the aesthetic attitude, which needs no social or spiritual justification for art, will be correct. For the visionary, however, committed to cultural transformation, there is hardly any point in making art just for the sake of making art, or writing just for the sake of writing. One has to want to do something important, to make something happen. We have made much of the idea of art as a mirror (reflecting the times); we have had art as a hammer (social protest); art as furniture (something to hang on the walls); and art as a search for the self. Perhaps we need another kind of art at this point as well—one that exercises its power to administer the social dreaming, through images which empower the collective unconscious. For me, this means art that speaks to the power of interconnectedness and establishes bonds, art that develops an active and practical dialogue with the environment, art that offers more dynamic and vivid ways of understanding the universe, and thus addresses our culture's failure to grasp what it means to be actively related to the cosmos.

12

POSTMODERNISM AND AESTHETIC SYMBOLISM IN JAPANESE SHINGON BUDDHISM

Steve Odin

In her book *Philosophy in a New Key*, Susanne Langer writes of a "great key change" in twentieth-century thought towards a "philosophical study of symbolism."[1] This key change or paradigm shift toward a philosophy of symbolism is truly postmodern, insofar as it breaks with the fundamental presuppositions formulated by such modern thinkers as Descartes, Hume, and Kant and constitutes a radically new point of departure for philosophical discourse. In Langer's words: "The study of symbol and meaning is a starting-point of philosophy, not a derivative of Cartesian, Humean or Kantian premises."[2] Langer credits Ernst Cassirer's *Philosophy of Symbolic Forms*[3] as among the first works to articulate a comprehensive theory of symbolism as the key to human mentality. Indeed, it was Cassirer who argued against the narrow Cartesian and Kantian view of the human being as an *animal rationale,* which itself accounts only for the intellectual and scientific activities of human existence, and instead framed a genuinely postmodern definition of the human being as an *animal symbolicum:* a symbol-producing, symbol-using, and symbol-reading animal who lives in a universe of symbolic forms. The symbolic universe of human existence includes not only the discursive aspects of experience, such as science, mathematics, and logic; it also includes those nondiscursive aspects such as art, myth, and religion. Following Cassirer, Langer argues that "symbolism is the recognized key to that mental life which is characteristically human and above the level of sheer animality."[4] Her polemic here is that *the human response is constructive, not passive, and that symbolization is the key to this constructive process.*

In order to demonstrate the "great key change," Langer cites as paradigm cases two disciplines arising in the twentieth century which are widely separate but nonetheless both rooted in the philosophical study of symbolism: depth psychology and symbolic logic. Langer primarily refers to depth psychology as developed by its founder, Sigmund Freud, who argues that all human experience is conditioned by symbolic images arising from erotic fantasy-processes of a personal subconscious. Since Freud, however, the field of depth psychology has undergone significant developments through the work of C.G. Jung and James Hillman. According to Jung, all human experience is also conditioned by archetypal "images of wholeness" which arise from the mythic imagination of a collective unconscious and which function as "symbols of transformation" aimed toward the production of "psychical totality" through a union of opposites. In contrast to Jung's monotheistic model of human development, in which psychic totality is produced by symbols of wholeness, Hillman frames a more pluralistic model which emphasizes the polytheistic, polycentric, and polymorphic nature of the human psyche as an irreducible multiplicity of archetypal images. Despite their individual differences, however, Freud, Jung, and Hillman have each converged upon the notion that human experience is always conditioned by symbolic images. They thereby stand in essential agreement with the postmodern definition of the human being as an *animal symbolicum* developed by Cassirer and Langer.

The theory of "symbolic reference" developed by Alfred North Whitehead is one of the most significant examples of what Langer has termed the "great key change" toward a philosophical study of symbolism in the twentieth century. Langer's book *Philosophy in a New Key* was in fact dedicated to Whitehead, and was profoundly influenced by his theory of symbolic reference as developed in his work *Symbolism:*

Its Meaning and Effect and in the chapter in *Process and Reality* entitled "Symbolic Reference." Insofar as Whitehead argues that the higher phases of experience characteristic of human perception are essentially symbolic in nature, his theory of symbolic reference represents yet another affirmation of the postmodern definition of the human being as an *animal symbolicum.*

In the present essay, I develop Whitehead's theory of symbolic reference as a Western hermeneutical framework capable of interpreting the Shingon (Sanskrit: *mantra*) sect of Esoteric Buddhism (*mikkyō*) in Japan. Kūkai (774-835), also known by his posthumous honorific title Kōbō Daishi, is the founder of the Shingon sect of Japanese Esoteric Buddhism. Kūkai declared that Buddhahood is achieved only through the medium of symbols (Japanese: *shōchō*), or what in the technical vocabulary of Shingon are referred to as expressive symbols (*monji*) and symbolic images (*sanmaya gyō*). He further proclaimed that the secret teachings of Esoteric Buddhism are so profound that they cannot be imparted through the discursive signs of written texts, but only through the aesthetic symbols of *maṇḍala* art. Shingon Esoteric Buddhism has therefore been characterized as a Way of Maṇḍalas which employs the aesthetic symbols and artistic images of *maṇḍala* pictures as a skillful means (Sanskrit: *upāya;* Japanese: *hōben*) for attaining enlightened wisdom. I will interpret Japanese Shingon Esoteric Buddhism in Whiteheadian terms as a system of symbolic reference. I then argue that Shingon Esoteric Buddhism, thus analyzed, holds for us an ancient key pointing the way to a truly postmodern philosophy of the human being as an *animal symbolicum.*

I. WHITEHEAD'S THEORY OF SYMBOLIC REFERENCE

According to Whitehead, there are three fundamental modes of perceptual experience, which he calls (1) causal efficacy, (2) presentational immediacy, and (3) symbolic reference. The most primordial level of experience, shared by all organisms, is causal perception, or perception in the mode of causal efficacy, which refers to the dim feelings of causal influence received from antecedent events. More evolved organisms develop perception in the mode of presentational immediacy, which designates the clear and distinct data of sense-perception, such as colors, sounds, tastes, and other vivid sensations as directly presented. In the higher phases of experience, characteristic especially of human organisms, arises symbolic perception, or perception in the mixed mode of symbolic reference, whereby the two pure perceptual modes of causal efficacy and presentational immediacy become fused. In symbolic reference, human mentality fuses the other two modes by using percepts in the mode of presentational immediacy as symbols for percepts in the mode of causal efficacy. As Whitehead writes in *Symbolism*: "The synthetic activity whereby these two modes are fused into one perception is what I have called 'symbolic reference.' "[5] In symbolic reference, he says, there is a "fusion of the two modes by one intensity of emotion."[6]

Whitehead further develops his theory of symbolism in the chapter entitled "Symbolic Reference" in *Process and Reality:*

> The first principle explanatory of symbolic reference, is that for such a reference a "common ground" is required. By this necessity for a "common ground" it is meant that there must be components in experience which are directly recognized as identical in each of the pure perceptive modes. In the transition to a higher phase of experience, there is a concrescence in which prehensions in the two pure modes are brought into a unity of feeling.[7]

The requisites for symbolism are therefore that there be two types of percepts, and that a perception of one type has some ground in common with a perception of the other type, so that a mutual correlation between the pairs of percepts is established. In such a manner, symbolic reference is said to produce a synthesis whereby percepts in the two modes are brought into a unity of feeling, fused into a single intensity of emotion, so that they enhance and intensify each other in a reciprocal way.

A significant feature of Whitehead's theory of symbolic reference is its insight that one can form a correlation or unity between two systems of perception, namely, causal perception (causal efficacy) and sense-perception (presentational immediacy), so that each system can be cognized in the light of the other. Although symbolic reference can work in either direction, usually we use the clear and distinct sensations of presentational immediacy to symbolize the vague and indistinct feelings experienced in the perceptual mode of causal efficacy.[8] Due to our preference for simplification, we tend to use the vivid data of sense-perception as symbols for the dim feelings of causal perception. Whitehead therefore writes:

> Thus symbolic reference, though in complex human experience it works both ways, is chiefly to be thought of as the elucidation of percepta in the mode of causal efficacy by the fluctuating interventions of percepta in the mode of presentational immediacy.[9]

Whitehead further argues that *it is possible to use certain sense-data arising in the perceptual mode of presentational immediacy as aesthetic symbols for deep religious emotions arising in the perceptual mode of causal perception.* To illustrate this form of symbolic reference, he cites the example of burning incense during sacred rituals in order to invoke intense religious feelings:

> It is easier to smell incense than to produce certain religious emotions; so if the two can be correlated, incense is a suitable symbol for such emotions. Indeed, for many purposes, certain aesthetic experiences which are easy to produce make better symbols than do words, written or spoken.[10]

In this case, because a correlation or unity of feeling has been established between the two pure modes of perception, the fragrance of burning incense arising as data in the mode of sensory perception can now function as an aesthetic symbol for deep religious emotions arising as data in the mode of causal perception. This doctrine of symbolic reference, whereby the percepts of sensory experience can function as aesthetic symbols for religious emotions arising as percepta in causal experience, will now be applied to Shingon Esoteric Buddhism in Japan.

II. SYMBOLIC REFERENCE AND ASIAN PHILOSOPHY

If used in the service of East-West comparative philosophy, Whitehead's theory of symbolic reference can be employed as a hermeneutic device for interpreting major Asian traditions, such as Taoism in China, or Tantric Buddhism in its Indo-Tibetan and East Asian variants. The first study to have applied Whitehead's technical theory of symbolic reference to Asian thought is an important essay by Chung-ying Cheng, entitled "Chinese Philosophy and Symbolic Reference." [11] Cheng interprets the *I Ching* and *Tao Te Ching* as systems of symbolic reference. He points out that in the *Tao Te Ching* Lao Tzu used the term *wu* (void) to refer to *tao,* and that *wu* means not simply nothingness but the indeterminate and formless creative ground which gives rise to the formation and determination of things. He then asks: "Given these characteristics of *tao,* how can we identify images of *tao*? Specifically, how do we identify images of *tao,* which is imageless?"[12] According to Cheng, the *Tao Te Ching* is best seen as a system of symbolic reference that provides five images symbolic of the *tao:* (1) water, (2) a child, (3) a mother, (4) a female, and (5) the uncarved block. After describing each image of *tao* separately, he asserts:

> In the preceeding we have discussed five main images of *tao* in the *Tao Te Ching*. Each of these images serves as a symbol for the *tao* and leads to a unity of feeling between the symbol and the meaning of *tao*.

He continues:

> This shows not only that there exists a common ground between our perception of the *tao* and our perception of the images of *tao*, but that *tao* itself illuminates these images of *tao*, which illuminates *tao*. One may even suggest that these images embody the *tao* itself just as *tao* presents these images, so that *tao* and these images shine forth through each other. This is what we call reciprocity of symbolic reference.[13]

According to Cheng, then, the *Tao Te Ching* is represented by a cluster of images which function as a system of symbols referring to the indeterminate void (*wu*) of *tao*. Each image is a symbol of *tao*, yet it does not merely point to *tao* but actually leads to a unity of feeling between the symbol and the meaning of *tao*. Each image embodies *tao* just as *tao* presents each image, so that they mutually illuminate one another in a reciprocity of symbolic reference.

The relevance of Whitehead's theory of symbolic reference to Chinese Taoism at once suggests applications to other Asian traditions. From the standpoint of this theory of symbolic reference, the tradition of Japanese Shingon Esoteric Buddhism is especially interesting in the light of Kūkai's fundamental doctrine that the emptiness of Dharmakāya Mahāvairocana Buddha can be revealed only through expressive symbols (*monji*). In contrast to the more apophatic or *via negativa* tradition of Japanese Zen Buddhism, which conceives of symbols and images as obstacles to enlightenment, the more kataphatic or *via affirmativa* tradition of Shingon Buddhism argues that symbolic images are in fact ultimate bearers of meaning in human experience. Shingon accordingly uses the contemplation of aesthetic symbols and artistic images depicted in *maṇḍala* paintings as its skillful means for attaining Buddhahood. Kūkai's explicit statement concerning the primacy of symbolism for conveying enlightened wisdom appears in his treatise entitled *Shōji jissō gi* (The Meaning of Sound, Word, and Reality), wherein he asserts: "The Tathāgata reveals his teachings by means of expressive symbols."[14] The

Shingon scholar Y.S. Hakeda, translator of Kūkai's major works, has explained this statement as follows:

Here the Tathāgata is the Dharmakāya Mahāvairocana Buddha. The original of "expressive symbol" is *monji,* which normally means a letter, character or ideograph. Kūkai's use of *monji* is not restricted to these ordinary meanings: objects of sight, hearing, smell, touch, taste and thought are regarded as *monji.*[15]

Elsewhere in the treatise, Kūkai says, "The six kinds of objects are expressive symbols," while further specifying that "the six kinds of objects are the objects of sight, hearing, smell, taste, touch and thought."[16] Indeed, Kūkai's doctrine concerning the symbolic nature of sensory perception in human experience stands in essential agreement with Susanne Langer's philosophy in a new key, which declares "the surprising truth that our sense-data are primarily symbols."[17] The idea that our sensory data are primarily symbols is also in concordance with Whitehead's doctrine of symbolic reference. What is most remarkable, however, is that both Whitehead and Shingon Buddhism have converged on the notion that *the data of sensory perception are primarily aesthetic symbols for the data of causal perception.* In the case of Shingon, the multivariate objects of sense-perception are expressive symbols making reference to emptiness (Japanese: *kū;* Sanskrit: *śūnyatā*), which designates the process of arising through chains of causation known as dependent cooriogination (Japanese: *engi;* Sanskrit: *pratitya-samutpāda*). Translated into the technical terms of Whitehead's theory of symbolic reference, this means that the clear and distinct sensory data of perception in the mode of presentational immediacy are aesthetic symbols referring to the dim and vague feelings of perception in the mode of causal efficacy.

III. THE MAHĀVAIROCANA SŪTRA AS A SYMBOLIC REFERENCE TEXT

The *Mahāvairocana Sūtra* (Japanese: *Dainichi Kyō*) and *Vajraśekhara Sūtra* (*Kongōkai Kyō*) are the two major Indian Sanskrit Tantric scriptures of Shingon Buddhism in Japan.[18] The *Taizokai,* or Womb-Realm *maṇḍala,* symbolically depicts the cosmology of the *Mahāvairocana Sūtra,* just as the *Kongōkai,* or Diamond-Realm *maṇḍala,* symbolically depicts the cosmology of the *Vajraśekahara Sūtra.* For purposes of analysis, I will focus on the *Mahāvairocana Sūtra* as a representative text of Shingon Buddhism. Throughout this work, *Mahāvairocana Tathāgata*

(Japanese: *Dainichi Nyōrai*), or the Buddha of Great Illumination, preaches in response to questions asked by Vajradhara-guhyapti, the Vajra Holder and Master of Mysteries. The representative ascetic practice of this work is the visualization of five mystic Sanskrit letters (A, Va, Ra, Ha, Kha) to symbolize the five elements of earth, water, fire, air, and space, the symbolic constituents of the universe. These elements and letters are visualized in five centers of the bodymind, from the soles of the feet to the crown of the head, thus uniting microcosm and macrocosm. The *Taizokai*, or Womb-Realm *maṇḍala*, is a pictorial representation of this microcosmic-macrocosmic cosmology, with Mahāvairocana Tathāgata at the center surrounded by a vast retinue of buddhas, bodhisattvas, and a polytheistic pantheon of deities. The Womb-Realm *maṇḍala* is therefore in fact a complex symbol system which is itself composed of myriad symbolic forms derived from the *Mahāvairocana Sūtra*, such as letters, elements, buddhas, bodhisattvas, and various other archetypal god-images. Furthermore, the *Mahāvairocana Sūtra* is the textual basis for the liturgical instructions and iconographic imagery of the *Taizokai* ceremony, which in accord with the three mysteries (*Sanmitsu*) of Shingon Buddhism is a symbolic ritual composed of *mudrā* (symbolic gestures), *mantra* (symbolic sounds), and *maṇḍala* (symbolic images). The three mysteries of *mudrā, mantra,* and *maṇḍala* thus lead to the symbolic transformation of experience, whereby one's body, speech and mind are transfigured into a microcosm reflecting the all-pervasive macrocosm of Mahāvairocana Buddha.

Along with all of these symbolic forms, the *Mahāvairocana Sūtra* propounds as one of its major skillful means the contemplation of Ten Images of the Void. The text reads:

> O Lord of the Mysteries, Bodhisattvas who practice the Bodhisattvah practices under the Shingon gate should deeply practice and observe Ten Images, and should deeply master Shingon practices and be enlightened. And what are the Ten Images? They are a phantom, heat waves, a dream, a shadow, Ghandarva Castle, an echo, a water moon, foam, a false flower in the sky, and a whirling ring of fire.[19]

In his famous commentary on the *Mahāvairocana Sūtra*, I-hsing (687-727) emphasizes the central importance of these Ten Images of the Void within the Shingon Buddhist contemplative tradition. I-hsing explains the basic meaning of these Ten Images in this way: "First, these Ten Images may be contemplated for curing us of attachment to fixed things by observing the functions of body and mind. According to this viewpoint, Illusion is Void Only."[20] On the basis of such passages from the *Mahāvairocana Sūtra,* together with I-hsing's commentary, Kūkai later composed his "Poems That Sing Ten Images." [21] Altogether, each of Kūkai's poems functions to break compulsive attachments to phenomenal objects by showing that all forms are empty, nonsubstantial, impermanent, and codependent on chains of causation. The Shingon contemplation upon Ten Images of the Void is thus designed to result in the fundamental Buddhist insight: "Form is Empty and Empty is Form" (Japanese: *shiki soku ze kū, kū soku ze shiki*).

When analyzed from the standpoint of Whiteheadian process cosmology, the *Mahāvairocana Sūtra* can be regarded as a symbolic reference text. Essentially, the *Mahāvairocana Sūtra* consists of aesthetic images derived from sense-perception being used as symbolic forms making reference to the formless void of *kū* or emptiness, in its strictly philosophical meaning of arising through dependent coorigination. The Ten Images of the Void from the *Mahāvairocana Sūtra,* including a phantom, heat waves, a dream, a shadow, Gandharva Castle, an echo, a water moon, foam, a false flower in the sky, and a whirling ring of fire, are all poetic images derived from sense-perception functioning as symbolic forms of formless emptiness and dependent coorigination. In terms of Whitehead's theory of symbolic reference, the Ten Images of the Void, like the various letters, elements, buddhas, bodhisattvas, and deities of the *Mahāvairocana Sūtra,* are all artistic or poetic images based on sense-data from the mode of presentational immediacy, which become aesthetic symbols for percepts in the more primordial mode of causal efficacy. Each image from the text is an object of sensory perception being used as an aesthetic symbol for the deep religious emotions of causal perception. However, although each image from the text functions as an aesthetic symbol of emptiness (*kū*), *it does not merely point to emptiness, but actually leads to a "unity of feeling" between the symbol and the meaning of emptiness.* By this view, there exists a common ground between our perception of emptiness and our perception of the images of emptiness, so that the symbol and the meaning of the symbol are fused by one intensity of emotion. Each image embodies the void just as the void presents each image, so that symbolic form and formless emptiness mutually illuminate one another in a reciprocity of symbolic reference.

IV. Maṇḍala Art and Symbolic Reference

According to Kūkai's doctrinal classification scheme (*hankyō*), the Buddhist teachings can be hierarchically ranked in ten stages, including three worldly stages, two pre-Mahāyāna stages, followed by *Yogacāra* (Japanese: *Hossō*), Madhyāmika (*Sanron*), T'ien-t'ai (*Tendai*), Hua-yen (*Kegon*) and Shingon Buddhism.[22] Hua-yen represents the ninth and culminating stage of Exoteric Buddhism (*Kengyō*), whereas Shingon marks the transition to Esoteric Buddhism (*mikkyō*). The basic concept of Hua-yen Buddhist metaphysics is the *dharmadhātu* (Japanese: *hōkai*), comprehended as *a cosmic net of causal interrelationships wherein there arises a complete harmonious interpenetration between the many and the one,* such that each event (*dharma*) both contains and pervades the entire universe as a microcosm of the macrocosm. This concept of *dharmadhātu* is summarized by the key Hua-yen doctrinal formulas of *riji muge* (interpenetration between particular and universal) and *jiji muge* (interpenetration of particular and particular). However, Kūkai argues that one must advance beyond the ninth and final stage of Exoteric Buddhism (*Kengyō*), represented by Hua-yen, to the tenth and ultimate stage of Esoteric Buddhism (*mikkyō*), represented by Shingon. According to Kūkai, while Hua-yen only *points to* the *dharmadhātu* of harmonious interpenetration between the many and the one, *Shingon actually reveals it* through the secret skillful means of meditation upon *maṇḍala* art. Thus Kūkai writes:

> In truth, the esoteric doctrines are so profound as to defy their enunciation in writing. With the help of painting, however, their obscurities may be understood. The various attitudes and *mudras* of the holy images all have their source in Buddha's love, and one may attain Buddhahood at the sight of them. Thus, the secret of the *sutras* and commentaries can be depicted in art, and the essential truths of the esoteric teachings are all set forth therein. Neither teachers nor students can dispense with it. Art is what reveals to us the state of perfection.[23]

In this passage, Kūkai formulates his famous principle that the esoteric teachings of Shingon cannot be imparted through words: Buddhahood can be attained only through meditation upon the aesthetic symbols and artistic images of *maṇḍala* paintings. Whitehead expresses a similar view in the passage cited previously from his chapter on "Symbolic Reference," wherein he argues that, in order to invoke deep religious emotions from causal perception, "certain aesthetic experiences *which are easy to produce* make better symbols than do words, written or spoken." [24] Whitehead's notion, that aesthetic symbols derived from sensory perception can function better than words to produce intense religious emotions from causal perception, is in general accord with the aesthetic foundations of his entire metaphysical system, thus standing in sharp contrast to modern Western philosophy since Descartes and Kant, which emphasizes the cognitive dimensions of human experience. In Whitehead's words:

> The metaphysical doctrine, here expounded, finds the foundations of the world in the aesthetic experience, rather than—as with Kant—in the cognitive and conceptive experience. All order is therefore aesthetic order and the moral order is merely certain aspects of aesthetic order. The actual world is the outcome of the aesthetic order and the aesthetic order is derived from the immanence of God.[25]

Elsewhere I have developed certain of the deep structural similarities between Whitehead's process metaphysics and Hua-yen Buddhism, insofar as both describe events in the aesthetic continuum of nature as arising through a causal process that fuses manyness into oneness, or multiplicity into unity, such that each moment of experience constitutes a microcosm of the macrocosm.[26] *The advance of Shingon Buddhism over both Hua-yen Buddhism and Whitehead's process metaphysics is its development of a practical technique designed to produce a direct visionary experience of this aesthetic continuum of harmonious interpenetration between the many and the one.* This technique is the contemplation of aesthetic symbols depicted by *maṇḍala* paintings, comprehended as archetypal symbols of wholeness that give pictorial representations of the cosmos as a unity in multiplicity.

The most simplified form of *maṇḍala* contemplation in Shingon Buddhism is known as *Ajikan,* or Ah-syllable visualization. The *locus classicus* for *Ajikan* meditation, like the Ten Images of the Void mentioned previously, is the *Mahāvairocana Sūtra,* although it is also described in the *Bodhicitta Śastra* and *Prajñāparamitā Sūtras.* The *Mahāvairocana Sūtra* says: "What is the *Mantra* Dharma? It is the teaching of the letter A."[27] The Japanese word *A-ji* literally means "letter A" or "Ah-syllable," and in this case specifically refers to the Sanskrit letter A depicted in the Shingon *Aji-maṇḍala.* In his work *Shingon Buddhism: Theory and Practice,* Minoru Kiyota explains the Buddhist symbolical meanings of the Sanskrit letter A as follows:

> *A-ji* symbolizes the *bija* (seed) of Dharmakaya Mahavairocana. 'A' has two meanings in Sanskrit: it is a sign of negation, symbolizing emptiness; it is a sign of all-pervasiveness, symbolizing the source of all things. It is the embodiment of emptiness and co-arising.[28]

In Shingon Buddhism, the Sanskrit letter A is therefore an expressive symbol (*monji*) for emptiness and dependent coorigination as well as for the all-pervasiveness of Dharmakāya Mahāvairocana Buddha. Or, in terms of Whitehead's theory of symbolic reference, the Sanskrit letter A depicted in Shingon *maṇḍala* art is an image derived from sensory perception which functions as an aesthetic symbol for the deep religious emotions arising from causal perception.

The *maṇḍala* painting used for *Ajikan* meditation is itself a composite image which includes three aesthetic symbols: (1) the moon-disc (*gatsurin*), symbolizing the clear and radiant Buddha Mind; (2) the lotus flower (*renge*), symbolizing purity; and (3) the Sanskrit "letter A" (*A-ji*), symbolizing emptiness, dependent coorigination, and all-pervasiveness. In his instructions for *Ajikan* practice, Kūkai first describes the preliminary meditation of *gatsurinkan,* or moon disc visualization, which uses only a simplified *maṇḍala* depicting the image of a full moon.

> The Buddhas of great compassion, therefore, with the wisdom of skillful means, taught them this profound Esoteric Buddhist yoga and made each devotee visualize in his inner eye the bright moon. By means of this practice each devotee will perceive his original Mind, which is serene and pure like the full moon whose rays pervade space without any discrimination.[29]

Kūkai next proceeds to give instructions for *Ajikan* using the more complex image of the Sanskrit letter A standing atop a pure lotus flower and encircled by a luminous full moon: "Visualize: a white lotus flower with eight petals [above which is a full moon disc] the size of a forearm in diameter [in which is] a radiant silvery letter A."[30] When one's visualization of the silvery letter A, white lotus flower, and full moon disc becomes clear, the technique of expansion (*kakudai hō*) is then added. Kūkai continues:

> If they gradually increase their competence in this meditation, they will finally be able to magnify it [the moon] until its circumference encompasses the entire universe and its magnitude becomes as inclusive as space. Being able freely to magnify or reduce it, they will surely come to be in possession of the all-inclusive wisdom.[31]

The Shingon technique of expansion consists of two parts: enlargement visualization (*kōkan*), and contraction visualization (*renkan*). It is precisely by magnifying the artistic image of a moon disc until its circumference encompasses the entire universe, with its magnitude becoming as inclusive as boundless empty space, through the enlargement technique of *kōkan,* then reducing it again, through the contraction technique of *renkan,* that the Shingon Buddhist envisions the Hua-yen *dharmadhātu* of total interfusion between one and many, whereby events both contain and pervade the whole space-time continuum as a microcosm of the macrocosm.

The first book written in the Japanese language by a contemporary Japanese scholar and priest of the Shingon tradition to describe the basic contemplative practices of Tantric Buddhist yoga in Japan is *Mikkyō meisō hō* (Secret Meditation Techniques of Shingon Buddhism) by Ajari-Master Yamazaki Taikō Sensei. In conjunction with the requisite oral transmission of teachings received directly from Yamazaki Taikō Sensei, I have translated a portion of his text which provides instructions for *Ajikan* meditation as follows:

> In the beginning it is all right to do just *Asokukan* (Ah-breathing meditation) or *gatsurinkan* (moon disc visualization). When this meditation becomes clear, visualize the Ah-syllable, lotus flower and moon disc in front of your eyes. When you have gradually progressed in this meditation, next put inside the region between your navel and your heart the Ah-syllable, lotus flower and moon disc.[32]

Yamazaki Sensei next describes the method for the technique of expansion:

> As for the "technique of expansion" (*kakudai hō*), it is a meditation method where you gradually enlarge your body to the size of the universe and visualize that your self and the vast universe have become one body (*kōkan* technique). After this, gradually contract it back again (*renkan* technique).[33]

He further describes the technique of expansion as a process of gradually magnifying and reducing the after-image (*zanzō*) of the moon disc by degrees through the power of mental visualization in the active imagination. In this context he writes:

> Enlarge the 26 centimeter moon disc in your heart gradually to 50 centimeters, one meter, as full as the room, as full as the house, finally making it as full as the universe. . . . After enjoying the state of expansion, slowly contract it back again into your heart, finally returning [the Ah-syllable, lotus flower and moon disc] to the meditation scroll. [34]

According to Yamazaki Sensei's explicit instructions for *Ajikan* practice, therefore, as a preliminary exercise one does moon disc visualization, followed by Ah-breathing meditation, whereby one intones the primordial Shingon *mantra* or symbolic incantation of "Ah." Proceeding to the actual practice of *Ajikan,* one sits before the meditation scroll (*honzon*) and focuses all attention on the *Ajikan-maṇḍala,* including the Ah-syllable, lotus flower, and moon disc. After concentrating on the *Ajikan-maṇḍala* until its aesthetic symbols are imprinted upon the memory, the eyes are closed and the eidetic after-image is *inwardly visualized in the mind's eye.* This is followed by the technique of expansion, whereby the mental after-image of the moon disc is magnified into the all-pervasive macrocosm through enlargement visualization, and then reduced again to a perspectival microcosm through contraction visualization. After this, additional esoteric techniques are incorporated into *Ajikan* meditation, including the technique of transformation (*tenjō-hō*),[35] whereby the Ah-syllable is visualized as changing into various other aesthetic symbols like the myriad archetypal God-images from the Shingon pantheon, and the technique of circulation (*junkan hō*)[36] whereby *mantra*-incantations are visualized as rotating between one's body and the imagined deity until an interfusion between subject and object occurs in a moment of ecstasy.

In a work entitled *The Bodymind Experience in Japanese Buddhism: A Phenomenological Study of Kūkai and Dōgen,* David Shaner develops a fascinating interpretation of Shingon *maṇḍala* contemplation from the standpoint of Husserlian phenomenology.[37] Shaner's contention is that, while in ordinary perception various "mental positings" constitute experience in such a way that awareness habitually intends mere focal objects, Shingon *maṇḍala* contemplation functions to neutralize all mental positings, thereby resulting in the bodymind awareness of an "expanded periphery and horizon *in toto.*" Furthermore, Shaner argues, the Shingon practices of *Ajikan* and *kakudai hō* function to neutralize compulsive mental discriminations so that one's bodymind awareness is no longer directed to a single privileged focus but instead makes present the total horizon surrounding focal objects as the boundless empty space of Dharmakāya Mahāvairocana Buddha.

As I have argued elsewhere, however, there are significant limitations to a purely Husserlian account of Shingon Buddhist *maṇḍala* contemplation.[38] For instance, although one can use Husserlian phenomenology to provide an illuminating description of how *maṇḍala* contemplation results in the bodymind experience of an expanded periphery and horizon *in toto*, it cannot explain *why* this is meaningful in terms of the realization of beauty or aesthetic value. Similarly, one cannot, using

Husserl's phenomenological framework alone, account for the Shingon Buddhist experience of expanded horizons phenomena in terms of a metaphysics of causal interdependence; just as one cannot sufficiently explain the function of symbolism in human perception. I suggest that Whitehead's process cosmology, with its doctrine of symbolic reference, provides a far more adequate account of Shingon Buddhism.

From a Whiteheadian perspective, the perceptual awareness of an expanded periphery and total horizon achieved through Shingon techniques of *maṇḍala* contemplation can be analyzed as *an immediate experience of the felt background of causal interrelationships which always encircles sensory objects discriminated in the foreground focus of attention.* For Whitehead, it is precisely this felt background of causal interrelationships encompassing sensory objects in the foreground that constitutes each occasion of experience as a felt whole with intrinsic beauty or depth of feeling. In a chapter entitled "Beauty" in *Adventures of Ideas,* Whitehead develops a phenomenological profile of the foreground/background structure of beauty in the perceptual field, wherein clear and distinct sensory objects articulated in the foreground gradually recede into a dim and vague field of causal interrelationships in the unarticulated background: "This is the habitual state of human experience, a vast undiscriminated or dimly discriminated background of low intensity, and a clear foreground."[39] Moreover, in a subsequent chapter entitled "Truth and Beauty," he goes on to describe the foreground/background structure of human art: "The type of Truth which human art seeks lies in the eliciting of the background to haunt the objects presented for clear consciousness."[40] By this view, the ultimate truth-function of *maṇḍala* art in Shingon Esoteric Buddhism would be to manifest the beauty of hidden depths, by eliciting the vast undiscriminated background of causal interrelationships which haunt those sensory objects clearly discriminated in the foreground focus of attention.

Whitehead further develops the foreground/background structure of beauty and art in terms of the metaphysical distinction between Appearance and Reality: "Thus it is Appearance which in consciousness is clear and distinct, and it is Reality which lies dimly in the background."[41] Moreover, he argues, Appearance signifies the clear and distinct sensory data in the foreground, whereas Reality designates the causal perception of a dim and vague background: "The Appearance is a simplification of Reality, reducing it to a foreground of enduring individuals and to a background of undiscriminated occasions. Sense-perception belongs to Appearance."[42] In this context he argues that every occasion of experience is a creative work of art, insofar as it interweaves Foreground and Background, Part and Whole, or Appearance and Reality into patterned contrasts with intrinsic beauty or aesthetic value.[43] Translated into Whitehead's theory of symbolic reference, a work of art is characterized by sensory objects clearly discriminated in the foreground which are surrounded by a vast undiscriminated field of causal interrelationships in the background. Moreover, the simplified Appearance of sensory objects in the foreground now become *aesthetic symbols* referring to the Reality of causal interrelationships which lie dimly in the background. Applying Whitehead's theory to the Shingon art form of the *Ajikan-maṇḍala,* the Sanskrit letter A becomes an image derived from sensory perception in the foreground, which functions as an aesthetic symbol for the deep religious emotions arising from causal perception in the background.

Whitehead's theory of symbolic reference results in the notion of art as an aesthetic symbol. In accordance with his postmodern view of the human being as an *animal symbolicum,* Cassirer defined art as a symbolic form.[44] Developing this notion further, Langer has written: "Art is the creation of forms symbolic of human feeling."[45] Similarly, Whitehead emphasizes the nature of art as a symbol for feeling, asserting that "the symbolic transfer of emotion lies at the base of any theory of the aesthetics of art."[46] Whitehead here interprets art in terms of his concept of symbolic reference, comprehended as a symbolic transfer of emotions from causal efficacy to sense-perception, and vice versa. From this perspective, then, the *maṇḍala* art of Shingon Esoteric Buddhism might be defined in terms of Whitehead's theory of symbolic reference as the creation of form symbolic of causal feeling.

V. Shingon Buddhism and the Cosmology of Imagination as Synthesis

In a book on Japanese Shingon Buddhism entitled *Mikkyō: The Universe of Tantric Buddhism,* Kimizane Yokoyama describes how intentional acts of consciousness can construct radically new experiential states through the visualization of symbolic *maṇḍala* images produced by the creative imagination. He writes:

> The world in which we live was created by this process of intention, imagination and construction. The magnificent world of spirit that appears in the Mikkyō practice hall is likewise realized by intention, imagination and construction through properly executed observances. Indeed, the phenomena of this entire universe grew out of the intention, imagination and construction of the Buddha Mind.[47]

By this view, the process of dependent coorigination (Japanese: *engi*; Sanskrit: *pratītya-samutpāda*), whereby moments of experience arise through chains of causation, can itself be ordered or controlled by meditation upon world-forming imagery depicted in the symbolic *maṇḍala* art of Shingon Buddhism. It is thus a fundamental doctrine of Shingon Buddhism that symbolic images visualized by imagination are normative for the process of dependent coorigination.

From the standpoint of Whiteheadian process thought, the most significant framework for interpreting the Shingon theories described above is the Axiological Cosmology of Imaginative Experiential Synthesis developed by Robert Neville in a remarkable book entitled *Reconstruction of Thinking*.[48] Throughout this work, Neville develops Whitehead's process theories based on the principle of Creativity, or Creative Synthesis, into a highly original Cosmology of Imagination as Synthesis which describes how symbolic images produced by imagination are normative for the experiential process of harmonizing multiplicity into unity. According to Neville's theory, the primary function of imagination as synthesis is to gather otherwise merely causal components into a background field for the foreground focus of attention; the irreducible harmonic contrast between foreground focus and background field is the elementary structure of beauty or aesthetic value. In Neville's words:

> Experience is distinguished by virtue of involving a synthesis of merely causal components into a unity. . . . The most elementary form of this is synthesis of the components into a field that serves as a background for focused attention.[49]

He continues:

> One way of answering the question why imagination as experiential synthesis occurs is to point out that when it does occur, experience can express the value of beauty. The contrast between background field and foreground focus of attention is the elementary structure of beauty.[50]

Neville further argues that images, or symbolic forms, are normative for imaginative experiential synthesis, thereby functioning to order the antecedent multiplicity of causal components into the primordial beauty of harmonic contrast between foreground focus and background field:

> An image is the form by which imagination synthesizes its components into experience. It is the selection of components whose inte-

grated presence allows the other components to be present in the synthesis, either as background or as focal elements. An image is thus normative for a particular synthesis.[51]

According to Neville's Axiological Cosmology of Imagination as Synthesis, religion is primarily concerned with the symbolic images with which we construct experience through synthesis in imagination. Art, especially religious art, has an extraordinary cultural importance as the conveyor and inventor of those symbolic images by means of which world-construction occurs through imaginative experiential synthesis. He argues that meditation upon symbolic images from religious art can radically transform experience through novel acts of imaginative synthesis:

> Consider this hypothesis: By repeated rehearsals and meditation upon significant religious images, a person can bring these images to dominate the basic structures in which the world appears.[52]

As an example of how meditation upon symbolic images from religious art can reconstruct experience through synthesis in imagination, Neville specifically refers to the Tantric Buddhist praxis of contemplation upon *maṇḍala* art: "An even more striking illustration of this hypothesis is found in Tantric Buddhism. By meditation on a *maṇḍala,* a person forms experience wholly by the world-structures of the *maṇḍala.*"[53]

Neville's doctrine of Imagination as Synthesis based upon Whitehead's process cosmology provides the theoretical foundations necessary to comprehend the dynamics of Shingon *maṇḍala* contemplation. By this view, the Shingon experience of an "expanded periphery and horizon *in toto* produced by *Ajikan,* or Ah-syllable visualization, along with *kakudai hō,* or the technique of expansion, itself arises through a process of gathering a multiplicity of causal components into a background field for the foreground focus of attention. From the axiological or value-centric standpoint of Neville and Whitehead, the teleological aim of synthesis in imagination is to realize the primordial beauty of harmonic contrast between foreground focus and background field. In this case, the *Ajikan-maṇḍala* is a symbolic image which becomes normative for a particular synthesis in imagination, thereby harmonizing multiplicity into unity with maximum beauty or aesthetic value. By repeated rehearsals and meditation upon symbolic images from religious art such as the *Ajikan-maṇḍala,* one can bring these images to dominate the basic structure of the perceptual field, thereby resulting in an immediate experience of the felt background of causal relationships which always surrounds the sensory objects discriminated in the foreground focus of attention.

VI. SUMMARY AND CONCLUSION

I have analyzed the tradition of Japanese Shingon Esoteric Buddhism in Whiteheadian terms as a system of symbolic reference. According to Whitehead's theory, symbolism is primarily concerned with the use of pure sensory perceptions in the character of symbols for more primitive causal elements in our experience. On this basis I have argued that the religious art and poetry of Shingon Buddhism consists of images derived from sensory perception functioning as aesthetic symbols for causal perception. That is to say, in Shingon Buddhism, poetic forms such as the Ten Images or the varieties of *maṇḍala* art are to be conceived as objects from sense-perception functioning as expressive symbols (*monji*) which refer to the formless void of emptiness (*ku*) and dependent coorigination (*engi*). However, from the standpoint of Whitehead's theory of symbolic reference, these images do not merely point to emptiness but actually lead to a unity of feeling between the symbol and the meaning of emptiness. By this view, there exists a common ground between our perception of emptiness and our perception of the images of emptiness, so that the symbol and the meaning of the symbol are fused by one intensity of emotion. Therefore, each image discloses the void just as the void reveals each image, such that symbolic form and formless emptiness shine forth through each other in a reciprocity of symbolic reference.

The major significance of Whitehead's theory of symbolic reference is that it undermines the false notion of symbolism in religious art whereby an aesthetic symbol merely points to the object which it symbolizes. Whitehead's view articulates instead *the genuine symbolic power of art as a bearer of ultimate reality.* This distinction between false and genuine symbolism in religious art has been concisely summarized by the Christian theologian Paul Tillich in an article entitled "Art and Ultimate Reality." Tillich writes:

> It is difficult to draw the line between an artificial symbolism and the symbolic power of things as bearers of ultimate reality. Perhaps one could say that wrong symbolism makes us look away from one thing to another for which it is a symbol, while genuine symbolic power in a work of art opens up its own depths, and the depths of reality as such.[54]

Whitehead's theory of symbolic reference is illuminating as a hermeneutic for the analysis of Shingon Buddhist symbolism precisely because it repudiates the false idea of an aesthetic symbol as pointing beyond itself toward the thing symbolized, and instead reveals the genuine symbolic power of Shingon *maṇḍala* art for opening up its own depths and the depths of ultimate reality as causal process, from which all emotion, including religious emotion, arises.

To conclude: the uniqueness of the Shingon sect of Japanese Esoteric Buddhism lies in its claim that enlightened wisdom can be obtained only through the secret *upāya* (skillful means) of meditation upon aesthetic symbols depicted by *maṇḍala* art. Analogously to twentieth-century Western thinkers in a "new key" such as Whitehead, Langer, Cassirer, Freud, Jung and Hillman, Japanese Shingon Buddhism has therefore recognized the profoundly symbolic nature of human experience. From the standpoint of the theory of symbolic reference, the Japanese tradition of Shingon Esoteric Buddhism holds an ancient key to a fully postmodern definition of the human being as an *animal symbolicum*. More than that, it provides a key for using symbols to realize experientially the ultimate depths of reality.

NOTES

1. Susanne K. Langer, *Philosophy in a New Key,* 3rd ed. (Cambridge, Mass.: Harvard University Press, 1942), xiii.

2. *Ibid.,* xiv.

3. Ernst Cassirer, *The Philosophy of Symbolic Forms,* 3 vols. (New Haven and London: Yale University Press, 1955).

4. Langer, *Philosophy in a New Key,* 28.

5. Alfred North Whitehead, *Symbolism: Its Meaning and Effect* (New York: Fordham University Press, 1985), 18.

6. *Ibid.,* 48.

7. Whitehead, *Process and Reality,* corrected edition, David Ray Griffin and Donald W. Sherburne, ed. (New York: The Free Press, 1978), 168.

8. Whitehead emphasizes that symbolic reference works both ways in human experience so that sense-perception and causal perception mutually enhance each other in a reciprocal way. This reciprocity of symbolic reference can also be seen in nonsubstantialist Asian traditions like Chinese Taoism and Japanese Shingon Buddhism. Curtis L. Carter has contrasted Whitehead's notion of a reciprocity of symbolic reference to Hegel's one-way function of symbolism:

> By his emphasis upon. . . . the fact that references between symbols and their meanings may incur double reference with respect to each other, Whitehead introduces a new approach to aesthetic symbols,

which offers a significant departure from Hegel. . . . Hegel believes that the reference of an aesthetic symbol runs *from* the work of art *toward* absolute spirit, but not the reverse ("Hegel and Whitehead on Aesthetic Symbols," in *Hegel and Whitehead,* ed. George Lucas, Jr. [Albany: State University of New York Press, 1984], 252).

In a one-way system of symbolic reference, as in Hegel's philosophy, an aesthetic symbol must point beyond itself to the object symbolized, while in a reciprocal system of symbolic reference, as developed by Whitehead or Shingon Buddhism, the work of art is itself the bearer of ultimate reality and value as directly presented.

9. Whitehead, *Process and Reality,* 178.

10. Ibid., 183.

11. Chung-ying Cheng, "Chinese Philosophy and Symbolic Reference," *Philosophy East and West* (July 1977), 307-22.

12. *Ibid.,* 316.

13. *Ibid.,* 320.

14. Y. S. Hakeda, *Kūkai: Major Works* (New York: Columbia University Press, 1972), 234.

15. *Ibid.,* 234.

16. *Ibid.,* 242.

17. Langer, *Philosophy in a New Key,* 21.

18. While the *Mahāvairocana Sūtra* (Japanese: *Dainichi Kyo*) tradition was introduced from India into China in 716 A.D. by Subhakarasima (637-735), the *Vajraśekhara Sūtra (Kongōkai Kyō)* tradition was introduced in 720 A.D. by Vajrabodhi (671-741) and later by his disciple Amogavajra (705-74). However, both traditions as represented by the "Womb-Realm" (*Taizokai*) and "Diamond-Realm" *(Kongōkai) maṇḍala* pictures were integrated into a unified system of Tantric Buddhism by the Chinese patriarch Hui-kuo (746-805). Kūkai (774-835) studied directly under Hui-kuo in China from 804-06 A.D., thus being initiated into the *ryōbu* or "dual transmission" of both traditions. Subsequently, Kūkai was appointed by Hui-kuo as the Eighth Patriarch of the lineage succession, whereupon he returned to Japan in 806 A.D. and founded the Shingon (Sanskrit: *mantra*) or True Word sect of Japanese Esoteric Buddhism two years later.

19. Morgan Gibson and Hiroshi Murakami, trans., *Tantric Poetry of Kūkai* (Bangkok, Thailand: Amarin Press, 1982), 39.

20. *Ibid.,* 45.

21. *Ibid.,* 23-24.

22. Hakeda, *Kūkai: Major Works,* 157-224.

23. Ryusaku Tsunoda, Wm. Theodore de Bary and Donald Keene, ed., *Sources of Japanese Tradition* (New York: Columbia University Press, 1964), 138.

24. Whitehead, *Process and Reality,* 183.

25. Whitehead, *Religion in the Making* (New York: Macmillan Co., 1960), 101.

26. See Steve Odin, *Process Metaphysics and Hua-Yen Buddhism* (Albany: State University of New York Press, 1982).

27. Minoru Kiyota, *Shingon Buddhism: Theory and Practice* (Los Angeles: Buddhist Books International, 1978), 71.

28. *Ibid.,* 71.

29. Hakeda, *Kūkai: Major Works,* 219.

30. *Ibid.,* 220.

31. *Ibid.,* 221.

32. Yamazaki Taikō, *Mikkyō meisō hō* (Kyoto, Japan: Nagata Bunshō Dō, 1974), 197. I gratefully acknowledge the assistance of Ajari Master Yamazaki Taikō Sensei, Dean of Esoteric Studies at Shuchin University and Professor of Shingon Buddhism at Kōyasan University, with whom I studied the theory and practice of *Ajikan* (Ah-syllable visualization) during the 1984-85 academic year at Tōji Temple in Kyoto, Japan.

33. *Ibid.,* 222.

34. *Ibid.,* 198.

35. *Ibid.,* 230-31.

36. *Ibid.,* 232-33.

37. David Edward Shaner, *The Bodymind Experience in Japanese Buddhism: A Phenomenological Study of Kūkai and Dōgen* (Albany: State University of New York Press, 1985).

38. See my review article, "David Edward Shaner's *The Bodymind Experience in Japanese Buddhism: A Phenomenological Study of Kūkai and Dōgen,*" *Philosophy East & West* 37/2 (April 1987), 202-06.

39. Whitehead, *Adventures of Ideas* (New York: The Free Press, 1967), 260.

40. *Ibid.,* 270.

41. *Idem.*

42. *Ibid.,* 281.

43. *Ibid.,* 267-81.

44. Ernst Cassirer, *An Essay on Man* (New Haven & London: Yale University Press, 1972), 148.

45. Susanne K. Langer, *Feeling and Form* (New York: Charles Scribner's Sons, 1953), 40.

46. Whitehead, *Symbolism,* 85.

47. Kimizane Yokoyama, *Mikkyō: The Universe of Tantric Buddhism,* trans. A. Gleason and E. Takeda (Tokyo, Japan: Tama Publishing Co., 1983), 8.

48. Robert C. Neville, *Reconstruction of Thinking* (Albany: State University of New York Press, 1981).

49. *Ibid.,* 17.

50. *Ibid.,* 18.

51. *Ibid.,* 19.

52. *Ibid.,* 261.

53. *Ibid.,* 262.

54. Paul Tillich, "Art and Ultimate Reality," in *Art, Creativity and the Sacred,* ed. Diane Apostolos-Cappadona (New York: Crossroad Publishers, 1985), 224.

NOTES ON CONTRIBUTORS
AND CENTERS

WILLIAM A. BEARDSLEE is author of *A House for Hope: A Study in Process and Biblical Thought* and *Literary Criticism of the New Testament*, and editor of *The Poetics of Faith: Essays Offered to Amos N. Wilder*. He is professor emeritus of religion at Emory University and director of the Process and Faith Program of the Center for Process Studies, 1325 North College Avenue, Claremont, California 91711.

JOHN B. COBB, JR., is author of *Process Theology as Political Theology*, *Beyond Dialogue: Toward a Mutual Transformation of Buddhism and Christianity*, *The Liberation of Life: From the Cell to the Community* (with Charles Birch), and *For the Common Good* (with Herman Daly). He is Ingraham professor of theology at the School of Theology at Claremont, Avery professor of religion at Claremont Graduate School, and director of the Center for Process Studies, 1325 North College Avenue, Claremont, California 91711.

RICHARD FALK is author of *This Endangered Planet*, *A Study of Future Worlds*, *Revolutionaries and Functionaries: The Dual Face of Terrorism*, and (with Robert J. Lifton) *Indefensible Weapons*. He is the Albert G. Milbank professor of international law and practice at Princeton University, Princeton, New Jersey 08544.

MATTHEW FOX, O.P., is the author of *A Spirituality Named Compassion*, *On Becoming a Musical, Mystical Bear*, *Original Blessing: A Primer in Creation Spirituality*, and *The Coming of the Cosmic Christ*. He is the director of the Institute in Culture and Creation Spirituality at Holy Names College, 3500 Mountain Boulevard, Oakland, California 94619.

SUZI GABLIK is author of *Progress in Art*, *Magritte*, *Has Modernism Failed?*, and *The Reenchantment of Art* (forthcoming). She teaches from

217

time to time at various universities (most recently Virginia Tech University in Blacksburg, Virginia) and resides at 5 Westmoreland Street, London, W.1., England.

DAVID RAY GRIFFIN is author of *God, Power, and Evil* and *God and Religion in the Postmodern World*, co-author of *Process Theology* and *Varieties of Postmodern Theology*, and editor of *The Reenchantment of Science* and *Spirituality and Society*. He is professor of philosophy of religion at the School of Theology at Claremont and Claremont Graduate School, founding president of the Center for a Postmodern World, and executive director of the Center for Process Studies, 1325 North College Avenue, Claremont, California 91711.

JOE HOLLAND is author of *Creative Communion: The Spirituality of Work* and (with Peter Henriot) *Social Analysis: Linking Faith with Justice*, and editor (with Anne Barsanti) of *American and Catholic: The New Debate*. He is an adjunct professor at New York Theological Seminary and president of The Warwick Institute, 257 Warwick Avenue, South Orange, New Jersey 07079.

CATHERINE KELLER is author of *From a Broken Web: Separation, Sexism, and Self*, as well as several essays, and is currently writing a book on feminist eschatology. She is associate professor of theology at The Theological School, Drew University, Madison, New Jersey 07940.

BERNARD J. LEE, S.M., is the co-editor of *Religious Experience and Process Theology* and author of *The Becoming of the Church* and *The Galilean Jewishness of Jesus*. He is professor of theology at the Institute for Ministry, Loyola University, New Orleans, Louisiana 70118.

JOANNA MACY is author of *Dharma and Development* and *Despair and Personal Power in the Nuclear Age* and co-author of *Thinking Like a Mountain: Towards a Council of All Beings*. Besides leading despair-and-empowerment workshops around the world, she is adjunct professor at Starr King School for Ministry, John F. Kennedy University, and the California Institute of Integral Studies, 765 Ashbury Street, San Francisco, California 94117.

STEVE ODIN is author of *Process Metaphysics and Hua Yen Buddhism: A Critical Study of Cumulative Penetration vs. Interpenetration* as well as numerous journal articles. He teaches in the philosophy department at the University of Hawaii at Manoa, 2530 Dole Street, Honolulu, Hawaii 96822.

FREDERIC TURNER, former editor of *The Kenyon Review* and a regular contributor to *Harper's* magazine, is author of *Natural Classicism*,

Shakespeare and the Nature of Time, *The New World: An Epic Poem*, and *Genesis: An Epic Poem*. He is founders professor of arts and humanities at the University of Texas at Dallas, Richardson, Texas 75083.

This series is published under the auspices of the Center for a Postmodern World and the Center for Process Studies.

The Center for a Postmodern World is an independent nonprofit organization in Santa Barbara, California, founded by David Ray Griffin. It exists to promote the awareness and exploration of the postmodern worldview and to encourage reflection about a postmodern world, from postmodern art, spirituality, and education to a postmodern world order, with all this implies for economics, ecology, and security. One of its major projects is to produce a collaborative study that marshals the numerous facts supportive of a postmodern worldview and provides a portrayal of a postmodern world order toward which we can realistically move. It is located at 3463 State Street, Suite 252, Santa Barbara, Calif. 93105.

The Center for Process Studies is a research organization affiliated with the School of Theology at Claremont and Claremont University Center and Graduate School. It was founded by John B. Cobb, Jr., Director, and David Ray Griffin, Executive Director. It exists to encourage research and reflection upon the process philosophy of Alfred North Whitehead, Charles Hartshorne, and related thinkers, and upon the application and testing of this viewpoint in all areas of thought and practice. This center sponsors conferences, welcomes visiting scholars to use its library, and publishes a scholarly journal, *Process Studies*, and a quarterly *Newsletter*. It is located at 1325 North College, Claremont, Calif. 91711.

Both Centers gratefully accept (tax-deductible) contributions to support their work.

INDEX

Values, 3, 7, 12, 155-61. *See also*
  Aesthetic; Beauty; Morality;
  Truth; Sacred
Via creativa, 27-29
Via negativa, 28, 198
Via positiva (affirmativa), 27-28,
  198
Via transformativa, 28-29
Violence, 4, 95, 97, 108, 112

Walesa, Lech, 90
Walker, R.B.J., 102n.18
Warrior, 65, 72-77
Watts, Alan, 37
Weber, Max, 18, 178, 184
Web: as sacred, 2, 94, 116; of
  interconnections, 2, 5, 6, 9, 11,

53-54, 71, 78; relational, 53-54,
  59, 61
Whitehead, Alfred North, 5, 7-8, 12,
  19, 174n.7, 194-99, 202-03, 207-12,
  212n.8
Wittgenstein, Ludwig, x
Woodruff, Sue, 32n.29
Work, 3, 103-22
Worldview, x; anti-, x; modern, 84,
  150, 179, 184. *See also* Dualism;
  Materialism; Postmodernism,
  constructive
Worship, 15, 17, 20, 30, 31n.5
Wright, James, 160

Yamazaki, Taiko, 205-06, 214n.32
Yokoyama, Kimizane, 208